SLAYER

The Totally Cool Unofficial Guide to *Buffy*

By the same author with Paul Cornell and Martin Day:

The New Trek Programme Guide
X-Treme Possibilities
The Avengers Dossier

By the same author with Martin Day:

Shut It!

SLAYER

The Totally Cool Unofficial Guide to *Buffy*

Keith Topping

First published in this form in 1999 by

Virgin Publishing Limited
Thames Wharf Studios
Rainville Road
London
W6 9HA

ISBN 0 7535 0475 8

A catalogue record for this book is available from the
British Library.

Typeset by Galleon Typesetting, Ipswich
Printed and bound in Great Britain by
Mackays of Chatham PLC

For Martin Day.
My Watcher. My guru, my brother and my friend.

And

Kathy Sullivan.
Without whom there would have been *no* book.

And

Lily Topping.

Acknowledgements

'I think I need help,' I said, and they came like bats out of the Hellmouth . . .

My thanks to the following for their encouragement and contributions to this, my first solo book: Ian Abrahams, Marie Antoon, Robyn Bennett, Jo Brooks, Kini Brooks-Smith, Keith RA DeCandido, Paul Gibson, Jeff Hart, Ian Hill, Theresa Lambert, Kevin Lamke, Andy and Helen Lane, Peter Linford, John and Lucy McLaughlin, Jon Miller, Steve 'Tiddler' Purcell, Justin Richards, Jim Sangster, Trina Short, Ruth Thomas, Samantha Warner and Simon Winstone; and to every-one at the 'Tenth Planet of Gallifrey One' convention in LA with whom I was able to share the news of *Slayer*'s commissioning.

Alan *Anime Nut* Hufana's website *Domain of the Slain* (http://www2.uic.edu/~ahufan1/btvs) helped enormously with the 'Logic, Let Me Introduce You to This Window' sections. For UK fans, Rob Francis's *The Watcher's Web* (http://www.users. globalnet.co.uk/~fraxis) is an invaluable source of information and analysis with a largely British perspective. Thanks also to the numerous website custodians who kindly spared the time to answer my e-mails. Details of these sites can be found in the chapter 'Buffy and the Internet'.

My gratitude to Tony Dryer, Beth Kiefner, Judy Pykala, Carol Stoneburner and Deb Walsh, who helped fill a few *vital* gaps.

A special thank-you to my Slayerettes, Ian Atkins (who gave me *all* of the best jokes, plus some impressive scone-related details), Daniel Ben-Zvi (for his amazing research work), Wendy Comeau, my editor Peter Darvill-Evans, Rob Francis (who went for the doughnuts), Liz Halliday, Paul Simpson (who provided unedited transcripts of his interviews with many of the cast), Susannah Tiller, Graeme Topping and Mark Wyman, all of whom lent me their enthusiasm and talent.

And to my family, who have supported my writing for the past decade.

Contents

Contents

Preface

When I first proposed *Slayer* to Virgin Publishing late in 1998, my main reason for wanting to write the book was that there was no episode guide to *Buffy the Vampire Slayer* available in Britain. By the time it was commissioned two months later, there were *three* in the shops. Such is the pace at which a cult can grow into a mainstream success. OK, so there *are* other *Buffy* books on the shelves and some of them are very good. *Slayer* is different from *all* of them, however. Certainly it covers the same episodes (though you'll find details of some that, at the time of writing, have yet to broadcast in the UK), but it covers them in very different ways. The aim of *Slayer* is to offer a British perspective to this most Californian of subjects, to recognise the sometimes very adult nature of the series and to provide a touch of critical analysis where other books fear to tread.

Buffy the Vampire Slayer is, on one level, a quasi-fairy tale in which a group of young people are the focus of a battle between the forces of good (as represented by themselves) and evil (represented, mostly, by an older generation). 'The Brothers Grimm' with a rock-and-roll soundtrack and its own syntax. Yet there is more to this series than sharp one-liners and eye-candy set pieces. Without getting too pretentious, *Buffy* has more in common with *Hamlet* than a blond hero and death on a large scale. *Buffy* is about growing up and facing the totally mundane horrors of the adult world. About a time when the game of life is still being played by *our* rules but with the knowledge that this is changing. It concerns the point where childhood ends and the ordinary, everyday realities of career, relationships and responsibilities appear on the horizon. Thus we as viewers explore Sunnydale seeing a world that we can, hopefully, recognise. Because it was *our* world too. A world of hormone-charged teenagers with their own secret language. A world where an educational establishment plays host to the epic battle between the forces of light and darkness. A world where the body count (physical *and* emotional) is astronomical. These are themes that are universal and timeless, not tied to a particular part of the United States in the final days of the twentieth century.

The story is simple: Buffy Summers and her mother move from Los Angeles to the small town of Sunnydale after her expulsion from a previous school (there was that nasty business of the gym burning down). On her first day at Sunnydale High, she befriends two local nerds, Xander Harris and Willow Rosenberg, a friendship that excludes her from the cool set led by the formidable Cordelia Chase. Buffy also meets her English Watcher, Rupert Giles, because, as we discover, she is a Vampire Slayer: a one-per-generation clan of stake-wielding super-babes who rid the world of vampires, demons and the forces of darkness. As *SFX* said, when placing the series in their 'Top Fifty SF TV Shows of All Time', '*Buffy* should be awful . . . In the land where the one-line pitch is king, *Buffy* rules . . .'

But *Buffy* is also a peek into a toy shop of magnificent conceit – a series fixated in equal measure by the claustrophobic 'outsider' constraints of the adolescent years and by the battle fought by a heroine, not because she *wants* to (indeed, she's initially a reluctant Slayer), but because she's good at it and because, as with most dirty jobs, *someone's* got to do it. Into this mix come elements of high (and sometimes extremely low) comedy and much confident and self-aware dialogue. *SFX* believes that the main reason for *Buffy*'s success is that it has 'the three cornerstones of quality TV: good writing, good characters and good acting. More to the point, *Buffy* is the perfect combination of both cynicism and quality; a well-written, well-acted series that just happens to star gorgeous teenagers in soap-style situations.' The heavyweight US critic Matt Roush also wrote of the series' genre-crossing appeal: 'A show as terrific as *Buffy*, with its kicky commingling of humor and horror, may be aimed at the youth market. But it deserves a following as wide as its buzz is loud. If only it could overcome the perception of its silly-sounding title . . . I'd argue that it has a bigger emotional resonance than any youth soap on the air.'

Anthony Stewart Head, who plays Rupert Giles, told *DreamWatch* about his first impressions of the script: 'I was sitting in the Border Grill in Santa Monica . . . I laughed out loud and suddenly found myself having to stop because people were looking at me! As I was reading it, I couldn't wait to turn the page and find out what happened next. I thought this is an extraordinary combination. I'm no judge of what is going to be a success on TV but this *has* to be a success.' And so it has proved. Along with series like *Xena: Warrior Princess*, *Buffy* has also brought an audience to mainstream SF that covers a wide demographic and gender range (put simply, lots of women like these series for their powerful female characters and hunky male icons). What follows may help to explain why:-

Headings

Dreaming (As Blondie Once Said) is Free: Lots of TV series do cool dream sequences. *Buffy* does *magnificent*, surreal, scary, funny ones – as you'll find listed here.

Dudes and Babes: Who's hot and who's not among the beautiful people of Sunnydale. Includes an occasional Drool Factor. I'm grateful to a plethora of fans (of various sexualities) for gleefully adding suggestions and the odd secret fantasy to this section.

Authority Sucks!: Which aspect of square conformity is trying to bring 'the kids' under its thumb? A category for would-be anarchists everywhere.

Mom's Apple Pie: Aspects of traditional family life shown or subverted. We also keep an eye on Buffy's (often tempestuous) relationship with her mother, Joyce. Brian Lowry writing in the *Los Angeles Times* noted: 'Parents on most of WB's teen-orientated shows – *Dawson's Creek*, *Buffy*, *Felicity* and *Zoe, Duncan, Jack & Jane* – aren't just absent or inept; rather, in the few scenes they're given they are frequently clueless, bullying or dysfunctional, in need of a stern lecture from their kids regarding morality.'

Denial, Thy Name is Joyce: A category that details Joyce Summers's amazing propensity for self-delusion. Kristine Sutherland, who plays the part of Joyce, in a thoughtful, revealing interview with Paul Simpson, confessed: 'A parent of an adolescent has to walk a very fine line, and sometimes what's called for is a healthy dose of denial, and looking the other way. Denial is an amazing . . . powerful thing. People have not let information in that is too big for them to handle in so much more amazing ways than Joyce not getting that Buffy is a Vampire Slayer. I really believe in the power of denial.' We've noticed.

It's a Designer Label!: Fashion statements, tips and victims are detailed here, along with the lengths of the skirts involved. And the bobble hats. As Jamie Diamond of *Mademoiselle* observed when interviewing Sarah Michelle Gellar: 'We meet at a Santa Monica café. Gellar, sporting a black cashmere sweater . . . and carrying a Prada bag.' *Buffy*'s costume designer Cynthia Bergstrom does, in fact, select clothes for the cast from LA fashion stores like Neiman-Marcus, Fred Siegel Flair, Tommy Hilfiger, Macy's, Contempo Casuals and Traffic.

References: Pop-culture, 'Generation X' and general homages to all things esoteric.

Bitch!: Girls will be girls . . . All those bitchy moments that make the boys twitch nervously.

Awesome!: The monsters that menace Sunnydale. The action sequences. The 'funny bits'. All of the things that make viewers say '*Cool!*'

Valley-Speak: For those who, *like*, don't understand what's, *you know*, being said. *Totally. Dude*. The series own unique teen-speak described by *Buffy*'s creator Joss Whedon as 'twisting the English language until it cries out in pain'.

Cigarettes and Alcohol: An occasional category dealing with teenage naughtiness of the nicotine-and-lager variety.

Logic, Let Me Introduce You to This Window: Goofs, plot holes and continuity errors.

I Just *Love* Your Accent: Examples of *Buffy*'s charmingly Californian view of Britain and the British. Joss Whedon spent part of his teenage years at school in England, so some of these observations are more accurate than you might think. Which other US series would include a reference to a sensationalist tabloid newspaper and then name-check the *Sun* rather than the *National Enquirer*?

Quote/Unquote: The dialogue worth rewinding the video for.

Other categories occasionally appear. Most should be fairly self-explanatory.

We begin each season with a list of the regular cast to help those of you who don't know who all of the actors are. Remember them – they are quite important. Sarah Michelle Gellar is Buffy, Nicholas Brendon is Xander, Alyson Hannigan is Willow, Anthony Stewart Head (usually referred to as Tony) is Giles, Charisma Carpenter is Cordelia, Kristine Sutherland is Joyce Summers, Seth Green is Oz and David Boreanaz is Angel (in several episodes in Season Two he plays a character called Angelus, who occupies the same body as Angel but is very different).

A Short History of the Vampire in Myth, Literature and Film

'The children of the night, what sweet music they make.'

'**Vampire** *n*. 1. (in European folklore) a corpse that rises nightly from its grave to drink the blood of the living. 2. a person who preys mercilessly upon others.' – *Collins Concise Dictionary*.

They've been with us for so long that it would require a book considerably larger than this to untangle the myriad legends and myths that concern them. They are the fabric of our nightmares. They are central to much of our literature and movie culture. 'Even today,' wrote the English priest and man of letters Montague Summers in 1928, 'in remoter districts of Europe, [like] Transylvania, Slovenia, the isles and mountains of Greece, the peasant will . . . utterly destroy the carrion who at night will issue from his unhallowed grave . . . Assyria knew the vampire long ago, and he lurked amid the primaeval [sic] forests of Mexico before Cortes came. He is feared by the Chinese, the Indian, and the Malay; while Arabian stories tell us . . . of the ghouls who haunt ill-omened lonely crossways.'

The origins of the word 'vampire' (or 'vampir', or 'vampyre') are hazy. Matthew Bunson notes in *Vampire: The Encyclopaedia*, that it 'may have come from the Lithuanian *wempti* ("to drink").' It arrived in the English language in 1732 via a translation of the case of the Serbian vampire Arnold Paole. As early as 1198, however, William of Newburgh's *Historia Rerum Anglicarum* recorded examples of vampiric activity in Northumberland. Other important historical works include Leo Allatius's *De Quorundum Graecorum Opinationibus* (on the Greek *vrykolakas* legends), Michael Ranftius's *De*

Masticatione Mortuorum in Tumulus Liber and Dom Augustine Calmet's *Traite sur les Apparition des Espirits, et sur les Vampires*.

Some scholars suggest ancient Egypt as the birthplace of vampirism (with so many death cults in Egyptian mythology, it's not an unreasonable starting point). Others look to India and the *bhuta* creatures of Hindu folklore, China and the Taoist *chiang-shi* or the Mesopotamian Empire. 'Bloodsuckers' (*sanguisugga*) are mentioned in the Old Testament (Proverbs 30:15), though the *utukku* of Assyria and Greek legends of the *callicantzaro* and the *vrykolakas* probably predate this. These myths of the Aegean are very different from the more familiar Slavic and Germanic tales of the walking dead that influenced Gothic literature, fascinated Paris in the 1820s and led (via a plethora of 'penny bloods') to Bram Stoker and *Dracula*.

The vampire in literature can be found in the work of German poets, such as Heinrich Ossenfelder's 'Der Vampir' and Gottfried August Bürger's 'Lenore', while Johann Wolfgang von Goethe's *Die Braut von Korinth* and Johann Ludwig Tieck's *Wake Not the Dead* are examples in the Gothic movement. But it was *The Vampyre* by John Polidori that caught the imagination of the public, particularly in England and France. Polidori was physician to Lord Byron and accompanied the poet on his notorious 1816 trip to Europe, before they parted company less than amicably. On the shores of Lake Geneva in June, they met Percy and Mary Shelley and a competition in writing ghost stories led to what Stephen King describes as 'one of the maddest British tea parties of all time'. The outcome is legendary: Mary Shelley wrote *Frankenstein*, while Byron's fragment ('The Burial') was acquired by Polidori and fleshed out into *The Vampyre* (as an act of revenge against his former employer). It was first published in the *New Monthly Magazine* in April 1819 under Byron's name before the true author took credit, and the charismatic 'Lord Ruthvan' was a thinly veiled caricature of Byron. Subsequent important vampire stories include Edgar Allen Poe's 'Ligeia', Tolstoy's 'Upry', the remarkable 'Varney the Vampire, or Feast of Blood' by James Malcolm

Rymer and Guy de Maupassant's 'Le Horla'.

Sheridan Le Fanu's *Carmilla*, first published in 1872, was one of the first novels to pursue the link between vampirism and sensuality, and in Carmilla Karnstein, Le Fanu created a lesbian icon of extraordinary power. The character was based on one of the Middle Ages' most notorious mass murderers, the Hungarian noblewoman Elizabeth Bathory (1560–1614), who was said to bathe in the blood of young women in an attempt to retain her youth. Bathory was one of two figures from the history of the Carpathians that became the basis for much of what we know today as the vampire genre. The other was Vlad Tepes (1431–76), the warlord prince of Transylvania. The son of Vlad Dracul of Wallachia, Tepes was a butcher who gained his sobriquet ('the impaler') from his delightful hobby of executing his enemies on wooden stakes. Now regarded in Romania as a symbol of nationalistic pride for his defeat of the Ottoman Turks, Vlad was also known by another name, in honour of his father. Draculae – Son of the Dragon.

Bram Stoker's 1897 novel is a stylistic summation of the genre. Influenced by Rymer, Poe and Le Fanu and with a majestic grasp of the Central European mythology, *Dracula* was an entirely new kind of vampire novel in which the combination of evil and human weakness continued to be exploited, but which also dealt with psychology and sex. In *Danse Macabre*, Stephen King discusses the most sexually explicit moment in the book (Harker's 'languorous ecstasy' as he encounters the voluptuous but lethal 'sisters'):

> In the England of 1897, a girl who 'went on her knees' was not the sort of girl you brought home to meet your mother; Harker is about to be orally raped, and he doesn't mind a bit. And it's all right because *he is not responsible*. In matters of sex, a highly moralistic society can find a psychological escape valve in the concept of outside evil.

These strong sexual overtones, notes King, are one reason why the movies based on Stoker's work have continued to be successful no matter how radical the treatment. AA Gill suggests that 'Dracula and his clan are all metaphors for sex, specifically virginal girls' yearnings and their consequent sense of guilt . . . Vampires have no reflections: being able to look yourself in the face is a sign of purity and innocence.'

Following Stoker's lead, the vampire novel has gone through a series of thematic changes but with, basically, the same ingredients that Stoker mixed in the 1890s. The early twentieth century saw such classics as Marion F Crawford's *For the Blood is the Life*, Algernon Blackwood's *The Transfer*, Reginald Hodder's *The Vampire* and MR James's *An Episode of Cathedral History*. One would have thought that the horrors of World War One would have ended the public's fascination with such stories but EF Benson's *Mrs Amsworth* was the first of a series of genre-stretching novels that have taken the vampire into the fabric of modern literature: *Revelation in Black* (Carl Jacobi), *The Cloak* (Robert Bloch), *Dreadful Hollow* (Irina Karlova), *The Devil is Not Mocked* (Manly Wade Wellman), *The Girl With the Hungry Eyes* (Fritz Leiber), *I Am Legend* (Richard Matheson), *Doctors Wear Scarlet* (Simon Raven), *'Salem's Lot* (Stephen King), *The Hunger* (Whitley Strieber), and the works of Anne Rice, beginning with *Interview with the Vampire*, are among the most celebrated of modern vampire texts.

Cinema's love affair with the vampire began as early as 1922 when FW Murnau's expressionist masterpiece *Nosferatu* (starring Max Schreck as the Dracula-like Count Orlok) suggested the enormous possibilities for cinematic horror. In America, Universal Films acquired the rights to Hamilton Deane's 1898 stage-adaptation of *Dracula* (directed by Tod Browning and starring Bela Lugosi) and fashioned a movie that, as Matthew Bunson notes, 'influenced the way the Count was forever after depicted, shaping the general style of succeeding Universal projects and proving the financial potential of horror'. The company went on to produce many variants on the theme before a dispiriting spiral into low-budget parody in the 1940s (e.g. *Abbott and Costello Meet Frankenstein*).

A decade later the British company Hammer revived the genre and produced a series of beautifully made bloodthirsty shockers on minimal budgets, in the process turning Peter Cushing and Christopher Lee into icons of equal status to Lugosi. Hammer's *Dracula* cycle, eight films between 1958's *Dracula* (US title: *Horror of Dracula*) and 1973's *Satanic Rites of Dracula*, are highly recommended to lovers of the genre, as is the company's 'Karnstein trilogy' (*The Vampire Lovers, Lust for a Vampire* and *Twins of Evil*). At the same time the French director Jean Rollin's series of vampire movies (which explored the sex angle to a greater degree than Hammer) were becoming both influential and popular.

Comedy and vampirism may seem strange bedfellows but Roman Polanski's 1967 *Dance of the Vampires* (US title: *The Fearless Vampire Killers*) showed that such a merging of seemingly incompatible genres *was* possible. RW Johnson noted in 1982, '. . . we have actually got round to really funny films about vampires – not burlesques, which refuse to take the myth seriously, but comedies which accept the myth head on, and still laugh at it.' In the 1980s – at the very moment when the vampire novel was becoming a serious literary subgenre with the success of Anne Rice's novels – numerous teenage vampire films were made in America. They were mostly low-budget, often sneered at by 'serious' critics who regarded the horror motif as not worthy of study, and equally loathed by horror fans for not including capes, castles and bats. But, from *Fright Night, Once Bitten, Vamp, The Lost Boys, Near Dark* and *Beverly Hills Vamp* it's only a very short step to *Buffy the Vampire Slayer*, a critical and artistic failure upon its release in 1992.

Did You Know?: Interviewed in 1996, Hammer's chairman Roy Skeggs noted that Miramax Films wanted to remake the camp classic *Dracula A.D. 1972* as '*Dracula 1999* reset in Los Angeles, [with] the modern whizz-kids fighting vampires.' Hang on, that sounds a bit like . . .

Awakenings

A shopaholic teenager discovers that she is the latest in a line of mythical warriors.

Whether *Buffy the Vampire Slayer* should be regarded as an example of Joss Whedon's talent or a triumph for his persuasive skills is unclear, but the fact that the concept ever made it beyond that one-line description suggests the latter.

Whedon is a third-generation Hollywood scriptwriter (his grandfather worked on *Leave it to Beaver*, his father wrote for *The Dick Cavett Show*). His education included a period at Winchester Public School and, after writing many speculative scripts in his teens, he landed a writing job on the enormously popular sitcom *Roseanne*. However, with his encyclopedic knowledge of horror movies and comics, Whedon had always wanted to write for that market, acknowledging the influence on *Buffy* of two modernist and stylistically fascinating vampire films, *The Lost Boys* and *Near Dark*. 'Sometimes we have fruity European Anne Rice-type vampires,' noted Whedon. 'Sometimes we have the dusty, western *Near Dark*-type vampires. And sometimes we just have a bunch of stuntmen.'

His script for *Buffy the Vampire Slayer* was hawked around the Hollywood studios and suffered four years of rejection before finding a supporter in the producer Howard Rosenman. Next to arrive was the Czech director Fran Rubel Kuzui (whose previous work included *Tokyo Pop*). She fell in love with *Buffy* as soon as she heard the preposterously silly title! Kuzui rewrote Whedon's script, introducing many of the elements that are now part of the mythos (like the John Woo-influenced martial-arts fight sequences).

What followed was an interesting failure – a false dawn that nevertheless contains moments that help to explain why nearly a decade later Buffy Summers is still around kicking vampire ass.

'Since the dawn of man, the Vampires have walked among us. Feeding. The only one with the strength or skill to stop their heinous evil is The Slayer. She who bears the birthmark, the mark of the coven. Trained by The Watcher, one Slayer dies and the next is chosen.'

A Kuzui Enterprises/Sandollar Production/ 20th Century Fox

M1
Buffy the Vampire Slayer – The Movie

Theatrical Release: September 1992; 86 minutes (rated PG-13)

Co-Producer: Dennis Stuart Murphy
Executive Producers: Sandy Gallin, Carol Baum, Fran Rubel Kuzui
Producers: Kaz Kuzui, Howard Rosenman
Writer: Joss Whedon
Director: Fran Rubel Kuzui

Cast:
Kristy Swanson (Buffy)
Donald Sutherland (Merrick)
Paul Reubens (Amilyn)
Rutger Hauer (Lothos)
Luke Perry (Pike)
Michele Abrams (Jennifer)
Hilary Swank (Kimberly)
Paris Vaughan (Nicole)
David Arquette (Benny)
Randall Bantinkoff (Jeffrey)
Andrew Lowery (Andy)
Sasha Jenson (Gueller)

Stephen Root (Gary Murray)
Natasha Gregson Wagner (Cassandra)
Candy Clark (Buffy's Mom)
Mark DeCarlo (Coach)
Tom Janes (Zeph)
James Paradise (Buffy's Dad)
David Sherrill (Knight)
Liz Smith (Reporter)
Paul M Lane (Robert Bowman)
Toby Holguin (Vampire Fan)
Eurlyne Epper-Woldman (Graveyard Woman)
Andre Warren (Newscaster)
Bob 'Swanie' Swanson (Referee)
Erika Dittner (Cheerleader)
JC Cole (Biker)
Michael S Kopelow (Student)
Ricky Dean Logan (Bloody Student)
Bobby Aldridge, Amanda Anka, Chino Binamo,
Al Goto, Terry Jackson, Mike Johnson, Sarah Lee Jones,
Kim Robert Kosci, Clint Lilley, Chi-Muoi Lo,
Jimmy N Roberts, David Rowden, Kenny Sacha,
Ben R Scott, Kurtis Epper Sanders, Sharon Schaffer,
Lincoln Simonds (Vampires)

Southern California – the 'Lite Ages': 'Killing time' takes on a whole new meaning at Hemery High when Buffy (a blonde-brained cheerleader) is told by the mysterious Merrick that she is the Chosen One – the Vampire Slayer. But, when Lothos and his cackling sidekick seek vengeance on The Slayer, Buffy finds herself up to her neck in trouble and battling against the undead – and against her rapidly dwindling popularity with her Valley girlfriends – with only the help of a seriously gorgeous drifter and a pointed stick. *Totally*.

Dudes and Babes: For the girls (and some of the guys), Luke Perry. Say no more.

Authority Spanks!: In Administrator Murray's office, a green spanking paddle is visible. Corporal punishment is supposed to be banned in California (see **9**, 'The Puppet Show').

A Little Learning is a Dangerous Thing: Buffy: 'Excuse me not knowing about El Salvador. Like I'm ever going to Spain anyway?' Cassandra's question about the ozone layer is met with Buffy's reply, 'Gotta get rid of that.'

Mom's Apple Pie: Buffy's mom (unnamed and clearly a *very* different character from Joyce in the TV series) calls Jeffrey 'Bobby'. Buffy offers the sulky opinion that she probably thinks Buffy's name is Bobby too. One of the best scenes of the film occurs when Buffy comes home extremely late and her mother apprehends her at the door asking if she knows what time it is. Buffy replies it's 'around ten', which her mom wanted to know because her watch had stopped and she's about to go out. (See **33**, 'Becoming' Part 1.)

It's a Designer Label!: Buffy's electric-blue cheerleader leggings and red flower-patterned miniskirt in the opening scenes are tame compared with her gym-wear during her first meeting with Merrick. Yellow sports bra, multicoloured pants, and shocking-pink leggings. Is she colourblind? (Possibly, if her desire for that lemon-yellow jacket is anything to go by.) The Grace Kelly-style prom dress and hairdo don't suit her, and when Pike stands on the end of the dress, ripping it, she's wearing jogging pants underneath. Which is *very* convenient.

References: 'It's time to put away such childish things' alludes to the Biblical passage I Corinthians 13:11 ('When I was a child, I spake as a child, I understood as a child, I thought as a child: but when I became a man I put away childish things.') 'The rest is silence' are the eponymous hero's dying words in *Hamlet*. Buffy sings a few lines from Louis Gost and Morris Albert's 1975 easy-listening standard 'Feelings'. There are references to Sting's battle to save the rain forests, the 'Elvis Lives' myth, the actor Christian Slater *(Heathers, Kuffs, Very Bad Things)*, *Kung Fu*, a misquote from *The Wizard of Oz*, and an oblique reference to the circumstances surrounding Jimi Hendrix's death.

The Drugs Don't Work: Administrator Murray claims to have 'done acid' at a Doobie Brothers concert and believed he was a giant toaster before freaking out when his friend Melissa's head turned into a party balloon.

'You May Remember Me From Such Films and TV Series As . . .': Kristy Swanson's film appearances include *Highway to Hell*, *Marshal Law*, *Flowers in the Attic*, *The Phantom*, *Bad to the Bone* and *The Chase*. She's now a regular on *Early Edition*, playing Erica Paget. Luke Perry was Dylan in *Beverly Hills 90210* and Sideshow Luke Perry in *The Simpsons*. Paul Reubens is best known as Pee-Wee Herman in *Pee-Wee Herman's Big Adventure*. Donald Sutherland's CV includes many of this author's favourite movies (*Dr Terror's House of Horror*, *The Dirty Dozen*, *M*A*S*H*, *Klute*, *Don't Look Now*, *The Eagle Has Landed*, *The First Great Train Robbery*, *Murder by Decree*, *Backdraft* and *JFK*). During the 60s, Sutherland was a British TV regular – he's the voodoo god Dwumbala in an episode of *The Champions* for instance, and also appeared in *Man in a Suitcase* and *The Avengers*. The Dutch actor Rutger Hauer is a cult figure in Britain via his adverts for Guinness during the 80s, and films like *Blade Runner*, *Ladyhawke*, *The Hitcher*, *The Osterman Weekend* and *Fatherland*. Hilary Swank played the lead in *The Next Karate Kid*. David Arquette was one of the stars of the *Scream* movies and also featured in *Muppets from Space*. Stephen Root's credits include *Crocodile Dundee II*, *Ghost* and *Robocop*, while he provides the voice of Bill Dauterive in *King of the Hill*. Candy Clark was Mary-Lou, Thomas Newton's girlfriend in *The Man Who Fell to Earth*. She's also in *Cat's Eyes*, *American Graffiti* and *Amityville 3-D*.

Don't Give Up The Day Job: Liz Smith is now a famous gossip columnist in the US. JC Cole's brief acting part was in addition to his production role on the film, as dolly grip.

Valley-Speak: The movie as a celebration and a critique of Valley-girl culture (or lack of it) is full of such contrivances as 'Mr Howard is *so heinous*!', 'This is *so lush*!', and 'Does the word "*Duh!*" mean anything to you?' all from Buffy.

Buffy and Jennifer, on why they aren't going to a movie theatre: '*Bogus* corn!'

Kimberly's opinion of the jacket Buffy wants: 'Pur-leeze. It's *so* five minutes ago!'

Surfer-kid: 'This party sucks, man.'

Pike: 'Pity, you seem like such a *flink*.'

Cigarettes and Alcohol: 'You're *thrashed*,' Buffy tells Pike. 'That', he says, 'would explain the slurred speech.'

Logic, Let Me Introduce You to This Window: When Pike fights the vampire wearing the varsity jacket, Buffy leaps on the vampire's shoulders and wraps her legs around his head. The next shot has her falling on Pike with the vampire nowhere to be seen. The implication is she's killed him – but how, exactly? (An answer is given in **2**, 'The Harvest', and it's not pretty.)

Quote/Unquote: Andrew, trying not to touch Buffy's bottom as she leans over him to kiss Jeffrey: 'I don't want to sound sexist or anything, but can I borrow her?'

Buffy's dad: 'Have fun. Be good. Stay away from the Jag.'

Buffy, on Merrick's claims: 'Does Elvis talk to you?'

Amilyn, after Pike has caused his arm to be severed: 'Kill him. A lot.'

Buffy on her ambitions: 'All I want to do is graduate from school, go to Europe, marry Christian Slater and die.'

Lothos, after Buffy has staked him: 'Now I'm *really* pissed off.'

Notes: 'I'm in a graveyard with a strange man, hunting for vampires, on a school night.' Imagine a cross between *Beverly Hills 90210*, *Clueless* and *Interview with the Vampire*, and you're about a third of the way to how weird *Buffy the Vampire Slayer* is. It's a badly plotted film (Whedon's script was extensively rewritten). Donald Sutherland is great but the movie dies on its feet the moment his character is written out with half an hour to go. It's also a very shallow tale: we care little about these people. This is particularly true of Buffy herself, who in this incarnation is a selfish moron.

hanging around with her sycophantic tittering girlfriends long after she realises that there are more important things in life. There *are* nice realistic moments, like her discussion with Merrick about suffering from the cramps ('my secret weapon is PMS').

Buffy owns a teddy bear (see **5**, 'Never Kill a Boy on the First Date'; **10**, 'Nightmares'; **21**, 'What's My Line?' Part 1). She used to do gymnastics, and still knows the moves. She wants a career as a 'buyer', even though she doesn't know what one does. She had the 'hairy mole' birthmark that identified her as The Slayer removed (an element that was, along with the PMS references, not picked up during the series).

Differences between the movie and the TV series: vampires can fly, and don't turn to dust when staked. They can't enter a building unless invited, including public areas like the school gym (see **7**, 'Angel'; **30**, 'Killed By Death') and leave no image on film (see **21**, 'What's My Line?' Part 1; **46**, 'Helpless'). Merrick (in a very confusing speech that suggests reincarnation, but also extreme longevity) says he has 'lived a hundred lifetimes' and that it's been the same life over and over with the knowledge to prepare The Slayer. But when he's killed by Lothos there's no evidence of soul transference, so maybe he's simplifying things for Buffy by not telling her there are other Watchers out there. The implication of Buffy's dreams (The Slayer is reborn each generation) also suggests reincarnation (we may see an example of this in **56**, 'Graduation Day' Part 2). Among the previous Slayers mentioned are a Magyar peasant girl, an Indian princess, a slave in Virginia and a serving girl (possibly in medieval England, certainly somewhere where there were knights). The Hemery High basketball team are called The Hogs. Much of the location filming took place in North Hollywood, Sherman Oaks and Pasadena.

Soundtrack: 'Keep it Comin' (Dance Till You Can't Dance No More)' by C&C Music Factory, 'In the Wind' by War Babies, 'Man Smart, Woman Smarter' by Dream Warriors, 'I Fought the Law (And the Law Won)' by Mary's Danish, 'I Ain't Gonna Eat Out My Heart Anymore' by Divinyls, 'Zap

City' by the Cult, 'Silent City' by Matthew Sweet, 'Inner Mind' by Eon, 'Little Haven' by Toad the Wet Sprocket, 'Party with the Animals' by Ozzy Osbourne, 'Light Comes Out Black' by Rob Holland and 'We Close Our Eyes' by Susannah Hoffs.

Did You Know?: One of the uncredited extras on the film was Seth Green, though the scenes in which he appeared were cut before release. His photo can be seen on the sleeve of the 1997 video of the movie.

The Comic: In an attempt to marry the continuity of the movie with the many variations of these events described in the TV series, January 1999 saw the publication by Dark Horse of a three-part comic, *Buffy the Vampire Slayer – The Origin*, adapted from Whedon's original screenplay by Daniel Brereton and Christopher Golden, pencilled by Joe Bennett and inked by Rick Ketcham. This drew heavily on the movie, but included elements subsequently changed by the series (such as Buffy's first meeting with Merrick, seen in **33**, 'Becoming' Part 1) and parts of the screenplay not used but alluded to in *Buffy* folklore (the burning down of the Hemery High gym). Some of the story is told in the form of a (possibly unreliable) narrative by Buffy's former friends, while an intriguing coda has Buffy telling Willow and Xander about a trip to Las Vegas with Pike before she came to Sunnydale.

U1
The untransmitted TV pilot

In 1996 Whedon (having worked on the scripts of *Speed, Twister, Waterworld, Toy Story* and *Alien: Resurrection*) was asked by Sandollar to revive *Buffy* as a TV format. Whedon wrote and (according to legend) partly financed a 25-minute 'presentation' showreel. This was to enable him to show interested networks what *Buffy* would look like. Since it features no on-screen credits it's impossible to give production details. What *is* clear is that the script (the first draft of which was dated 26 January 1996) was a work-in-progress version of **1**, 'Welcome to the Hellmouth' (some scenes are word-for-word and shot-for-shot identical with the broadcast version). Tony Head has indicated that Whedon also directed the 'presentation', recalling that 'he's now an incredible director, but he had a fairly unhelpful crew'.

Head, Sarah Michelle Gellar, Nicholas Brendon, Charisma Carpenter, Mercedes McNab and Danny Strong were all present, although there was a different Willow, a different Principal Flutie and no trace of Angel. The editing was, according to *The Watcher's Guide*, the work of the future co-producer David Solomon. Head also remembers that, 'it wasn't as polished as the pilot became. The effects were great but it was all very strange. The end scene that I did was horrible.'

The Blonde Leading the Blonde: Here, Buffy is a brunette.

No Fat Chicks!: The script describes Willow as: 'Bookish and very possibly dressed by her mother. The intelligence in her eyes and the sweetness of her smile belie a genuine charm that is lost on the unsubtle highschool [sic] mind.' Casting her as a shy obese girl with a *very* unfortunate skirt length, and then (when a series was commissioned) dropping her in favour of someone thinner, was unfortunate. Who knows what a self-esteem boost for millions of fat kids an overweight character could have achieved? (Given that the entire population of the USA will, according to recent statistics, be clinically obese by the year 2032, how likely is it that a group of high school misfits like the Scooby Gang would all be slim to the point of anorexia?) That said, Riff Regan is clearly nervous, fluffing some of her lines badly.

It's a Designer Label!: The girl vampire's flowery dress and black leggings clash with the faded 80s soul-boy look of her male counterpart. Buffy's blue-suede shoes, ginger miniskirt and Technicolor-yawn top show little sign of what we would come to expect, though in this incarnation Willow *does* seem to have seen 'the softer side of Sears'. Harmony's black and white miniskirt is nice. If the 'presentation' shows one thing that the series needed to get sorted, it's what they were trying to say about clothes. As Cordelia notes, 'I know flannel is *so* over, but I can never tell what's coming next.' Taste, seemingly.

References: Name checks for the fashion guru Laura Ashley (see **11**, 'Out of Sight, Out of Mind') and Martha Stewart (see **37**, 'Faith, Hope and Trick'), the Beach Boys' 'Surf's Up', *The Muppets Take Manhattan*, *Crossroads* and Lionel Ritchie; allusions to *Terminator II: Judgment Day* ('She's back, and this time it's personal'), *Bambi*, the Smiths' 'Meat is Murder' and *The Flintstones*. Giles quotes Hamlet ('There are more things in heaven and earth . . . than are dreamt of in your philosophy'). A poster of FW Murnau's vampire classic *Nosferatu* decorates the final scene.

Bitch!: Cordelia to Xander: 'Has any girl ever spoken to you of her own free will?'

Awesome!: Loads of cool images (like the close-up on a skull in the opening scene) and Buffy's fight with three vampires in the auditorium is probably what sold the show. Her gymnastic way of getting from the first floor of the library to the ground is a particular highlight. There's a terrific sequence (sadly dropped from **1**, 'Welcome to the Hellmouth') in which Xander shows Buffy around school.

'You May Remember Me From Such Films As . . .': Stephen Tobolowsky, who plays Principal Flutie, appeared in *Thelma and Louise*, *Spaceballs*, *Single White Female* and *Basic Instinct*. Readers may know him best as 'Ned the Insurance Man' in *Groundhog Day*.

'Is The Band Any Good?': Long before their debut on the series (see **16**, 'Inca Mummy Girl') Dingoes Ate My Baby are mentioned. One of Cordelia's friends think 'They Rock!' but Xander tells Buffy 'they don't know any actual chords yet, but they have *really* big amps.' (See **50**, 'Dopplegangland'.)

Dust to Dust: Only one vampire death is seen in close-up and it's interesting to compare the rather slow and ordinary 'crumbling skeleton' effect seen here with the beautifully realised explosion of dust featured in the series itself.

Valley-Speak: Girl #2: 'Chatter in the caf is that she [Buffy] got kicked out and that's why her mom had to get a new job.' Girl #1: '*Neg!*' Girl #2: '*Pos!*'

Buffy: 'I was *totally* phasing.' And 'I'm *way* sure'. And 'I'm *totally jammin'* on your dress'. And 'It's *lush*'. And 'I've both been there, and done that . . .' Anybody think someone was trying too hard?

Cordelia: 'Grunge! Wow! *What* a new look.'

Xander: '*Dudes!* Surf's always up somewhere in the world.'

Logic, Let Me Introduce You to This Window: Why does Buffy immediately assume, when Xander tells her that Willow has a date, that the boy in question is a vampire?

You Can See Why They Dropped *That* Idea: Flutie's habit of calling Buffy 'Bunny', 'Bambi', 'Betty' and 'Wilma'. They would have run out of pun names by episode three.

What A Shame They Dropped . . .: This gem from the shooting script. Guy: 'My parents grounded me! It's *so* not fair.' Other Guy: 'You should sue.' Guy: '*No way*. My dad's lawyer is *way* better than mine!'

Quote/Unquote: Xander: 'Those guys are the Howzers. They'd be total hardcore gangstas except for the Upper-Class White-Guy stigma. Total wannabes, but they're OK.'

Flutie's 'School Rules': 'No gang colours. No fur. No hanging from the rafters in the cafeteria screaming "Meat is Murder" during Sloppy Joe day.'

And: 'We *almost never* have dead kids stuffed in the locker.'

Buffy: 'What is it with vampires and clothes? You always think the march of fashion stopped dead the day you did.'

Notes: Buffy: 'Relax. The world's in beauty hands.' One has to agree with Tony Head's assessment of this oddity – that is, nice ideas and effects (and clearly with potential) but *how* did they sell a series out of it? It's unfair to apply the same criteria to something that was never intended for public consumption as to the actual series, but there was obviously still much to be done.

The characterisation is rather odd too, although Cordelia and especially Xander are excellently played (*love* Nick Brendon's demonstration of Buffy's 'crane technique').

The school is Berryman High, whose football (or basketball) team are called The Bulls. Buffy chews gum (a habit we've never seen her repeat). She is taking 'Eurocentric history' (it's not her best subject). She was thrown out of her last (unnamed) school for 'causing trouble' (there's no reference to burning down the gym). She implies to Giles that her last Watcher died (is it Merrick she's talking about?). Buffy was on the student council at her previous school. She mentions the football team and Xander jokingly asks if she was on that too. She seems to be referring to her time as a cheerleader (see **M1**, and **3**, 'The Witch'). The history teacher is Mr Bron, and Mr Worth teaches maths.

Of course, the series *was* picked up. As Tony Head told *DreamWatch*: 'Several people have said it's one of the few instances where a TV spin-off improves on what people originally knew as the project. It's basically what Joss [Whedon] originally envisaged. He was twenty-one and a writer. He had no real say in the way the movie was made, in the way that writers *do* have very little say . . . I'm just glad to be part of what he eventually got made.'

Did You Know?: 'Mutant Enemy', the name of Joss Whedon's production company, is from a line in the song 'And You, And I' by the prog-rockers Yes.

'We can do this the hard way, or . . . Actually,
there's just the hard way!'

– 'Welcome to the Hellmouth'

*'In every generation there is a Chosen One. She will
stand against the vampires, the demons and the forces
of darkness. She is The Slayer.'*

First Season (1997)

**Mutant Enemy Inc./Kuzui Enterprises/
Sandollar Television/20th Century Fox**
Created by Joss Whedon
Producer: Gareth Davies
Co-Producer: David Solomon
Executive Producers: Sandy Gallin, Gail Berman, Fran
Rubel Kuzui, Kaz Kuzui, Joss Whedon
Co-Executive Producer: David Greenwalt

Regular Cast:
Sarah Michelle Gellar (Buffy Summers)
Nicholas Brendon (Xander Harris)
Alyson Hannigan (Willow Rosenberg)
Charisma Carpenter (Cordelia Chase, 1–5, 7, 9–12)
Anthony Stewart Head (Rupert Giles)
David Boreanaz (Angel, 1–2, 4–5, 7, 11–12)
Mark Metcalf (the Master, 1–2, 5, 7, 10, 12)
Ken Lerner (Principal Flutie, 1–2, 4, 6)
Kristine Sutherland (Joyce Summers, 1–3, 7, 9–10, 12)
Julie Benz (Darla, 1–2, 7)
Mercedes McNab (Harmony, 2, 11)
Elizabeth Anne Allen (Amy Madison, 3)
Amanda Wilmshurst (Cheerleader, 3[1])
William Monaghan (Dr Gregory, 3–4)
Andrew J Ferchland (the Anointed One, 5,[2] 7,[3] 10, 12)
Robia LaMorte (Jenny Calendar, 8, 12)
Dean Butler (Hank Summers, 10)
Armin Shimerman (Principal Snyder, 9, 11)

1

Welcome to the Hellmouth

US Transmission Date: 10 Mar. 1997
UK Transmission Date: 3 Jan. 1998 (Sky),
30 Dec. 1998 (BBC2)

Writer: Joss Whedon
Director: Charles Martin Smith
Cast: Brian Thompson (Luke), J Patrick Lawlor (Thomas),
Eric Balfour (Jesse), Natalie Strauss (Teacher),
Amy Chance (Girl #1), Tupelo Jereme (Girl #2),
Persia White (Girl #3), Carmine D Giovinazzo (Boy)

On her first day at Sunnydale High, the Vampire Slayer Buffy
Summers befriends Xander and Willow, to the chagrin of the
resident snob, Cordelia. In the library, Buffy meets Mr Giles,
who reveals he is her Watcher. A corpse is discovered and
Buffy finds that the victim was killed by a vampire. She argues
with Giles about her responsibilities, both unaware that
Xander has overheard. On her way to the Bronze Club Buffy
encounters a stranger who warns her that she is living at 'the
mouth of Hell'. He gives Buffy a crucifix and tells her that 'the
Harvest' is coming. At the cemetery Willow is attacked by a
female vampire, Darla, who has also brought another offering
to the Master, Xander's friend Jesse. Buffy and Xander over-
power Darla, just as the Master's henchman, Luke, appears.

Dudes and Babes: Angel's first appearance set a million
female hearts aflutter (Buffy describes him as 'dark, gorgeous
in an annoying sort of way'). Darla's cute until she turns all
vampiry, at which point the attraction becomes somewhat
obscure (see **7**, 'Angel'). But Miss Summers in *that* skirt . . .
Hubba. Xander's fumbling attempts to chat her up are a comedy highlight (particularly 'you forgot your . . . stake').

Authority Sucks!: Principal Flutie ('All the kids here are
free to call me Bob. But they don't') seems prepared to let
Buffy's past lie until he reads about the gym burning down.

A Little Learning is a Dangerous Thing: Xander tells Willow he has a problem with 'the math'. When she asks which part, he replies 'the math'. We're informed that 25 million people died in the Black Death and that it was 'an early form of germ warfare'.

Mom's Apple Pie: Joyce's plea to Buffy before she starts her first day at Sunnydale High is, 'Honey, try not to get kicked out.' Buffy says stakes are being used for self-defence in LA as pepper sprays are 'so passé'.

It's a Designer Label!: Cordelia would kill to live in LA to be so close to 'that many shoes'. Buffy recognises a vampire by his jacket, noting that only someone who has 'lived underground for ten years' would wear something so unfashionable. Willow's white tights are functional rather than sexy and her dress was one that her mom picked out for her. Buffy's red miniskirt and knee-length leather boots are smashing, but the two skirts she considers wearing to the Bronze make her look, she believes, like either a slut or a Jehovah's Witness.

References: Cordelia's 'coolness factor' test includes what Buffy thinks of James Spader (*Pretty in Pink*, *Less than Zero*, *sex, lies and videotape*, *Stargate* and *Crash*) and the former TV host and musician John Tesh. There are references to the department stores Neiman-Marcus and Sears, the Jehovah's Witness magazine *The Watchtower* and the 80s pop group De Barge.

Awesome!: The montage that forms Buffy's nightmare (many fans believe these to be scenes from the movie – they aren't). Buffy's fight with Luke in the mausoleum is impressive, though her first meeting with Angel tops it for emotional impact, *and* gymnastic stunts.

'You May Remember Me From Such Films and TV Series As . . .': Sarah Michelle Gellar was a child star, appearing in Burger King adverts as a four-year-old and having a starring role in *Swans Crossing*. She won a Daytime Emmy for her role as Kendall Hart in the soap *All My Children*. Her movies include *I Know What You Did Last Summer*, *Cruel Intentions* and *Scream 2*. Alyson Hannigan was also a child actor, making her movie debut in *My Stepmother is an Alien*. She has had many guest slots on series as diverse as *Roseanne*, *Picket Fences* and *Touched By An Angel*. Anthony Stewart Head will be known to British audiences for his Gold Blend commercials opposite Sharon Maughan in the 1980s (the adverts were also popular in the US where the coffee is called Taster's Choice). He played Adam Klaus in the pilot of *Jonathan Creek* and appeared in two *The Comic Strip Presents* . . . Fans of *The X-Files* will know Brian Thompson as the enigmatic Alien Pilot. He was also in *The Terminator* and *Star Trek: Generations* (playing a Klingon). J Patrick Lawlor has a small role in *Pleasantville*.

Don't Give Up The Day Job: The director Charles Martin Smith is also an actor appearing in *Deep Impact*, *The Untouchables*, *Starman*, *American Graffiti* and *Pat Garrett and Billy the Kid* and TV series including *The X-Files*, *The Outer Limits* and *The Twilight Zone*.

Valley-Speak: Buffy: 'OK? What's the sitch?' And: 'I'm *way* sure.'

Cordelia: '*Totally* dead. *Way* dead.'

'The wiggins' is Buffy's personal version of 'the willies'. Subsequent episodes often feature it, or a variation.

Xander on Buffy: 'Pretty much a *hottie*.'

Willow: 'I could *totally* help you out.'

Logic, Let Me Introduce You to This Window: In the library, Giles piles several books into Buffy's arms, while telling her about all of the mythical creatures that exist. He stacks them so that the bindings are facing Buffy. Before she gives them back, Buffy raises the pile into shot, and the bindings are facing Giles. When she hands them over, they are again facing her. When Buffy looks for Willow in the Bronze, she breaks off a stool leg to use as a weapon. Next time we see her, it has become a stake.

I Just *Love* Your Accent: Giles was the curator at a British museum or, 'possibly *the* British Museum'. His ideal night is staying home with a cup of Bovril (can you *get* Bovril in the

US?) and a good book (see **8**, 'I Robot . . . You Jane'). The producer Gareth Davies worked for the BBC in the 1960s on *The Wednesday Play* (including Dennis Potter's ground-breaking dramas *Vote, Vote, Vote For Nigel Barton*, *Alice, Where the Buffalo Roam*, *Message for Posterity*, *Angels Are so Few* and the notorious *Son of Man*). He subsequently produced *Tales of the Unexpected* and *Boon* before moving to America to work on *Remington Steele*.

Motors: Joyce Summers drives a Jeep Cherokee Sport (see **40**, 'Band Candy').

Quote/Unquote: Giles on zombies, werewolves, incubi and succubi: 'Everything you ever dreaded was under your bed but told yourself couldn't be in the light of day. *They're all real!*'

Buffy's reply to Giles's surprise that the vampire she's tracking isn't dead: 'No, but my social life is on the critical list.'

Notes: 'This is Sunnydale. How bad an evil can there be here?' A great first episode, well paced, superbly characterised (we already feel as if we'd known these people for *years*) and with a wicked sense of humour, 'Welcome to the Hellmouth' is an intricate doll's house of a plot, with many clever moments and knowing winks to the audience. If you don't find something of interest in this, you're probably dead.

Buffy's previous school was Hemery High in Los Angeles (see **M1**). She burned down the gymnasium because 'it was full of vampires' (real reason), or 'asbestos' (official excuse). Xander's skateboarding skills leave much to be desired. Xander and Willow used to go out, but split up when he stole her Barbie doll (they were five). Willow says that when she's with a boy it's hard for her to say anything 'cool or witty. Or at all. I can usually make a few vowel sounds and then I have to go away.' The book Giles shows Buffy to establish his Watcher credentials is an ancient volume called *Vampyr*. When Giles tells Buffy about all of the mythical creatures that exist, she asks, 'Did you send away for the *Time Life* series?' Giles confirms he *did* and that he received the free calendar instead of the free phone. The Bronze is in 'the bad part of town', which is 'half a block from the good part of town'. It is said that the whole of Sunnydale can be seen from the top of the gym, which ties in with there not being 'a whole lot of town' (see **15**, 'School Hard'), even if it has got an airport (see **21**, 'What's My Line?' Part 1). If a vampire sucks someone's blood, this will kill the person being attacked. The victim will turn into a vampire themselves only if they suck the vampire's blood in return (see **33**, 'Becoming' Part 1, though the series occasionally contradicts this: see **46**, 'Helpless'). The vampires refer to themselves as 'the Old Ones' (as does Giles in **2**, 'The Harvest'). The history teacher is called Mr Chopski. The female gym coach, Foster, has 'chest hair' according to Cordelia.

US transmissions are accompanied by a pre-episode caption: 'Tonight's presentation is rated TV-PG, and contains action scenes which may be too intense for younger viewers'. When the BBC purchased the series, they edited the episodes with a blunt hacksaw instead (notably any fight sequences). Overseas prints of the episode do not feature the voice-over concerning two previous Slayers – Lucy Hanover in Virginia in 1866, and a nameless woman in Chicago in 1927. The theme music is by Nerf Herder, whose name is an insult Princess Leia hurls at Han Solo in *The Empire Strikes Back*. The high school used is Torrance High. It's also the location used for *Beverly Hills 90210* and *She's All That*.

Nick Brendon, interviewed by *Spectrum*, noted: 'Being on a network like WB at the time was beneficial for both parties. I think that *Buffy* has helped to launch that network and make it the fastest-growing on TV.'

Soundtrack: Sprung Monkey perform 'Believe', 'Swirl' and 'Things Are Changing' in the Bronze. Another song, 'Saturated', is heard when Buffy tries to decide which dress to wear.

Did You Know?: David Boreanaz's audition scene was the sequence in which Angel warns Buffy about the coming Harvest. The scene was shot at two in the morning 'in some god-awful street' according to Boreanaz.

2
The Harvest

US Transmission Date: 10 Mar. 1997
UK Transmission Date: 10 Jan. 1998 (Sky),
30 Dec. 1998 (BBC2)

Writer: Joss Whedon
Director: John T Kretchmer
Cast: Brian Thompson (Luke), Eric Balfour (Jesse),
Deborah Brown (Girl), Teddy Lane Jr (Bouncer),
Jeffrey Steven Smith (Guy in Comp. Class)

Buffy escapes from Luke and saves Xander and Willow, but Jesse has been taken by the vampires. Luke and Darla tell the Master about Buffy. Suspecting she may be The Slayer, they use Jesse as bait. Buffy and Xander return to the cemetery and meet the stranger who warned Buffy about the Harvest. He introduces himself as Angel and tells her that it will take place that night. They find Jesse, but he's now a vampire. Buffy and Xander escape through a ventilation duct. At the Bronze, Luke begins to drain victims of their blood, becoming the Master's 'Vessel'. Buffy battles with Luke as the others lead the frightened teenagers out of the Bronze. Xander fights Jesse, and kills him. Buffy tricks Luke into believing it is sunrise and, with the Vessel dead, the Harvest is prevented.

Dudes and Babes: Xander's inadequacy when Buffy won't let him help is touching, and makes his actions at the end all the more impressive. Buffy complains about Angel's 'cryptic wiseman act'. For the boys, there's Cordelia dancing. Oh baby.

Mom's Apple Pie: Buffy's mom grounds her for skipping class. 'If you don't go out it'll be the end of the world? *Everything*'s life or death to a sixteen-year-old girl.'

A Little Learning is a Dangerous Thing: Cordy discovers how to save a computer file. Not.

It's a Designer Label!: Willow's dungarees are horrible. *Love* Angel's disco threads. Buffy's Raybans and her leather jacket give the final scenes a touch of class.

References: Luke burning himself on Buffy's cross mirrors a plot device used in many vampire films, notably Hammer's *Dracula, Prince of Darkness*. Buffy mentions Sam Peckinpah's notoriously violent *The Wild Bunch*.

Bitch!: Cordelia: 'Hello, Miss Motormouth, can I get a sentence finished?' Cordelia and Harmony discussing what a 'psycho loony' Buffy is, matched by Cordy asking Willow: 'Excuse me, who gave you permission to exist?'

Awesome!: When Xander and Buffy are climbing to the surface after the failed attempt to rescue Jesse, watch Xander's left hand grabbing Buffy's breast after the vampire reaches out for her foot. The Buffy–Luke fight is sensational.

'You May Remember Me From Such Film and TV Series As . . .': Both Nick Brendon and David Boreanaz made guest appearances on the popular sitcom *Married: With Children*. Charisma Carpenter had a small part in an episode of *Baywatch* (probably the only time you'll see 'Baywatch' and 'small part' in the same sentence). Mark Metcalf played Doug Neidermeyer in the classic *National Lampoon's Animal House*. Kristine Sutherland was Matt Frewer's wife in *Honey I Shrunk the Kids*. Ken Lerner appeared in dozens of films, including *Robocop 2* and *The Running Man*, and was Fonzie's love rival Rocko in *Happy Days*. Mercedes McNab played the young Sue Storm in *The Fantastic Four* and was in both *The Addams Family* and *Addams Family Values*.

Don't Give Up The Day Job: John T Kretchmer was assistant director on the first two *Naked Gun* movies and *Jurassic Park*.

Valley-Speak: Buffy: 'We *so* don't have the time . . .' And: 'God, I'm *so* mentally challenged.'
  Buffy's description of the Harvest: 'A suck-fest.'

Logic, Let Me Introduce You to This Window: Why is that globe spinning in the library while Giles is talking about the

Earth's ancient history? In the computer class, Harmony asks: 'Are we going to the Bronze tonight?' Cordelia: 'Of course we're going to the Bronze. Friday night, no cover.' If it's Friday night, why are they at school the next day? And, as we see, there clearly *is* a cover charge.

I Just *Love* Your Accent: Flutie refers to the British royal family and to 'all kinds of problems' in the UK. Oh really? Wish we had a crime rate as low as California, mate. Giles hates computers, an attitude he describes as 'a bit British', which is pretty insulting to perfectly respectable UK-based Net nerds like this author. And most of his friends. (See **8**, 'I Robot . . . You Jane'.)

Quote/Unquote: Buffy notes that the first time she saw a vampire, she tried to rationalise their existence: 'Once I'd done with the screaming part.' (See 'Becoming' Part 1.)

Luke on Jesse: 'I thought you were nothing more than a meal, boy. Congratulations, you've just been upgraded. To "bait".'

Xander, on how his life has changed: 'Yesterday, "Uh-oh Pop Quiz". Today, it's "rain of toads".'

Buffy asks Giles what he can say that will make the day any worse. 'How about the End of the World?'; '*Knew* I could rely on you.'

Notes: 'Buffy is a Slayer . . . Don't tell anyone.' This concludes the first part with an apocalyptic storyline, a dark atmosphere and lots of cool jokes. You can get hooked on this series *very* quickly.

Giles indicates that the world is older than most people realise and is dismissive of Christianity, noting that 'contrary to popular mythology' it did not begin with a paradise. (This doesn't fit with a crucifix and holy water being deadly to a vampire, not to mention the very quasi-Christian presentation of Hell in the series, the plethora of biblical lore either quoted or alluded to and references to the crucifixion in **15**, 'School Hard'. See **44**, 'Amends'.) Willow has 'accidentally' decrypted the city council's computer security system allowing her access to all sorts of classified material. Luke recounts the last time someone attacked him and survived·

'1843, Madrid. He caught me sleeping.' Things that will kill a vampire (aside from a wooden stake) include garlic, fire, holy water, sunlight and beheading. Buffy has done a little of the last of these, including, in the story she tells Xander, hacking off a varsity football left-tackle's head with a small penknife. (So *that* explains that garbled scene in **M1**.) She beheads a vampire in this episode, using a cymbal (unless you were watching on BBC2). There was an earthquake in Sunnydale in 1937 during the Master's last bid for freedom (since California is on the San Andreas fault, that isn't so surprising; see **12**, 'Prophecy Girl'). Sunnydale is the 'Hellmouth', originally named by Spanish settlers: a portal between this world and the next ('other dimension' references crop up regularly too). When the BBC broadcast 'The Harvest' (as a double feature with **1**, 'Welcome to the Hellmouth'), several cuts were made, including the almost complete ruination of the 'Just say you're sorry' eye-poking sequence between the Master and one of the vampires. Thankfully, Sky left it in uncut. The first two episodes were novelised by Richie Tankersley Cusick as *The Harvest*, published by Pocket Books in September 1997, which included scenes and dialogue cut from the episodes.

Soundtrack: Sprung Monkey's 'Right My Wrong' and the Dashboard Prophets' 'Ballad for a Dead Friend' and 'Wearing Me Down'.

3

The Witch

US Transmission Date: 17 Mar. 1997
UK Transmission Date: 17 Jan. 1998 (Sky),
6 Jan. 1999 (BBC2)

Writer: Dana Reston
Director: Stephen Cragg
Cast: Robin Riker (Catherine), Jim Doughan (Mr Pole),
Nicole Prescott (Lishanne)

It's the cheerleading tryouts, and Buffy hopes to make the squad. However, horrible things happen to leading contenders (including the blinding of Cordelia). Willow's friend Amy, whose mom was a great cheerleader, is an obvious suspect and, when Buffy, Xander and Willow perform an experiment to confirm if Amy is a witch, the test is positive. Amy concocts a spell that will kill Buffy. Desperate to reverse it, Giles and Buffy meet Amy's mom, Catherine, and discover that Catherine has switched bodies with her daughter so that she can relive her glorious past. While Giles prepares the reversal, 'Amy' realises what is happening. She attacks Buffy, but Giles completes the spell. Catherine, back in her own body, unleashes an energy bolt as Buffy kicks out the support of a mirror, which traps the witch in her own cheerleading trophy.

Dudes and Babes: 'You were pretending seeing scantily clad girls in revealing postures was a spiritual experience,' Willow tells Xander, who spends the episode trying to date Buffy, including giving her a chain with 'Yours Always' written on it. He says it 'came that way'. Poor lad, he obviously has a lot on his plate once Buffy tells him he's '*totally* one of the girls' (a reversal of his informing Willow she is 'like a guy'). Let's not forget that Buffy has needs too, as we're reminded by her reaction to an African fertility statue: 'Jeepers!'

Authority Sucks!: Giles forbids Buffy to join the cheerleading squad, to which she replies, 'And you'll be stopping me, how?' Saucy minx.

Mom's Apple Pie: The issue of parental pressure is central (with the implication of child abuse in Buffy's description of Catherine as 'Nazi-like'). Joyce (who is seemingly more concerned with her gallery's first exhibition than with Buffy) doesn't come out of the episode too well, but the closing scenes are well done as she admits she doesn't understand her daughter. She says she wouldn't want to be sixteen again (judging by the uncool 'wannabe' girl we see glimpses of in **40**, 'Band Candy', it's obvious why not).

It's a Designer Label!: Let's start with Buffy's cheerleading outfit (those red sports knickers they wear are *outstanding*)

Many discerning male viewers will also be pointed in the direction of Cordelia's jogger shorts. Minus points for Amy's horrible sweatshirt, with a CND logo.

References: 'Count the ways' is a reference to Elizabeth Barrett Browning's love poem *Sonnets from the Portuguese*. Also name-checked are the LA Lakers, *Sabrina the Teenage Witch*, the biography of Joan Crawford (*Mommie Dearest*), Marvel's *Fantastic Four* character Johnny Storm the Human Torch and HG Wells's *The Invisible Man*. Buffy sings a couple of lines from the Village People's 'Macho Man'.

There's an oblique reference to Farrah Fawcett Majors (of *Charlie's Angels*) when Buffy looks at her mom's yearbook photo and says, 'I've accepted that you've had sex; I am not ready to know you had Farrah-hair.' Joyce says it was actually '*Gidget*-hair', referring to the Sally Fields sitcom based on the *Gidget* novel by Frederick Kohner. Giles gives a precise little essay on Spontaneous Human Combustion.

Bitch!: Cordelia's response to Willow saying Amber is on fire. 'Enough of the hyperbole.'

Willow, when Giles wonders why anyone would want to harm Cordelia: 'Maybe, they *met* her?'

Awesome!: Giles's reaction to Buffy enslaving herself 'to this cult'. Which turns out to be the cheerleading squad. Plus the bits with Amber's hands on fire, and the girl with no mouth.

'You May Remember Me From Such Films and TV Series As . . .': Robin Riker was the female lead in the seminal 1980 horror movie *Alligator*. She's also made guest appearances on *M*A*S*H*, *The A-Team* and *Murder She Wrote*.

Don't Give Up The Day Job: The writer Dana Reston was story editor and producer on the Fran Drescher sitcom *The Nanny*.

Valley-Speak: Buffy: 'Get *down* with your bad self.'

Cordelia: 'You're going to be so very *beyond* sorry.' Followed by a fluttering of eyelashes and 'have a nice day'.

Cigarettes and Alcohol: Willow says Amber got detention only once, for smoking. ('Regular smoking . . . With a cigarette.')

Logic, Let Me Introduce You to This Window: Sunnydale must have the most dangerous parcel-delivery service in America. One would have expected the van driver to at least slow down after crashing into a parked car and nearly running a blind girl down. Maybe he was on a time bonus. Amber's hair is significantly shorter when seen from behind as Buffy is putting out the fire on her hands. When Giles and Buffy arrive at the Madison home, Giles's car is missing its front licence plate. (This 'error' was spotted by lots of American fans, which is odd because in many states such plates are not required by law. The same thing crops up in **26**, 'Innocence', and **27**, 'Phases'). When and how did Amy steal Buffy's bracelet? On overseas prints, the end credits list the band who play the theme tune as 'Nerfherder' (one word).

Motors: A first look at Giles's 1963 Citroën DS Coupé, one of the most desirable cars ever designed. There is no cooler vehicle. Unfortunately, Giles's has fallen into disrepair.

Quote/Unquote: Xander tells Buffy he laughs in the face of danger. 'Then, I hide until it goes away.'

Giles, at the cynical looks the others give him as he talks enthusiastically about the 'cornucopia of fiends, devils and ghouls' that inhabit the Hellmouth: 'Pardon me for finding the glass half full.'

Notes: 'Let me make sure I have this right? This witch is casting horrible and disfiguring spells so that she can become a cheerleader?' One of the lesser episodes of the first season, though it *does* improve with repeated viewing. Giles gets most of the best lines but half the episode is made up of non sequiturs. The black cat in Amy's room ('nice kitty') is a highlight.

Xander has taken several books on witchcraft out of the library. ('It's not what you think.') To look at the seminude engravings. ('OK, maybe it *is* what you think.') Willow describes herself and Xander as 'the Slayerettes'. The sign in the gym at the beginning reads, 1996 CHEERLEADING TRY-OUTS, which indicates that the first season of *Buffy* is set during the autumn of 1996 (see **33**, 'Becoming' Part 1). Sunnydale's basketball team are The Razorbacks.

Soundtrack: 'Twilight Zone' by the Dutch techno duo 2 Unlimited.

What's In A Name?: Willow shares her unusual name with the character played by Britt Ekland in Robin Hardy's dream-like horror masterpiece *The Wicker Man*. The name Cordelia first appeared in Holinshed's *Chronicles* and was used by Shakespeare in *King Lear*. It's also the name given to the smallest of Uranus's moons, discovered by *Voyager 2* in 1986. Variations on the surname Giles appear in England as far back as the Domesday Book in 1086. St Giles lived as a hermit in France and the name derives from the Celtic word for 'servant'. A large number of English churches were dedicated to him, though the name itself was not popular, possibly because of St Giles's association with beggars and cripples, of whom he is the patron saint.

4
Teacher's Pet

US Transmission Date: 25 Mar. 1997
UK Transmission Date: 24 Jan. 1998 (Sky),
13 Jan. 1999 (BBC2)

Writer: David Greenwalt
Director: Bruce Seth Green
Cast: Musetta Vander (She-Mantis), Jackson Price (Blayne),
Jean Speegle Howard (Natalie French),
Jack Knight (Homeless Guy),
Michael Robb Verona (Teacher), Karim Oliver (Bud #1)

When the biology teacher, Dr Gregory, goes missing, the school assigns a substitute, the alluring Ms French. Dr Gregory's body is found in the cafeteria, minus his head. Believing

a clawed vampire who attacked Angel to be responsible, Buffy
sees him about to attack Ms French, then flee in terror. Buffy
concludes that Natalie French is a disguised She-Mantis. Giles
calls a friend – who went mad hunting such a creature – for
details on how to kill it. At Natalie's home Xander is drugged
and locked in a cage in the basement, next to another boy from
school, Blayne. When Xander awakens, he sees Ms French in
her true form. Blayne says she has already eaten the head of
her mate. Buffy uses the clawed vampire to lead her to the She-
Mantis. With Giles and Willow's help, she breaks in and hacks
the creature to death.

Dudes and Babes: Xander is jealous of Angel. Easy, tiger.
Mind you, anybody who has dreams like young Mr Harris
(finding time to 'finish my solo and kiss you like you've never
been kissed before') deserves what they get, frankly. He may
have been distracted by the cheerleaders modelling their 'new
short skirts' (see **3**, 'The Witch'). Giles's description of Natalie
is 'lovely, in a common, extremely well-proportioned way'.
Her slinky black dress reveals *how* well proportioned. As
Xander says, 'It's a beautiful chest . . . dress.'

A Little Learning is a Dangerous Thing: How ants commu-
nicate. With other ants. The sexually charged lesson on the
praying mantis and its wily ways is interesting: there are
1,800-plus species worldwide, in most of which the females
are larger and more aggressive.

School Dinners: The following items are on a notice board
in the cafeteria: 'salad bar, meat loaf, lasagna, sloppy joes,
macaroni and cheese, fajitas, cheese burger, blueberry pie,
orange jello, brownies'. Buffy and Willow are horrified to
find out they're getting 'hot-dog surprise' for lunch. Cordelia
has a medically prepared lunch, prescribed by her doctor
(implication: it's to keep her weight steady), but finding Dr
Gregory's body in the kitchen seems to put her off her food.
Anybody eating during this episode, beware of Natalie's
insect sandwich.

It's a Designer Label!: Buffy's red dress in Xander's dream
and her extremely short, light-blue skirt are impressive, but

the highlight is her yellow stretchpants. Angel gives Buffy his leather jacket. The She-Mantis's fashion sense is described as 'predatory'.

References: Xander's flashbacks bear similarity to techniques used in another seminal high school series, *Parker Lewis Can't Lose*. There are name checks for *The Exorcist*, the legends of 'virgin thieves' (the Greek sirens and the Celtic maidens) and an oblique reference to *Godzilla* and its sequels ('We're on Monster Island').

Awesome!: Buffy's fight with the claw-handed vampire. Twenty seconds of unrestrained violence. Or, in the case of the BBC edit, *five* seconds of unrestrained violence.

'You May Remember Me From Such Films As . . .': Jean Speegle Howard is the mother of Ron Howard and has a great role in his movie *Apollo 13* (as Jim Lovell's confused mom).

'You May Remember Me From Such Video Games As . . .': Musette Vander had a starring role in the *Voyeur* computer game (circa 1991), which received a lot of bad publicity owing to its tacky and voyeuristic nature. She also plays Munita in *The Wild Wild West*.

Don't Give Up The Day Job: One of writer David Greenwalt's first jobs was as Jeff Bridges' body double before becoming a director on *The Wonder Years*, preceding a period as writer and producer on *The X-Files* and *Doogie Howser M.D.* His film credits include the scripts of *Class*, *American Dreamer* and *Secret Admirer* (which he also directed) and *one* acting role as 'Uniformed Cop' in a 1981 horror-spoof movie called *Wacko*. The director Bruce Seth Green's TV work includes series such as *Knight Rider*, *Airwolf*, *MacGyver*, *She-Wolf of London*, *V*, *seaQuest DSV*, *Xena: Warrior Princess*, *Hercules: The Legendary Journeys* and *American Gothic*.

Cigarettes and Alcohol: Xander drinks the Martini that Ms French gives him.

Logic, Let Me Introduce You to This Window: Xander throws a chair leg into a vampire's chest during his dream. It goes into the right side of the chest, as opposed to where the heart is. Since it's a dream, we could excuse this as Xander's naïveté in the ways of killing (though he's already staked one vampire: Jesse in **2**, 'The Harvest'). The door shouldn't be left open during a private session with a counsellor. Dr Gregory's narration on the ant features a slide of a beetle, not an ant. As Natalie eats her insect sandwich, for most of the scene her sweater sleeves are pulled up to her elbows. However, for the close-up of her hands pouring the insects on to the bread, the cuffs cover her wrists. When Xander is tied up in Natalie's basement, he has a flashback to her first class with him. If Blayne was heading straight to biology when Buffy and friends were sitting outside, we can assume that it was the first class of the day. Certainly the group are seen at lunch *afterwards*. However, as Natalie approaches Xander, the clock behind him says 1.45. After Buffy hacks the She-Mantis to death, she wipes the machete blade on the seat of her pants. Bet she caught it from her mom on the next washing day (see **34**, 'Becoming' Part 2). Angel's scar from his encounter with the clawed vampire: although vampires seem to heal quickly (Angel being shot in 'Angel', for instance), this doesn't always work (see **43**, 'The Wish', and **55**, 'Graduation Day' Part 1).

I Just *Love* Your Accent: Giles's former colleague, Carlisle, first discovered references to the She-Mantis in old German texts. He tried to hunt her after boys were murdered in the Cotswolds, but went insane. (Giles tells him in a telephone call that he *was* right about the She-Mantis, but probably wrong about his mother being reincarnated as a Pekinese).

Quote/Unquote: Giles on bat sonar: 'Soothingly akin to having one's teeth drilled.'

Notes: 'A perfect end to a wonderful day.' Quite fun, this one. The She-Mantis is played so over-the-top that it transcends parody and moves into areas of grand kitsch. Isn't the monster costume gloriously pants? Proof that in the best traditions of *Doctor Who* a witty, intelligent and entertaining series can still do crap monsters on a budget and get away with it.

Xander's middle name is LaVelle (he's embarrassed by it). He says he likes cucumber. He's also a virgin (which we *all* knew anyway). The real Natalie French's address is 837 Weatherley Drive. This episode was one of three stories novelised by Keith RA DeCandido as part of the Pocket Books anthology *The Xander Years [Vol. 1]* first published in February 1999.

Soundtrack: Super Fine perform 'Already Met You' in the Bronze. Their song, 'Stoner Love', is also featured.

Critique: *Buffy* received its first UK publicity with this episode, as 'Today's Choice' in the satellite section of *Radio Times* (though it had been previously mentioned in the magazine's John Peel column). It was described as 'a huge hit in the States', a 'supernatural drama' and 'a sort of *Beverly Hills 90210* meets *The X-Files*.' Extremely 'sort of . . .'

Did You Know?: One of David Boreanaz's few previous movie roles had been playing 'Vampire Victim' in a movie called *Macabre Pair of Shorts* (1996).

5

Never Kill a Boy on the First Date

US Transmission Date: 31 Mar. 1997
UK Transmission Date: 31 Jan. 1998 (Sky),
20 Jan. 1999 (BBC2)

Writers: Rob Des Hotel, Dean Batali
Director: David Semel
Cast: Christopher Wiehl (Owen),
Geoff Meed (Andrew Vorba),
Paul-Felix Montez (Mysterious Guy),
Robert Mont (Van Driver)

Giles discovers that a dead vampire's ring belongs to the Order of Aurelius, just as Buffy's crush, Owen Thurman, arranges a date. Unfortunately, Buffy learns that an ancient prophecy, the rising of the Anointed, will be fulfilled tonight and by the time she has finished her patrol she finds Owen dancing with Cordelia at the Bronze. A shuttle bus crashes and all of the passengers are killed by the vampires. Giles asks Buffy to check out the funeral home where the bodies were taken. She refuses, saying that she needs a break. Giles goes himself and encounters two vampires. Xander and Willow alert Buffy, though she is unable to get rid of Owen. Buffy finds Giles in the storage room, and she and Owen fight the vampire, whom Giles believes to be the Anointed One. Enraged when Owen is hurt, Buffy tosses the vampire into the incinerator. Owen wants to go out with Buffy again, but only to relive the adrenaline rush, and Buffy refuses. Meanwhile, the Master meets the *real* Anointed One.

Dudes and Babes: Owen seems a little bookish for Buffy (and Cordy for that matter), despite Buffy's brattish outburst to Giles ('Cute guy; teenage post-pubescent fantasies').

Cordelia on Angel: '*Hello*, salty goodness!'

A Little Learning is a Dangerous Thing: Owen's 'Emily Dickinson for beginners' gives a nice introduction to the works of the poet (1830–86). It's certainly a more impressive overview than Giles stuffily noting that she was 'quite a good poet . . . for an American'.

School Dinners: There's a big discussion on what the 'green stuff' served in the cafeteria is.

It's a Designer Label!: Buffy's green and white dress ('Does this outfit make me look fat?'). Let's heave a sigh of delight for her tigerskin anorak, too.

References: Nick Brendon impersonates Jerry Seinfeld: 'Everyone forgets, Willow, that knowledge is the ultimate weapon.' Vorba sings the hymn 'Gather at the River'. There are references to *Soylent Green*, *The Untouchables* ('Here endeth the lesson') and *Superman* ('even Clark Kent had a job'). Xander has a Tweety Pie wristwatch. There's a possible reference to Patrick McGoohan's 1960s series *Danger Man*, but, as that show was called *Secret Agent* in the US, it's more likely a coincidence.

Bitch!: Buffy: 'Boy, Cordelia's hips are wider than I thought.'

Awesome!: Buffy's fight with Vorba in the funeral home ('you killed my date').

Valley-Speak: Buffy: 'I *totally* blew it.' And her legendary taunt to Vorba: 'Bite me!'

Logic, Let Me Introduce You to This Window: If a vampire's clothes turn to dust when they are killed, why does the ring remain intact? In the first shot of the shuttle bus, we can see the interior lights illuminated. When the scene cuts inside, all of its lights are off. As Buffy tells Giles 'if the Apocalypse comes, beep me', she reaches forward, grabs her pager and holds it up. The next shot is from the side and there is no table or platform on which the pager could have been resting.

Quote/Unquote: Buffy, when Giles shows an interest in the ring of the dead vampire: 'That's great. I kill 'em, you fence their stuff.'

Giles: 'I'll just jump into my time machine, go back to the twelfth century and ask the vampires to postpone their ancient prophecy for a few days while you take in dinner and a show?'

Notes: 'Prophecy. Anointed One. Yadda yadda yadda.' A solid, if rather uneventful episode, with not much to get excited about except for the usual array of great one-liners. The ending, however, is clever as the identity of the Anointed One is revealed.

Giles was ten when his father told him he was destined to be a Watcher (as part of a 'tiresome speech about responsibility and sacrifice'). Giles had plans to be a fighter pilot (or a grocer). At least two previous members of the Giles family were Watchers: Giles's father, and his paternal grandmother. He has volumes of lore, prophecies and predictions, but he says he doesn't have an instruction book on how to be a Slayer (but, see **22**, 'What's My Line?' Part 2).

Soundtrack: Three Day Wheely's 'Rotten Apples', Rubber's 'Junkie Girl' and 'Let the Sun Fall Down' by Kim Richey. Velvet Chain perform 'Strong' and 'Treason' in the Bronze.

6

The Pack

US Transmission Date: 7 Apr. 1997
UK Transmission Date: 7 Feb. 1998 (Sky),
3 Feb. 1999 (BBC2)

Writers: Matt Kiene, Joe Reinkemeyer
Director: Bruce Seth Green
Cast: Eion Bailey (Kyle), Michael McRaine (Rhonda),
Brian Gross (Tor), Jennifer Sky (Heidi),
Jeff Maynard (Lance), James Stephens (Zookeeper),
Gregory White (Coach Herrold),
Jeffrey Steven Smith (Adam), David Brisbin (Mr Anderson),
Barbara K Whinnery (Mrs Anderson),
Justin Jon Ross (Joey), Patrese Borem (Young Woman)

On a zoo trip, Kyle and his gang of bullies are confronted by Xander in the quarantined-hyena house. All of the teenagers leave with yellow eyes and changed personalities, Xander acting cruelly particularly to Willow. Buffy and Giles discover an African tribal legend concerning hyena spirits that possess men. The pack find Herbert, the school's pig mascot, and eat him. Buffy is attacked by Xander but she locks him in the book cage. The rest of the pack are sent to the principal's office, where they eat Flutie. Buffy and Giles talk to the zookeeper, who describes a way of reversing the curse. Buffy leads the pack, including Xander, to the zoo, where the keeper plans to create a transfer to gain the hyena spirits himself. He is successful but is tossed into the hyena pit by Buffy and a recovered Xander.

Dudes and Babes: Willow tells Buffy that Xander makes her head 'all tingly'. Xander seems similarly excited by the sight of zebras mating. He says he's been waiting for Buffy 'to jump on my bones'.

A Little Learning is a Dangerous Thing: Willow's attempts to teach Xander basic geometry are hindered by his possession.

School Dinners: Xander's hunger isn't satisfied by Buffy's croissant or various hotdogs so he goes for a giant, uncooked bacon sandwich. Without the bread. As Buffy asks: 'Didn't your mom teach you, don't play with your food?'

It's a Designer Label!: Ouch! The Rupert Bear pants on the girl walking behind Buffy in the opening scene and Xander and Willow's near-matching Nerds-On-Tour gear. Reference is made to Buffy wearing the jacket Angel gave her (see **4**, 'Teacher's Pet'). It goes with her shoes, she says. It may, but her pink miniskirt definitely doesn't go with the black ski-cap she's wearing in the final scene.

References: The signs in the zoo are in the same font as those in *Jurassic Park*. The line 'all shiny and new' *may* be a nod to Madonna's 'Like A Virgin'. Noah's Ark is referred to (see Giles's Christianity-baiting speech in **2**, 'The Harvest'). There are references to *The X-Files* ('I can't believe you, of all people, is trying to Scully me'), *The Wizard of Oz* ('Oh great, it's the Winged Monkeys'), and *The Silence of the Lambs* ('a bottle of Chianti'). Buffy makes a sarcastic comment about Yanni, the notorious US easy-listening synth-musak guy.

Bitch!: Without Cordelia, the episode is somewhat flat, although Rhonda and Heidi do their best to make Buffy's life a misery in the opening scene.

Awesome!: Buffy's practice session with Giles. His reaction to her aggression is priceless.

'You May Remember Me From Such Films As . . .': David Brisbin seems to have made a career of small roles in blockbusters: he's in *Twin Peaks: Fire Walk With Me* and *Forrest Gump* (as 'Newscaster'), and plays Nicholas Cage's landlord in *Leaving Las Vegas*.

Valley-Speak: Buffy: 'Xander has been acting *totally* wiggy since that day at the zoo.'

Logic, Let Me Introduce You to This Window: When Xander is locked in the cage, Willow watches a documentary about hyenas. However, while the first clip shows a pack of hyenas, all subsequent ones depict African wild dogs (you can tell by the white fur at the end of their tails). Why would Willow keep viewing this, especially with Xander caged behind her? Seems a touch masochistic.

Cruelty to Animals: Two words: bacon sandwich (see **School Dinners**).

Quote/Unquote: Giles, upon being told that Xander has been teasing the less fortunate, has a noticeable change in demeanour, and is spending his time lounging about: 'It's devastating. He's turned into a sixteen-year-old boy. Of course, you'll have to kill him.'

Willow: 'Why couldn't Xander be possessed by a puppy? Or some ducks?'

Notes: 'Once they separate them, the pack devours them.' The silliest episode of the season, though, in a lot of ways the most disturbing. Xander makes an extremely credible bully (it's in the eyes). There's not enough plot to fill the screen-time requirements, however, and what there is is often a bit inconsequential (an act closing with the implied death of a pig is hardly the height of terror). But it's an amusing piece and occasionally scary.

Buffy seems to have an affinity with pigs. Willow knows Xander's blood pressure is 130 over 80. There are references to Buffy rescuing Willow and Xander in **2**, 'The Harvest', and Xander's knowledge of guitar music (given his daydream in **4**, 'Teacher's Pet', we assume he can play, but, see **47**, 'The Zeppo'). The Razorbacks is not only the name of the Sunnydale High basketball team (see **3**, 'The Witch'), but also their football team (using the same name for all sports teams is not uncommon in US high schools). Wretched Refuse are a rock band. The incidental music is some of the best of the season.

Soundtrack: Sprung Monkey's 'Reluctant Man', Dashboard Prophet's 'All You Want' and Far's 'Job's Eyes'.

7
Angel

US Transmission Date: 14 Apr. 1997
UK Transmission Date: 14 Feb. 1998 (Sky),
17 Feb. 1999 (BBC2)

Writer: David Greenwalt
Director: Scott Brazil
Cast: Charles Wesley ('Meanest Vamp')

The Master sends the Three (a trio of vampire super warriors) after Buffy, who is saved by Angel. He tells Buffy that he is attracted to her, and they kiss. Angel suddenly reveals that he is a vampire, and Buffy screams as he escapes through her window. Giles discovers that Angel's real name is Angelus, and he and Xander believe it's Buffy's duty to kill the vampire. Angel meets Darla, who suggests Angel tell Buffy about his 'curse'. Darla goes to Buffy's house and attacks Joyce, leaving her for Buffy to find in Angel's arms. Buffy hunts down Angel, and finds him in the Bronze. They fight. Angel tells Buffy that this is a trap, just as Darla shoots him. During the struggle Angel kills Darla with a crossbow bolt.

Dudes and Babes: Drool factor eleven, on a scale of one to ten as far as *everybody* is concerned. Xander dancing is a bit special . . . In terms of comedy. Darla's 'Catholic schoolgirl' look is disturbingly effective.

Denial, Thy Name is Joyce: Joyce believes her neck wounds were caused by her passing out and falling on a barbecue fork, despite the fact that she doesn't own one.

It's a Designer Label!: Xander's greeny-yellow shirt and Willow's horrible stripy top clash for the worst clothes of the season. Cordy is horrified that somebody has a carbon copy of her Todd Oldman 'one-of-a-kind' dress: 'This is exactly what happens when we sign these free-trade agreements.' She tells Xander to 'please get your extreme oafishness off my two-hundred-dollar shoes.'

References: Friar Tuck from the Robin Hood legends. The Master's line 'out of the mouths of babes' is from the biblical passage 'out of the mouth of babes and sucklings hast thou ordained strength' (Psalms 8:2). The Darla/Angel reminiscences about their past may have been conceptually inspired by *Highlander* and *Forever Knight*. Watch out for a SMOKING SUCKS poster, and issues of the fanzine *Twisted* on the wall at the Bronze.

Bitch!: Xander, telling Cordelia, 'I don't know what everybody's talking about. That outfit doesn't make you look like a hooker.'

Surprise!: End of act one: Angel turns towards Buffy with his face contorted and fangs bared. *Gasp.* One of the most shocking and brilliantly timed moments of 90s television that has every viewer shouting 'But . . .?' at their TV sets.

Logic, Let Me Introduce You to This Window: When Angel hears Joyce scream from inside the Summers's home, Sarah Michelle Gellar's scream from earlier in the episode is used on the soundtrack. Just before Buffy is attacked by the Three, she passes a green-lit window. After Angel saves her, the pair run off in the opposite direction to that which Buffy arrived, but pass the same window. The strange case of the disappearing lipstick: when Buffy takes Angel dinner in her bedroom, she is wearing a shiny-red lipstick; after the discussion about her diary, she isn't. As noted in **4**, 'Teacher's Pet', vampires' healing properties are sometimes spectacular. The cross mark on Angel's chest is missing from future barechested scenes. At what point did Buffy tell Giles about the Three so that he could research them 'from midnight until six'? How did Darla know when Angel would arrive at Buffy's home for her plan to work? Does Darla have an unlimited supply of ammunition during the climax?

Quote/Unquote: Willow on 'speaking up': 'That way lies madness, and sweaty palms.'

Darla: 'It's been a while.' Angel: 'A lifetime.' Darla: '. . . Or two, but who's counting?'

Willow: 'So he *is* a good vampire? I mean on a scale of one to ten. Ten being someone who's killing and maiming every night. One being someone who's . . . not.'

Notes: 'You're living overground. Like one of *them*.' *The* revelation of *Buffy*'s first season. (See **Surprise!**) *Everything* you know is wrong. Beautifully filmed and acted. The highlight of the year.

Buffy and Joyce live at 1630 Revello Drive. Giles is a master with the quarterstaff (except when fighting Buffy). Angel confirms the legend about a vampire being unable to enter a building unless invited (see **M1**), though this doesn't apply to public domain (see **15**, 'School Hard', **30**, 'Killed By Death'). Angel says his family are dead, killed by vampires long ago. In fact, *he* killed them. And their friends. And their friends' children. Angelus is approximately 240 years old and was 'made' by Darla in Ireland (see **33**, 'Becoming' Part 1). He spent decades creating havoc in Europe (the Master regards him as 'the most vicious creature I ever met'). Eighty years ago (actually 98, see **33**, 'Becoming' Part 1, **44**, 'Amends') he left Europe after killing a Romany gypsy girl whose clan cursed him and restored his soul, giving him a conscience. He came to America but shunned other vampires. He drinks refrigerated blood, the implication being it's not human (see **11**, 'Out of Sight, Out of Mind', **21**, 'What's My Line?' Part 1, **54**, 'The Prom'). He has a tattoo on his back. Angel and Darla last met in Budapest, Hungary, at the turn of the century; his reference to kimonos indicates they may also have both been in Japan. Darla is approximately 400 years old. (Buffy says she's been 'around since Columbus' but then Buffy's history isn't too great, because that would make Darla 500 years old.) Bullets can't kill vampires, but they can 'hurt like hell'. This episode was novelised by Nancy Holder as one of three stories in the Pocket Books anthology *The Angel Chronicles [Vol. 1]*, first published July 1998.

Soundtrack: 'I'll Remember You' by Sophie Zelmani.

8

I Robot . . . You Jane

US Transmission Date: 28 Apr. 1997
UK Transmission Date: 21 Feb. 1998 (Sky),
24 Feb. 1999 (BBC2)

Writers: Ashley Gable, Tom Swyden
Director: Stephen Posey
Cast: Chad Lindberg (Dave), Jamison Ryan (Fritz),
Pierrino Mascarino (Thelonius),
Edith Fields (School Nurse), Damon Sharp (Male Student),
Mark Deakins (Voice of Moloch)

Cartona, Italy, 1418: A horned demon, Moloch the Corrupter, is trapped in a book. Sunnydale 1997: The computer-science teacher, Ms Calendar, and her students are scanning books on to computer. Buffy finds the book that Moloch was trapped in and Willow scans the pages. Some time later Willow tells Buffy she has met a guy called Malcolm on line. Buffy asks a computer nerd, Dave, to find out more about Malcolm, but he warns her to stay away from Willow. Buffy follows Dave to a computer facility. After Buffy survives near electrocution, and Dave apparently kills himself, Willow suspects that Malcolm is not all he seems, but she is kidnapped by his human acolyte, Fritz. Willow discovers that Moloch has created a robotic body for himself as Buffy and Xander break into the facility. Giles informs Ms Calendar that a demon is loose on the Internet. She tells him that she was already aware of this. In an attempt to trap Moloch, they recant the spell that traps Moloch in his robot body. Enraged, he attacks Buffy, but she electrocutes him.

Dudes and Babes: 'That dreadful Calendar woman' – a technopagan babe ('there's more of us than you think'). How come we never had teachers like her at my school?

A Little Learning is a Dangerous Thing: Buffy: 'Woah! I *got* knowledge!' 'Nazi Germany was a model of a well-ordered society,' we are informed, which is *technically* correct. It was only when it came to the 'murdering half of Europe' thing that it all went pear-shaped.

It's a Designer Label!: Buffy's white vest-type T-shirt and *tiny* skirt in the opening scene. If Giles is ever on the *Jerry Springer Show* episode 'My Slayer Dresses Like A Hooker', this will be Exhibit A. The skirt puts in another appearance later, accompanied by a black T-shirt that leaves little to the imagination either. Her private investigations' dark glasses and trench coat are much more restrained.

References: Buffy's 'pop-culture reference' to her 'spider sense' concerns *Spider-Man*. The title is a homage to *Tarzan* and Isaac Asimov. It could be coincidental, but there are lots of references to *Macbeth* ('I'll see you anon', 'we three', Malcolm.) Xander refers to 'With a little help from my friends', which seems a bit retro for him. Maybe his parents have *Sgt. Pepper's Lonely Hearts Club Band*. Or, given his misquoting 'I Am the Walrus' in **22**, 'What's My Line?' Part 2, more likely *The Beatles 1967–70*. His self-aware 'for those in our studio audience who are me' is a homage to the many US sitcoms that were 'videotaped before a live studio audience' (*Happy Days, Cheers* etc.). The voice synthesiser that Moloch uses has more than a touch of *2001* about it.

Fritz cutting a message into his arm: while self-mutilation is by no means rare (Elizabeth Wurtzel's *Prozac Nation* contains a harrowing autobiographical account of the disorder), one cannot help but think of the Manic Street Preachers' guitarist Richie Edwards and his carving the slogan '4-Real' into his arm during an interview with *NME* in the early 90s. There was a well-reported case about a US Internet couple who fantasised about the man murdering the woman, to the point where she went knowingly to her death at his hands. Had she deleted his e-mails as he requested, the crime would probably never have been discovered. It's possible that Buffy and Xander are thinking of this case, prompting their hysterical discussion about Willow's Net friend (believing she may be 'axe-murdered by a circus freak').

'You May Remember Me From Such TV Series As . . .': Chad Lindberg was excellent as the moody teenager Bobby Rich in the *X-Files* episode 'Schizogyny'.

'You May Remember Me From Such Pop Music Videos As . . .': Aside from a brief stint in *Beverly Hills 90210*, as Jill Fleming, Robia LaMorte's main claim to fame is as 'Pearl' in the Artist Then Quite Happy To Be Known As Prince's video 'Diamonds and Pearl'.

Don't Give Up The Day Job: Stephen Posey was cinematographer on *Friday The 13th Part V: A New Beginning*, *The Slumber Party Massacre* and *Bloody Birthday*.

Valley-Speak: Buffy: 'Let's focus here, OK?'

Not Exactly A Haven For The Bruthas: Jenny's angry rant about knowledge being kept for 'a handful of white guys'. Political correctness aside, there *is* an undercurrent of racial tension in *Buffy*. Has anyone else noticed how few non-Caucasian people there are in Sunnydale? (See **37**, 'Faith, Hope and Trick'.)

Logic, Let Me Introduce You to This Window: Buffy's status changes from 'sophomore' to 'senior', between the records that Moloch accesses and those Fritz is looking at. Her date of birth also changes from 24 October 1980 to 6 May 1979 (see **10**, 'Nightmares'). Buffy attempts to delete Willow's file from the computer. However, when Buffy turns on the monitor, the folder is already open. Watch the handheld scanner Willow is using – it doesn't cover more than two-thirds of the page width, yet scans the entire text of Moloch. How did Buffy keep track of Dave if he drove off in his car? And why didn't she see Dave's hanging body as soon as she entered the lab? Buffy is focused on through the PC camera. If such cameras had a focusing element, it would be manual. More significantly, the camera centres on her. Not possible. The cameras have no motors and, if this was some Moloch magic, you'd think Willow would notice the movement of a nonmovable object. Malcolm Black? OK, it's close to Moloch but what kind of a name is that for a demon to choose? 'Malcolm' is Gaelic – 'the followers of St Columbus'. Four kings of Scotland used it, and it's a character name in *Macbeth* (see **References**), but still . . .

Buffy telling Giles to call Willow at home seems dumb, when she's already talked to Willow earlier about her being inaccessible when she's on the Net. If Willow *was* at home at this point (in fact, where *was* she?) then they wouldn't be able to talk to her. When Giles leaves the library following his discovery of the blank book, why don't we see him through the window of the room he goes into? 'I know the secrets of your kings' – what is Moloch on about? He's become modern enough to hold convincing conversations with Willow, but he's unaware of a lack of kings in the modern world? As in many TV shows, there is a naïve correlation between the Internet and sources of all knowledge. Confidential information isn't stored on the Internet because it is not a safe medium (as the publishing of the Stephen Lawrence inquiry report in the UK proved).

I Just *Love* Your Accent: 'How am I going to convince her there's a demon on the Internet?' is an amusing (if probably unintentional) reference to the UK-based Internet provider Demon.

Quote/Unquote: Jenny: 'I know our ways are strange to you, but soon you will join us in the twentieth century, with three whole years to spare.'

Giles: 'I'll be back in the Middle Ages.' Jenny: 'Did you ever leave?'

Moloch: 'Right now a man in Beijing is transferring money to a Swiss bank account for a contract on his mother's life. Good for him.'

Notes: 'He's gone all binary on us.' Another top-drawer classic and easily the funniest episode of the first season. *Buffy* proves it can do sitcom, taking a technophobe's view of the Internet and having fun with it. Clever and intelligent characterisation (Giles's horror of a world without books) adds a dose of realpolitik to the fantasy elements. With the millennium bug almost upon us . . .

Buffy's Grade Point Average is 2.8, according to her school record, which destroys the whole 'Buffy is doing lousy at school' idea. A 2.8 GPA, while not in Willow's league, still corresponds to C+ or B– level (see **42**, 'Lover's Walk'). Willow keeps a picture in her locker of Giles and herself. Xander has an uncle who worked at Computer Research Development (CRD), 'in a floor-sweeping capacity'. There are references to Buffy and Xander's disastrous crushes on nonhumans in **7**, 'Angel', and **4**, 'Teacher's Pet', respectively. Giles says he has a 'childlike terror' of computers, and still prefers a good book (see **1**, 'Welcome to the Hellmouth').

Cool in-joke: Fritz uses the camera and a program called Watcher Pro Security. Elmwood, where Malcolm claims to live, is eighty miles from Sunnydale. The announcer's voice heard while Giles listens to the radio is, apparently, Joss Whedon. Among the news items reported are all the FBI's serial-killer files being downloaded on to the Net and a fragment concerning financial irregularities involving an archbishop.

9
The Puppet Show

US Transmission Date: 5 May 1997
UK Transmission Date: 28 Feb. 1998 (Sky),
3 Mar. 1999 (BBC2)

Writers: Rob Des Hotel, Dean Batali
Director: Ellen S. Pressman
Cast: Richard Werner (Morgan),
Burke Roberts (Marc), Lenora May (Mrs Jackson),
Chasen Hampton (Elliott),
Natasha Pearce (Lisa),
Tom Wyner (Voice of Sid),
Krissy Carlson (Emily (Dancer)),
Michelle Miracle (Locker Girl)

Giles is assigned by Principal Snyder to produce the annual 'Talent(less) Show'. Snyder forces Buffy and friends to participate as punishment for their regular absences. They meet Morgan, who is doing a ventriloquist act with his puppet Sid. One of the dancers is killed in the changing room, and Morgan seems a likely killer. Buffy breaks into his locker, but finds his puppet is missing. Buffy discovers Morgan's dead body with its brain removed. In her bedroom, Buffy is attacked by the puppet, and he later tries to stab her. They realise both believed they were fighting a demon. Sid explains that he is a demon hunter who is cursed to live inside a puppet's body. Marc, the real demon, straps Giles into a guillotine. Buffy saves Giles's life aided by Sid, who kills the demon, freeing himself from his wooden existence.

Authority Sucks!: The appointment of the new school *Führer* (sorry, principal) gives plenty of opportunity for power-crazed megalomania. His line 'Sunnydale has touched and felt for the last time' serves notice that Buffy and her friends have more than vampires and demons to worry about. And Xander asks, 'Whatever happened to corporal punishment?' (see **M1**). However, Snyder's dialogue suggests that he is less knowledgeable about the Hellmouth than he will subsequently become. 'There's something going on here' seems genuine. At this point he may be on the outside of whatever conspiracy it is that he is most certainly on the inside of by **15**, 'School Hard'. (See **31**, 'I Only Have Eyes for You', **34**, 'Becoming' Part 2, **53**, 'Choices'.)

A Little Learning is a Dangerous Thing: Giles tells Willow, 'Concentrate on reanimation theory, I'll poke about in organ harvesting.' Mrs Jackson's history class gets a minimal overview of the 'Monroe Doctrine', as well as a (somewhat simplistic) definition of the word 'eponymous'. Willow knows the square root of 841 is 29 off the top of her head.

Mom's Apple Pie: Buffy appeals to her mother *not* to attend the talent show.

It's a Designer Label!: Buffy's slip-on tortoiseshell dress is great, compared with Willow's duck T-shirt. But, what *are* they all wearing at the end?

References: Cordelia sings 'The Greatest Love of All' (*very* badly). Originally a hit for George Benson, it's probably more familiar via Whitney Houston's cover version. Xander's cries of 'Redrum' are from Stephen King's novel *The Shining*. 'Does anyone else feel like we've been Keyser Soze'd' concerns the mysterious (and possibly fictitious) villain in *The Usual Suspects*. There's a reference to *The Sting*, while aspects of the plot may have been influenced by the 'Prey' segment of the 1975 TV movie *Trilogy of Terror* or any number of other 'devil-doll' stories (e.g. *Magic*).

Bitch!: Xander, replying to Cordelia's self-pitying whinge that the murdered Emily could have been her. 'We can *dream.*'

Awesome!: Buffy's fight with Marc while Xander and Willow struggle to free Giles from the guillotine. Xander's double-take when discovering Sid is missing. Pure *Tom and Jerry*.

'You May Remember Me From Such TV Series As . . .': Armin Shimerman played Pascal in *Beauty and the Beast* and then became a TV comedy icon as the Ferengi bar owner Quark in *Star Trek: Deep Space 9*. He also has a semiregular role as a judge in *Ally McBeal*. Krissy Carlson has recently joined the cast of *Sunset Beach*.

Valley-Speak: Buffy: 'However did you finagle such a permo assignment?'
    Willow: 'Creep factor is also heightened.'

Logic, Let Me Introduce You to This Window: While Buffy says, 'I'm never going to stop washing my hands', you can hear Willow typing and the computer beeping. However, the monitor is visible and there is no program running.

    Buffy lives a fair distance from school (established by the fact that her mom drives her there each day) and Sid's got only little legs, so how did he manage to get all the way from school to Buffy's house and back in a night? After Sid stabs the demon, the knife is left sticking out of Marc's body. When Buffy picks up Sid, the knife has disappeared. Why would the teacher let Morgan keep his puppet on his desk during class? Where were the rest of the talent-show participants when Buffy was fighting the demon just before the curtain opened?

Quote/Unquote: Snyder: 'There are things I will not tolerate. Students loitering on campus after school. Horrible murders with hearts being removed. And also smoking.'

And on where Flutie went wrong: 'That's the kind of woolly-headed liberal thinking that leads to getting eaten.'

Giles advises a nervous Cordelia on overcoming stage fright by imagining all of the audience in their underwear. Cordelia: 'Euw! Even Mrs Franklin?' Giles: 'Perhaps not.'

Notes: 'I don't get it. What is it, avant garde?' Outrageously over the top, the impression of 'The Puppet Show' is of nearly everyone being out of character; but it's a memorable debut for Armin Shimerman, the jokes are good and the direction is top-quality.

Willow plays the piano, though not in public. Snyder is obviously well read on the events of previous episodes, making specific reference to the death of his predecessor in **6**, 'The Pack', and the case of 'spontaneous cheerleader combustion' in **3**, 'The Witch'. Buffy has never liked ventriloquists' dummies (there is no story behind it, she just doesn't). The day before these events Buffy, Willow and Xander left school to fight a demon. Since this doesn't sound like the plot of **8**, 'I Robot . . . You Jane', we must assume there's at least one missing adventure in between.

Sid says he knew a Slayer in the 1930s who was a Korean girl. After Willow flees the stage during the *Oedipus Rex* sequence, Xander and Buffy move together. Their pose is an imitation of the *American Gothic* painting (see **10**, 'Nightmares', for Willow suffering stage fright again). There's a rivalry between the dancers and the school band.

Critique: Peter Fairly reviewed this episode in *The Journal*: 'Last night, they stretched the plot line, in a series in which the credibility factor is rapidly approaching warp nine, to breaking point. Take a school play, another corpse – Buffy's school has already seen its headmaster eaten alive and various staff and pupils dispatched in unsavory ways – and a moody scholar with headaches whose best friend is a wooden ventriloquist's dummy, and you have a ready-made scenario for Buffy to strut her ghoul-slaying stuff.'

10

Nightmares

US Transmission Date: 12 May 1997
UK Transmission Date: 7 Mar. 1998 (Sky),
10 Mar. 1999 (BBC2)

Writer: David Greenwalt
From a story by Joss Whedon
Director: Bruce Seth Green
Cast: Jeremy Foley (Billy Palmer), Justin Urich (Wendell),
J Robin Miller (Laura), Terry Cain (Ms Tishler),
Scott Harlan (Aldo Gianfranco), Brian Pietro (Coach),
Johnny Green (Way-Cool Guy),
Patty Ross (Cool Guy's Mom), Dom Magwili (Doctor),
Sean Moran (Stage Manager)

Everyone is having nightmares, and some of them are starting to affect reality, but only Buffy can see the strange little boy hanging around school. A girl, smoking in the boiler room, is attacked by an ugly man saying 'Lucky nineteen'. Buffy and Giles learn that the girl is the second victim of the same attacker. The first was a Junior League baseball player, Billy Palmer, currently in a coma. Giles theorises that Buffy saw an astral projection of the comatose boy. Buffy finds Billy, who explains that he is trying to hide from 'the Ugly Man'. Buffy dreams that the Master is free and, when Giles, Willow and Xander find Buffy, she has become a vampire. They rush to the hospital to try to wake Billy. The Ugly Man appears again, and Buffy fights and kills him, restoring reality.

Dreaming (As Blondie Once Said) is Free: Among the night-mares-made-flesh are Buffy walking into the Master's lair but being powerless against him. She also has fears concerning a history test she hasn't studied for, her father telling her that *she* was the reason for her parents' divorce and being turned into a vampire. Giles's two nightmares are probably the most emotionally effective: losing his ability to read and Buffy's death. Xander faces twin fears – nakedness (except, fortunately, for his underwear) in class and a clown who terrorised him at his sixth-birthday party (that this is a dream sequence is evidenced by the swastikas, echoing Xander's earlier comment about being more frightened of Nazis than spiders). Willow suffers from stage fright (as we already knew from **9**, 'The Puppet Show'), while Cordelia is having a bad-hair day and turns into a chess-club geek. Wendell's arachnophobia is understandable once he explains the background and the Way-Cool Guy's fear of his mom embarrassing him in front of his friends is one we've all shared. But, *come on*, who dreamed about giant flies destroying Sunnydale? Own up . . .

A Little Learning is a Dangerous Thing: Xander didn't pay much attention in Ms Tilsher's 'active-listening' class, being more interested in the midnight-blue angora sweater she was wearing. He is surprised to find that spiders are 'arachnids' ('They come from the Middle East?'). Buffy shouldn't find this too amusing ('What am I, knowledge girl now?'). She gets 'astral' and 'asteroid' mixed up. Giles can read five languages. On a normal day.

Mom's Apple Pie: Xander's birthday party sounds like the kind of nightmare many children suffer; but a darker side to the competitiveness of American life is highlighted when Billy is beaten by his baseball coach for dropping a catch that lost the game. Joyce's attempts to convince Buffy that her father loves her, without weakening her own position ('no more than I do'), are hilarious, if a bit scary.

It's a Designer Label!: Buffy's T-shirt manages to take our attention away from Xander's horrible shirt (does he get them in bulk?), Cordy's pink pants and Willow's yellow tights.

References: Visual references to Poe's 'The Premature Burial' and the Grimms' 'Hansel and Gretel' (Xander following a trail of chocolate; see also **45**, 'Gingerbread'), as well as dialogue sampled from *The Wizard of Oz* ('You were there, and you.'), *Star Trek* ('Red alert'), *Cinderella* ('a dream is a wish your heart makes') and *Rosemary's Baby* ('This *isn't* a dream'). *Evita* is mentioned concerning Cordelia's delusions of grandeur. The opera that Willow dreams herself into is Puccini's *Madame Butterfly* (as Cio-Cio-San).

Bitch!: Cordelia's reply to Buffy's panic over how she'll be able to pass a test she hasn't studied for: 'Blind luck?'

'You May Remember Me From Such TV Series As . . .': Dean Butler is best known as Almanzo in *Little House on the Prairie*.

Don't Give Up The Day Job: Sean Moran was one of the dancers in *Grease* (1978). Dom Magwili is also a writer – his credits include the movie *Bikini Hotel*.

Valley-Speak: Xander: 'Which is a fair wiggins, I admit . . .'

Logic, Let Me Introduce You to This Window: When Buffy is talking about her parents' separation, Willow slips her backpack off. In the next shot, it is on her shoulder again. How did Buffy get to the hospital in daylight if she had become a vampire?

Quote/Unquote: Xander tells the clown how rotten he was: 'Your balloon animals were *pathetic*. Anyone can make a giraffe.'

Notes: 'Our nightmares are coming true.' A surreal and well-structured episode with some of the most memorable images of the season. The highlights of 'Nightmares' are in the area of characterisation, subtly playing with secret fears.

Buffy has a red stuffed animal (see **M1**). Her parents divorced last year, although they were separated for some time before that (see **33**, 'Becoming' Part 1). Willow says *her* parents don't bicker, though they do occasionally 'glare'. Given that Buffy was born in both 1979 and 1980 in **8**, 'I

Robot . . . You Jane', it's little surprise to see her gravestone read 'Buffy Summers 1981–1997'. Though, as this takes place as part of Giles's nightmare, it's possible this is his mistake. Similarly, when Buffy sees the Master in the graveyard he says, 'You're prettier than the last one,' indicating that he met The Slayer before Buffy. But we have to ask ourselves if this is a *real* conversation or just Buffy's overactive imagination. Willow has a Nerf Herder sticker on the inside of her locker door. She attended Xander's sixth-birthday party at which he ate a chocolate hurricane and was chased by the clown (we never find out exactly why, or what happened, but the experience has scarred Xander's life).

11

Out of Sight, Out of Mind
[a.k.a. Invisible Girl]

US Transmission Date: 19 May 1999
UK Transmission Date: 14 Mar. 1998 (Sky),
17 Mar. 1999 (BBC2)

Writers: Ashley Gable, Tom Swyden
Story: Joss Whedon
Director: Reza Badiyi
Cast: Clea DuVall (Marcie Ross), Ryan Bittle (Mitch),
Denise Dowse (Ms Miller), John Knight (Bud 1),
Mark Phelan (Agent Doyle), Skip Stellrecht (Agent Manetti),
Julie Fulton (FBI Teacher)

Cordelia's boyfriend Mitch and her friend Harmony fall victim to attacks by an invisible force as Cordy is running for May Queen. Willow and Buffy link the attacks to a missing student, Marcie Ross, whom no one can remember. Buffy finds Marcie's yearbook, the entries in which suggest that Marcie had no friends. Cordelia, having worked out that she may be the next target, asks Buffy for help. Marcie sets a trap for Giles, Willow and Xander in a gas-filled basement. While Angel saves their lives, Buffy and Cordelia wake up in the

Bronze, tied to chairs. Marcie has gone mad during her isolation, and wants to disfigure Cordelia, but Buffy overcomes the difficulties of fighting an opponent she cannot see. Two FBI agents take Marcie into custody, and tell Buffy and Cordelia to forget what happened. Cordelia thanks Buffy and her friends for their help, though she is still unable to publicly admit this.

Dudes and Babes: Naked-guys alert. Plus Angel in leather-jacket-and-vest mode. Xander says he would use the power of invisibility to 'guard the girls' locker room'.

Authority Sucks!: Snyder's hysterical reaction to Harmony breaking her ankle is to tell her not to sue the school.

A Little Learning is a Dangerous Thing: Ms Jackson's English class is doing *The Merchant of Venice*, focusing on 'the anger of the outcast', which is this episode and, indeed, this series all over. Xander's research leads him to note: 'Great myths speak of cloaks of invisibility, but they're usually for the gods.'

It's a Designer Label!: Cordelia says she's having her May Queen dress specially made as off-the-rack clothes give her 'the hives'. Check out Harmony's kitten T-shirt, Willow's Tasmanian-devil T-shirt, Buffy's pink skirt and the peach skirt she wears in the final scene.

References: The writer and scholar Helen Keller (1880–1968), *Poltergeist*, *The Merchant of Venice*. 'Gee, it's fun we're speaking in tongues,' says Buffy, referring to the spiritual state of glossolalia. 'Crush! Kill! Destroy!' was the catchphrase of the robot in *Lost in Space*. On the blackboard, there's a reference to the Irish playwright Samuel Beckett (1906–89).

Bitch!: Even when she's trying to be nice Cordy asks Buffy, 'You were popular? In what alternate universe?' And, in response to Giles's comment that he doesn't recall seeing her in the library before, 'Oh no. I have a life.' And, when seeing a picture of Marcie, 'Oh my God. Is she *really* wearing Laura Ashley?'

'You May Remember Me From Such Films As . . .': Clea DuVall's film appearances include *The Faculty* and *Can't Hardly Wait* (with Seth Green).

Valley-Speak: Cordelia on Shylock: 'Colour me *totally* self-involved . . .'

Buffy: 'I think I speak for everyone here when I say, "*Huh*?" '

Willow, on Marcie: 'No wonder she's miffed.'

Logic, Let Me Introduce You to This Window: As Giles says, 'I've never actually heard of anyone attacked by a lone baseball bat before,' Xander puts a potato chip in his mouth. In the next shot from a slightly different angle Xander is holding a sandwich as he says, 'Maybe it's a vampire bat.' There is clearly something strange going on in the cafeteria, as Buffy's French fries change into a drink during the same scene. After Snyder announces Cordelia as May Queen, he steps to the left as Cordelia comes to the microphone. For the distance shots, Snyder is standing behind Cordelia's left shoulder, but in close-up Cordy is the only person in shot. The board at the Bronze reads, CLOSED FOR FUMIGATION (stock footage from 7, 'Angel'). How does Angel get to the school during daylight? After Marcie slashes Cordelia's face, Buffy kicks the instrument table, knocking Marcie out of the way. Buffy rushes to Cordelia's chair and tries to loosen the rope. As Buffy is attacked by Marcie, the rope around Cordy's left hand comes free. For the rest of the scene, however, the rope is still tightly tied. Why did Marcie's clothes become invisible as well as her body? If it's something to do with their being in contact with her body then why isn't the knife she holds also invisible? How did Marcie get Cordelia and Buffy to the Bronze without anyone noticing? When Marcie goes into the classroom full of other invisible students, how does she know the chair she sits on isn't occupied?

Quote/Unquote: Angel's Byronic anguish: 'Looking in the mirror every day and seeing nothing there. It's an overrated pleasure.'

Giles: 'Once again, I teeter on the precipice of the generation gap.'

Notes: 'Being this popular is not just my right, it's a responsibility.' An intriguing and mysterious opening gives way to a snail's-pace middle ten minutes (full of bad jokes and no tension) before the episode comes to an excellent climax with a powerful series of set pieces. Great direction, particularly during the flashbacks. The scene between Giles and Angel is one of the most well written in the show (Giles noting that Angel and Buffy's affection is 'rather poetic, in a maudlin sort of way').

There's also the rehabilitation of Cordelia Chase. This is very much Cordy's episode and we see a first hint that, far from being a simpering bad girl with mush for brains, she is actually a tough cookie. Her eyes are hazel. She once 'sort of' ran over a girl on a bicycle in her car (she must, therefore, have passed her driving test sometime after **3**, 'The Witch', and prior to this episode). Willow and Xander tell a (seemingly amusing) story about something that happened to Cordelia in sixth grade that involves antlers and a man in a hat. Sounds like quite a back-story to *that* one. Cordelia refers to Buffy 'attacking' her in **1**, 'Welcome to the Hellmouth'. Buffy was the equivalent of May Queen at Hemery. When Giles suggests witchcraft may be involved Willow says, 'We can fight a witch' (see **3**, 'The Witch'). It is confirmed that Angel casts no reflection and that he hasn't fed from a human for 'a long while' (see **7**, 'Angel', **33**, 'Becoming' Part 1). Xander invites Willow home for dinner. 'Mom's making her famous "phone call to the Chinese place".' Willow doubts the Harrises even *have* a stove.

Mitch's dad is Sunnydale's most powerful lawyer if Willow and Xander aren't lying to Snyder. Angel tells Giles that the Master is planning something big (see **12**, 'Prophecy Girl', for the climax to *that* story arc). Salient books of Slayer prophecy have mostly been lost, including *The Tiberius Manifesto* and *The Pergamum Codex*, which Angel manages to acquire. Did he get it from the demon bookseller in **53**, 'Choices'? Giles is currently reading the Hindi text, *Legends of Vishnu*. When Buffy shows Marcie's yearbook picture to Cordelia, Willow's photo is next to Marcie's, which makes the fact that Willow can't remember Marcie even sadder. Page 54 of the textbook at the end of the episode contains the heading: 'Chapter 11: Infiltration and Assassination'. The subheading says, 'Case D: Radical Cult Leader as Intended Victim'. The paragraph begins, 'August 2nd 19XX'. The rest of the page consists of lyrics from the Beatles' 'Happiness is a Warm Gun'.

12
Prophecy Girl

US Transmission Date: 2 Jun. 1997
UK Transmission Date: 21 Mar. 1998 (Sky),
31 Mar. 1999 (BBC2)

Writer: Joss Whedon
Director: Joss Whedon
Cast: Scott Gurney (Kevin)

Xander asks Buffy to the Spring Fling but is turned down. Giles translates an ancient codex, and discovers a prophecy predicting the death of The Slayer as Jenny tells him that portents suggest the apocalypse is coming. As Giles and Angel discuss the prophecy Buffy overhears them. She says she doesn't want to be a Slayer any more. When Cordelia and Willow discover several murdered students, Buffy decides she must follow her destiny, entering the Master's lair alone. Xander and Angel find Buffy's drowned body but Xander performs mouth-to-mouth resuscitation and revives her. An army of vampires attack Giles, Cordelia, Willow and Jenny in the library as the Hellmouth is about to open. Buffy faces the Master again and pushes him through the library skylight, where he is impaled on a beam of wood. With the Hellmouth closed, at Xander's suggestion they all leave for the Bronze.

Dudes and Babes: Poor Xander, he hasn't got a *clue* has he? ('Just *kill* me.') Trying to get Willow on the bounce from Buffy is dumb. There's a fragile beauty to Buffy that can inspire exchanges like Angel: 'You're in love with her'. Xander: 'Aren't you?'

Mom's Apple Pie: The dress Joyce buys her daughter is, indeed, beautiful. Joyce tells Buffy that she attended Homecoming during her freshman year without a date. (*With* 'Gidget-hair'? See **3**, 'The Witch'.) It was horrible for an hour until she met Buffy's father (who *did* have a date). This fits in with the uncool girl that Joyce describes herself as in **3**, 'The Witch', and whom we see in **40**, 'Band Candy'.

It's a Designer Label!: Buffy's grey T-shirt and blue skirt, plus Willow's green trainers and zigzag jumper.

References: Xander describes country as 'the music of pain'. The Master's 'where are your jibes now?' is a question Hamlet asks Ophelia in *Hamlet*. A few seconds of a *Porky the Pig* cartoon are seen on the TV in the room where the vampires killed the boys. There's a quotation from Isaiah 11:6 ('The wolf shall lie with the lamb'). Xander refers to the *Star Trek: The Next Generation* episode 'The Best of Both Worlds': 'Calm may work for Locutus of the Borg.' The rising of the dead and their descending on the library owes much to Romero's *Night of the Living Dead*, while the Master's death may have been suggested by the climax to Hammer's *Dracula Has Risen from the Grave*, in which Dracula is impaled on a cross.

Bitch!: Cordelia being 'nice' to Willow (to gain her help in setting up the sound system for the dance). Well, at least she's honest about it. Indeed, the stunning scene between the pair as they discover the bodies of Kevin and his friends is so well played, it's almost voyeuristic. In no other series would we be made to care so much about Cordelia's loss.

Awesome!: The pre-title sequence of Buffy taking on a vampire mostly in slow motion. Her twin duels with the Master are equally spectacular. The scene of Xander asking Buffy out to the dance is both sweet and heart-rending because you *know* what the answer is going to be.

That **Scene:** Highlight of the episode is the sequence where Cordelia and Willow find the bodies of the boys (see **Bitch!**). Alyson Hannigan, interviewed by *DreamWatch*, noted: 'We did two different versions of the scene where we walk into a room and find a bunch of dead kids. We did the tame version for America and . . . a bloodier version that we thought we could get away with in Europe. We poured blood everywhere . . . It's probably non-existent now.'

Valley-Speak: Buffy: 'What on earth is her deal?'

Xander, on the results of asking Buffy for a date: 'On a scale of one to ten? It sucked.'

Willow, on Xander's revelation that Buffy died: 'Wow. Harsh.'

Logic, Let Me Introduce You to This Window: While Buffy is walking in the tunnels the shadow of one of the production team can be seen on the wall. When Xander asks Buffy to the prom, keep an eye on his backpack. In distance shots it's resting on the bench beside his legs; in close-ups, the strap is on his right shoulder. When Buffy falls into the pool, her arms are under her body while her hair is tied up in a ponytail. But when Angel and Xander find her, her arms are spread out and her hair is undone and floating in the water. Everyone leaves for the Bronze at the end of the episode. However, it's clearly daylight outside the library (Angel should burn to death from the sun coming through the broken skylight). How does Angel pay his phone bills? Or his rent for that matter? (Direct debit, probably.) How could Angel and Giles not notice Buffy coming into the library? Did Buffy *really* tell Xander where Angel lives? (How else would he know?)

Quote/Unquote: Buffy; 'I'm sixteen years old. I don't want to die.' And, after knocking Giles unconscious: 'When he wakes up, tell him . . . Think of something cool, tell him I said it.'

Willow on finding the bodies: 'It wasn't our world any more. They [the vampires] made it theirs. And they had fun.'

Notes: 'By the way, I like your dress.' A staggering season finale, though with some flaws (the Xander/Buffy subplot gets irritating after the superb initial scene). Impressive direction, which features a circular feeling, as elements from the initial episodes are again referred to. One of the finest aspects is the juxtaposition of Giles and Jenny talking about Armageddon, and Cordelia and Kevin discussing their trivial dance.

Willow checks with Xander that nerds are still 'in'. Xander doesn't handle rejection well which, he notes, is odd since he's had a lot of practice at it. Giles finally realises that the vampire Buffy killed in **5**, 'Never Kill a Boy on the First Date', *wasn't* the Anointed One. Among the portents of the 'end days' are a cat giving birth to a litter of snakes, a boy being born with his eyes facing inwards and blood pouring from the sink in the girls' bathroom. This was the first episode to be rated TV-14.

Soundtrack: 'I Fall to Pieces' by Patsy Cline, and 'Inconsolable' by Jonathan Brooke.

Buffy the Vampire Slayer **Will Return . . .:** At this point the production team and cast didn't know whether *Buffy* would be picked up for a second season (indeed, the lateness of the renewal is why Anthony Stewart Head had to vacate his potentially recurring role in *Jonathan Creek*). Therefore, the final scenes have an added poignancy since (at the time of shooting) this might have been our last look at the characters. Fortunately, a second season *was* eventually commissioned.

Did You Know . . .?: Sarah Michelle Gellar originally screen-tested for the role of Cordelia (we get a vague idea of how she might have played the role from her performance in the film *Cruel Intentions*).

'I wish dating was like slaying. Simple, direct, stake to the heart . . .'

– 'Bewitched, Bothered and Bewildered'

Second Season (1997–8)

**Mutant Enemy Inc./Kuzui Enterprises/
Sandollar Television/20th Century Fox**
Created by Joss Whedon
Producer: Gareth Davies
Co-Producer: David Solomon, Gary Law (19–34)
Consulting Producer: Howard Gordon (13–25)
Executive Producers: Sandy Gallin, Gail Berman,
Fran Rubel Kuzui, Kaz Kuzui, Joss Whedon
Co-Executive Producer: David Greenwalt

Regular Cast:
Sarah Michelle Gellar (Buffy Summers)
Nicholas Brendon (Xander Harris)
Alyson Hannigan (Willow Rosenberg)
Charisma Carpenter (Cordelia Chase)
Anthony Stewart Head (Rupert Giles)
David Boreanaz (Angel/Angelus[1] 13–15, 17–34)
Kristine Sutherland (Joyce Summers, 13, 15–16, 23–6, 28–30, 33–4)
Julie Benz (Darla, 33)
Mercedes McNab (Harmony, 25,[2] 28)
Elizabeth Anne Allen (Amy Madison, 28)
Amanda Wilmshurst (Cheerleader, 14)
Andrew J Ferchland (The Anointed One, 13, 15)
Robia LaMorte (Jenny Calendar, 13–15, 19, 23, 25–6, 28–9, 34)
Dean Butler (Hank Summers, 13)
Armin Shimerman (Principal Snyder, 13, 15, 18, 21, 31–4)
James Marsters (Spike, 15, 18–19, 21–2, 25–6, 28–9, 31, 33–4)
Juliet Landau (Drusilla, 15, 18–19, 21–2, 25–6, 28–9, 31, 33–4)
Brian Reddy (Bob, 15, 31)
Seth Green (Oz, 16, 18, 21–2, 25–8, 33–4)
Jason Hall (Devon, 16, 28)
Danny Strong (Jonathan, 16–17, 22,[3] 24, 29,[4] 32)
Larry Bagby III (Larry, 18, 27)

Robin Sachs (Ethan Rayne, 18, 20)
Julia Lee ('Chanterelle'/'Lily', 19)
Bianca Lawson (Kendra, 21–2, 33)
Eric Saiet (Dalton, 21, 25)
Saverio Guerra (Willy, 21–2)
James G MacDonald (Detective Stein, 23, 34)
Jeremy Ratchford (Lyle Gorch, 24)
James Lurie (Mr Miller, 26,[5] 31)

13

When She Was Bad

US Transmission Date: 15 Sep. 1997
UK Transmission Date: 28 Mar. 1998 (Sky),
8 Apr. 1999 (BBC2)

Writer: Joss Whedon
Director: Joss Whedon
Cast: Brent Jennings (Absalom), Tamara Braun (Tara)

Buffy's back from summer vacation, but to Giles's surprise
she recommences her training immediately. Buffy suffers a
nightmare and awakens to find Angel in her room. He warns
her that the Anointed One has been gathering vampires, but
Buffy is dismissive. Willow, Xander and Cordy all realise
that Buffy is not acting like herself. Cordelia and Jenny are
kidnapped by vampires and Buffy is told to go to the Bronze.
Assuming she is walking into a trap, Buffy realises too late
that it is actually a diversion to allow the abduction of Giles
and Willow, as the blood of the people closest to the Master
when he died is needed for his revivification. With Angel and
Xander's help, Buffy tracks the vampires to a warehouse and,
in a whirlwind of violence, deals with the 'issues' that Giles
believes she still has outstanding.

Dreaming (As Blondie Once Said) is Free: Buffy's nightmare features the Master (wearing Giles's face) trying to
strangle her.

Dudes and Babes: Buffy working out. Oh, sweet mother . . . Lads, if you *have* access to a cold shower, now might be a good time. Buffy and Xander dancing is erotic in all sorts of ways but is clearly designed to make Angel jealous. It's actually a nasty, cruel trick Buffy pulls since Willow doesn't look too pleased, while poor Xander is left completely baffled as to where he stands. 'I'm a man,' he says. 'I have certain needs.'

Authority Sucks!: Snyder: 'That Summers girl. I smell trouble. I smell expulsion and just the faintest whiff of jail.'

A Little Learning is a Dangerous Thing: Xander has genuine trouble working out what 'B-I-T-C-H' spells.

Mom's Apple Pie: Joyce tells Hank that she hasn't been able to get through to Buffy for a long time, and that she'll be happy if Buffy gets through the year without getting expelled. (See 'Becoming' Part 2.)

It's a Designer Label!: Cordy's pants in the final scene. *Hot damn.* Willow sports yet another pair of *horrible* tights (these are yellowy-green).

References: The title is an allusion to the nursery rhyme 'Jemima': 'There was a little girl, and she had a little curl, right in the middle of her forehead. When she was good, she was very very good, but when she was bad, she was horrid.' Xander and Willow's 'dumb game' includes dialogue misquotes from *The Terminator*, *Planet of the Apes*, *Star Wars* and *Witness*. Xander refers to Giles as 'G-Man', a nickname given to the FBI and first used (allegedly) by the bank robber Machine Gun Kelly in 1934. Cordy cites Dumas's Three Musketeers as an insult. After Willow points out that they were actually quite cool, Xander suggests the Three Stooges would have been more appropriate. Again, it's possible to spot the influence of Hammer's *Dracula, Prince of Darkness* (both contain a victim suspended above a vampire's corpse so that their blood can be used to reanimate it).

Bitch!: Buffy telling Cordelia, 'Your mouth is open, sound is coming from it. This is never good.' And, 'You won't tell

Slayer

anyone that I'm The Slayer. I won't tell anyone you're a moron.'

Cordy considers that Buffy is 'really campaigning for Bitch of the Year', to which Buffy replies, 'As defending champion, are you nervous?'

Awesome!: The opening: Buffy kicking the crap out of a vampire and throwing him against a tree with a conveniently placed stake-shaped branch with a cheeky, extremely post-modern nod to the audience: 'Hi guys. Miss me?' You've *gotta* love this girl, haven't you?

Subtext: the audience assume that Buffy is addressing *them*, but actually the theme of the story is the fear of rejection and of finding that your friends don't need you any more. Buffy is actually addressing Willow and Xander, and she needs them to say that, yes, they have missed her.

Act Naturally?: A bit of bad acting can slip into even the classiest of productions. When Xander is telling Cordelia not to mention Buffy's Slaying abilities in public, watch the guy in the blue shirt on the right of screen. Is that the most dreadful piece of ham you've seen this side of a bacon commercial? He does another little cameo of scene-stealing a moment later, walking behind Willow as she says, 'A little too good?'

Valley-Speak: Xander: 'Please, I'm *so* over her.'

Logic, Let Me Introduce You to This Window: Watch the tree with the conveniently stake-shaped branch in the pre-titles. In the preceding scene the pointed branch is missing. The morning after Angel's visit, Buffy rides to school with her mom. In the car, Buffy is wearing a pink camisole. However, in her next scene at the school, Buffy sports a white tank top. The pink camisole shows up again the next day. Nobody seems to notice Cordelia or Jenny's absence for an entire day. As Buffy, Angel and Xander spy on the revivification ritual, the vampires gather around the Master's skeleton. The long-haired vampire moves into position; to his right stands the vampire wearing the tan jacket. Moments later as Buffy stakes the long-haired vampire, all the other vampires turn towards her. The tan-jacket vampire is now on the opposite side to where he was earlier. As Giles hangs above the skeleton, his left hand brushes over its ribcage and the 'bones' bend. Buffy's sledgehammer skills leave a bit to be desired. Her first blow destroys the skull. The second smashes the left side of the ribcage. The next nine occur off screen. When we see the skeleton again during sledgehammer blow twelve, it still looks remarkably intact. Did she miss a lot? Buffy tells Giles, 'I put my best friends in mortal danger on the second day of school.' Willow later confirms it's Wednesday. However, Buffy actually put her friends in mortal danger on the *third* day of school, so it should be Thursday. The Anointed One sees the remains of the Master's skull at the climax, but Buffy smashed it earlier.

Quote/Unquote: Hank: 'At least when she was burning stuff down I knew what to say.'

Snyder: 'There are some things I can just smell. It's like a sixth sense.' Giles: 'Actually, that would be one of the five.'

Cordy's advice: 'Whatever's causing the Joan Collins 'tude, dcal with it. Embrace the pain. Spank your inner moppet. Whatever.'

Xander telling Buffy: 'If they hurt Willow, I'll kill you.'

Notes: 'Come on. Kick my ass.' A slow but effective start. Good fight sequences aside (see **Awesome!**), the best bits are the Buffy/Cordelia scenes, which add depth to both characters. It's just a pity that after some fine approach play, several goal-scoring opportunities are missed until the exciting climax. And is it just me or does this episode look *cheap*?

Buffy spent the summer in LA with her dad, partying and shopping. She says she never thanked Xander for saving her life in **12**, 'Prophecy Girl'. Xander always does 'scissors' in 'rock-scissors-paper'. He bets Willow that Giles will need to 'consult his books' within ten minutes of the start of school. He wins, with over a minute to spare. Cordy spent the summer with her parents in Tuscany. Suffering, apparently. Jenny says she went to a couple of 'stirring' festivals (including naked mud dancers, which sounds like fun).

Two pieces of stock footage are used across a scene break.

The first (the front of the school with a bus passing in the foreground) crops up in many episodes. The second shows the water fountain in the plaza. The guy walking away in a purple shirt is Owen from 5, 'Never Kill a Boy on the First Date', which gives us a clue where this came from.

Soundtrack: 'It Doesn't Matter' by Alison Krauss and Union Station, and 'Spoon' and 'Sugar Water' by Cibo Matto (who perform in the Bronze and get name-checked by both Xander and Willow).

Did You Know?: Sarah Michelle Gellar has a phobia about cemeteries. As she told *FHM* (in the issue in which readers voted her top of 1999's '100 Sexiest Women'), 'I used to cry if I went near one . . . The first series was a horrible nightmare, so for the second they had to build fake cemeteries.'

14
Some Assembly Required

US Transmission Date: 22 Sep. 1997
UK Transmission Date: 4 Apr. 1998 (Sky),
14 Apr. 1999 (BBC2)

Writer: Ty King
Director: Bruce Seth Green
Cast: Angelo Spizzirri (Chris), Michael Bacall (Eric),
Ingo Neuhaus (Daryl), Melanie MacQueen (Mrs Epps)

After the discovery of the robbed graves of three cheer-leaders, suspicion falls on two of Willow's acquaintances from the science club, Chris and the ghoulish Eric. In their lab, the boys require only a head to perfect a mate for Chris's formerly dead brother, Daryl. Daryl kidnaps Cordelia during a football game, but Buffy defeats him and Xander rescues Cordelia from the burning lab. Cordelia tries to express her gratitude to Xander for saving her life, but he brushes her off.

Dudes and Babes: Eric's pornography collection is so huge it scares even Xander. Cordelia hangs on to Angel's arm when Buffy enters the library and gets him to take her home – 'I always pegged him as a one-woman vampire.'

A Little Learning is a Dangerous Thing: Buffy is worried that Slaying is interfering with her trigonometry homework. As Cordelia notes, 'I don't think anyone should be made to do anything educational in school if they don't want to.'

It's a Designer Label!: Check out Eric's nasty shirt, Willow's multicoloured patterned blouse and Jenny's tight cream stretchpants. When Eric ties Cordelia up, he lifts her skirt and we get a look at those red cheerleader knickers again (see **3**, 'The Witch').

References: Giles refers to Cyrano de Bergerac while Buffy provides an oblique reference to the film critics Gene Siskel and Roger Ebert. There's a homage to *Batman* ('it's the Bat signal'). Eric sings a few lines from the Temptations' 'My Girl'.

Bitch!: Another episode full of glorious Cordy/Xander exchanges. Cordelia: 'Why are these terrible things always happening to me?' Xander: 'Karma?'

Awesome!: Buffy falling into the grave in the pre-titles. Top comedy. Buffy's fight with Daryl in the burning lab, while Xander and Cordy escape on the medical trolley through the flames, is pure James Bond.

Surprise!: The first appearance of Daryl.

'You May Remember Me From Such Films As . . .': Michael Bacall played Petry in *Free Willy*.

Valley-Speak: Xander describes Jenny as 'dollsome'.
   Buffy's advice on dating to Giles: 'Just say "Hey, I gotta *thing*, you maybe have a *thing*. Maybe we could have a *thing*."'
   Jenny: 'Is this normal strategy for a first date? Dissing my country's national pastime.'

Logic, Let Me Introduce You to This Window: The cheer-leaders were students at Fondren High so why do they have the letter 'J' on their uniforms? None of the pictures that Eric develops matches the shots he took: there was no boy in a striped shirt walking on the stairs behind Buffy; Willow was looking at her clipboard when she was photographed; and Cordelia's eyes were aimed away from the camera for the first two shots, then her hand covered her face for the last photo. How did the keys roll that far under Cordelia's car? Look at the depressions in the earth caused by dragging the body from the grave. Either the ground was *immensely* soft, or the body was that of the world's first thirty-two-stone cheerleader.

I Just *Love* Your Accent: Buffy: 'Speak English, not what-ever it is they speak in . . .' Giles: 'England?'

Quote/Unquote: Buffy refuses to dig graves: 'Sorry, but I'm an old-fashioned gal. I was raised to believe that men dig up the corpses and women have the babies.'

Cordelia: 'Hello, can we deal with my pain, please?' Giles (uninterestedly patting her on the back): 'There, there.'

Giles on American football: 'I just think it's rather odd that a nation that prides itself on its virility should feel compelled to strap on forty pounds of protective gear just in order to play rugby.'

Notes: 'Love makes you do the wacky.' An overt homage to *Frankenstein*, which takes longer to get to the point than it should (in a series as sharp as this, it's surprising somebody doesn't say, 'This is just like *Frankenstein*'), but which includes lots of cool bits that transcend the disappointingly obvious nature of the denouement.

Buffy owns a yo-yo. There are references to Buffy's dance with Xander in 13, 'When She Was Bad'. Jenny likes Mexi-can food (Buffy somehow guessed she would). Willow believes she's the only girl in school who has the coroner's office website bookmarked. Her science project is 'Effects of subviolet light spectrum deprivation on the development of fruit flies'. That sounds a more likely winner than Cordelia's

'The Tomato – fruit or vegetable?' When Cordy asks for help, Willow tells her, 'It's a fruit.' There's at least one issue of *Scientific American* that Willow hasn't read. Angel reveals that he is 241 years old (see **33**, 'Becoming' Part 1). Giles assumed that Jenny spent her evenings downloading incantations and casting bones. In fact, she *does*, but she likes football too. She tells Giles that 'Ms Calendar' is her father's name. This may imply a sex-change operation but as Calendar isn't her real surname (see **25**, 'Surprise') she's almost certainly teasing.

Tony Head's voice replaces the original narrator in the opening monologue.

15
School Hard

US Transmission Date: 29 Sep. 1997
UK Transmission Date: 11 Apr. 1998 (Sky),
15 Apr. 1999 (BBC2)

Writer: David Greenwalt
Story: Joss Whedon, David Greenwalt
Director: John T Kretchmer
Cast: Alexandra Johnes (Sheila), Keith Mackechnie (Parent),
Alan Abelew (Brian Kirch),
Joanie Pleasant (Helpless Girl)

Snyder assigns the organisation of Parent–Teacher Night to his two worst students, Sheila and Buffy. The vampire couple Spike and Drusilla arrive in town but are coldly received by the Anointed One. The Night of St Vigeous will occur on Saturday, the time when a vampire's strength is at its peak. Spike watches Buffy at the Bronze and tells her that he will kill her on Saturday. He then lures Sheila to his warehouse and feeds her to Drusilla. At Parent–Teacher Night Buffy is unable to keep Snyder and Joyce apart and is in big trouble with her mom until Spike and an army of vampires attack the school. Buffy herds the parents into a room, while Willow and Cordelia hide in a nearby cupboard, and Giles, Xander and Jenny barricade the library. Buffy takes on the vampires, including Sheila. After an angry confrontation with his former guru, Angel, Spike almost kills Buffy, but Joyce smashes an axe over Spike's head. Joyce tells Buffy how proud she is of her daughter's bravery and says that those qualities are more important than her problems at school. Spike and Dru, however, are here to stay and end the 'Annoying' One's term as leader.

Dudes and Babes: Buffy worries about whether she has a split end. Some people are just never satisfied. Xander, once again, dances like somebody trying to crush cockroaches.

Authority Sucks!: Snyder says he wants his students to think of him not as their pal but as their judge, jury and executioner.

A Little Learning is a Dangerous Thing: Xander learns a very important lesson in this episode: never rummage through a girl's handbag because you don't know what you might find. It's a little mousie, right?

Mom's Apple Pie: 'In the car, now.' Buffy and Joyce have a mini-argument about Parent–Teacher Night, including the explicit threat that Buffy will be stopped from going out with her friends. However, despite Snyder's attempts to paint Buffy as a troublemaker, Joyce comes to realise that Buffy is a resourceful and brave girl who cares about other people (but, see **24**, 'Bad Eggs'). Snyder now has *two* problems called Summers: 'I'm beginning to see a certain mother–daughter resemblance,' he says.

It's a Designer Label!: What *is* Xander wearing? That shirt should carry a public-health warning. Willow's dungarees also deserve attention. Buffy has a cute purple top. Sheila has one of the same colour, but several degrees sluttier, and an extremely short skirt to match.

References: Spike's bravado in front of the other vampires (see **Valley-Speak**) may be an oblique reference to the famous 'Show us your yarbles' scene in *A Clockwork*

Orange. The title and aspects of the plot are taken from the classic action movie *Die Hard*. The works of the novelist Anne Rice (*Interview with the Vampire* et al.) are referred to in a derogatory way. Spike calls Angel 'my Yoda' (from *The Empire Strikes Back*) and 'an Uncle Tom', a cynical term normally applied to a black whose behaviour towards whites is regarded as servile after the character in HB Stowe's novel *Uncle Tom's Cabin* (1852). There are possible references to the Beatles' 'From Me to You' and 'Jack and the Beanstalk'.

Bitch!: Xander: 'Does anybody remember when Saturday night meant date night?' Cordelia: '*You* sure don't.'

Awesome!: Giles swearing for the first time ('*Bloody* right I will . . .'). Buffy's fight with the vampire behind the Bronze is so good it gets a round of applause from Spike. The massive fist fight at the end has more in common with the Western genre than horror. Cordy's prayer in the final scene is one of the funniest sequences they've ever done and Willow crowning a vampire with a bronze bust is another delightful moment.

The Drugs Don't Work: Spike says he was at Woodstock (presumably he had a tent and slept through the day). He fed on a flower person and spent the next six hours 'watching my hand move'. Snyder and Bob's 'official' explanation for the outbreak of violence at the school is: 'gang-related; PCP' – a reference to the hallucinogenic narcotic phencyclidine, the street name of which is angel dust.

'You May Remember Me From Such Films As . . .': Juliet Landau (Drusilla), despite appearances in films like *The Grifters* and *Pump Up the Volume*, is best known for her performance opposite her father Martin in Tim Burton's *Ed Wood*.

Valley-Speak: Spike: 'Any of you wanna test who's got the biggest wrinklies around here, step on up.'

Cigarettes and Alcohol: Willow says that Sheila was already smoking in fifth grade (age ten).

Logic, Let Me Introduce You to This Window: Buffy and Willow leave their books on the table as they dance at the Bronze. These have vanished when Xander returns to the table to fetch a stake from Buffy's bag. Of course, someone may have stolen them, but why not take the bag too? Why does Buffy not confront Spike when he tells her he is going to kill her? Willow and Cordelia run into a room next to a trophy cabinet to hide from the vampires. When we see them inside the cupboard, the cabinet is nowhere near the door. It is located on the opposite side of the hall. The vampires cut the power in the school, so why is the cabinet still illuminated? Why was Snyder turning off all the lights in the lounge while some of the parents were still there?

Motors: Spike's 'deathmobile' is a 1963 DeSoto.

Quote/Unquote: Spike: 'If every vampire who said he was at the crucifixion was actually there, it would have been like Woodstock.'

Jenny tells Giles: 'You have *got* to read something that was published *after* 1066.'

Joyce's triumphant: 'Nobody lays a hand on my little girl.'

Notes: 'So, who do you kill for fun around here?' A *gorgeous* episode. Funny in all the right places, but with a real tension and menace. The introduction of Spike and Drusilla is the point at which *Buffy* went from being merely a good show to being a great one.

In reply to Snyder referring to Buffy burning down a school building, Buffy says this was never proved (the fire marshal said it could have been mice). Given that she freely admitted to burning down the Hemery gym in **1**, 'Welcome to the Hellmouth', and that she later tells Sheila she burned down more than one building, are we to assume that this refers to the destruction of the old science lab in **14**, 'Some Assembly Required'? Spike's reference to the crucifixion begs the question: were the vampires who attended afraid of crosses? This is the first time that Mrs Summers is referred to as Joyce. Sheila stabbed a horticulture teacher with some pruning shears, which seems to put Buffy's antisocial activities into context.

Spike, also known as 'William the Bloody' (he gained his nickname by torturing his victims with railroad spikes), is younger than his mentor and hero Angelus, who 'sired' him (a term Angel is reticent to explain to Xander). Giles notes he is 'barely two hundred'. He has killed two Slayers in the last century. One was during the Boxer Rising, which *just* fits into that timescale (this was an anti-Western uprising in China during the years 1898–1900). He says that the last Slayer he killed begged for her life. His (childlike) lover, Drusilla, collects dolls. Before coming to Sunnydale they were in Prague. This episode includes the first hints that Snyder, in collaboration with others (in this case Bob), knows *something* odd is occurring in Sunnydale, but that they are actively engaged in a cover-up (see **31**, 'I Only Have Eyes for You'). According to the sign Spike's car knocks down, Sunnydale has a population of 38,500. And decreasing (see **42**, 'Lover's Walk'). The French teacher is called Mr Dujon.

Soundtrack: Nickel perform '1,000 Nights' and 'Stupid Thing' in the Bronze.

16
Inca Mummy Girl

US Transmission Date: 6 Oct. 1997
UK Transmission Date: 18 Apr. 1998 (Sky),
5 May 1999 (BBC2)

Writers: Matt Kiene, Joe Reinkemeyer
Director: Ellen S Pressman
Cast: Ara Celi (Ampata), Henrik Rosvall (Sven),
Joey Crawford (Rodney), Kristen Winnicki (Gwen),
Gil Birmingham (Peru Man), Samuel Jacobs (Peruvian Boy)

Sunnydale's student-exchange programme brings the beautiful Ampata to town. Unbeknown to her new friends, Ampata is a mummy-girl who escaped from her tomb when the seal was stolen. While Xander and Ampata develop a mutual attachment, Giles asks Ampata to translate the pictograms on the seal fragment, but she is frightened by the object and tells him to destroy it. Buffy and Giles discover that the mummy has the ability to drain the life force of its victims. Buffy finds a shrivelled corpse in Ampata's trunk proving that her new friend is the mummy. Giles begins to piece together the broken seal fragments to send Ampata back to her mummified state. Ampata attacks him, also throwing Buffy into an open tomb. But Xander tells her that if she wants another life it must be his, and Buffy pulls the disintegrating Ampata apart in her hands.

Dudes and Babes: A Xander love story that lets us see the sensitive and vulnerable side of X-boy. Ampata's gorgeous and Xander can't believe how lucky he is – 'You're not a praying mantis?' he asked, referring to **4**, 'Teacher's Pet'. There's a severe lack of Angel, however.

A Little Learning is a Dangerous Thing: Willow helps the inordinately stupid Rodney with his chemistry. He says he's almost memorised the 'fourteen natural elements'. Willow notes there are 103. However, since the discovery of the 103rd (lawrencium in 1961), a further eight had been identified by 1998.

Mom's Apple Pie: Is Joyce's pleasure at how quickly Ampata is fitting into Sunnydale society a sly dig at her daughter's inability to do likewise?

No Fat Chicks!: Buffy is seen drinking a can of (non-diet) Pepsi. She should have a look over her shoulder at the three girls with enormous bottoms who wobble through shot and reflect on America, the land of the pancake breakfast.

It's a Designer Label!: Good stuff: Buffy's very low-cut top in the scenes investigating Rodney's disappearance and her kick-boxing vest and stretchpants, Ampata's night shorts, Cordelia's blue miniskirt. *Very* bad stuff: Buffy's 'whitetrash' look, Willow's bobble-hat. Willow's Eskimo costume could also be a contender but it seems to do something for Oz, so the jury is still out on that one. Xander says lederhosen makes his calves look fat. There's also a delicious double entendre between Buffy and Giles over the word 'trunks'.

References: Willow makes specific reference to the mummy-film genre and the plot bears a slight similarity to Hammer's *Blood From the Mummy's Tomb*. Buffy makes a pun concerning *Mommie Dearest*. The name of Oz's band, Dingoes Ate My Baby, is a reference to the case of an Australian mother, Lindy Chamberlain, wrongly imprisoned for murdering her infant daughter. Readers may be familiar with the film dramatisation *A Cry in the Dark*. Xander's '*Ay carumba*' is a probable nod to *The Simpsons*, while 'I am from the country of Leone – it's in Italy pretending to be Montana' identifies somebody as a fan of Sergio Leone's spaghetti Westerns.

Bitch!: Cordelia on Willow's Eskimo suit: 'Near *faux pas*. I nearly wore the same thing.'

Awesome!: A big girly cat fight. Encore! Also Xander's fight with the bodyguard is rather good (if short). He's beginning to be able to handle himself (in a Xander kind of way . . .).

'You May Remember Me From Such Films and TV Series As . . .': Seth Green's movies include *Stephen King's It*, *Radio Days*, *Can't Hardly Wait*, *Idle Hands*, *Enemy of the State*, *Austin Powers: International Man of Mystery*, *Austin Powers: The Spy Who Shagged Me* (as Scott Evil) and *My Stepmother is an Alien* (as Alyson Hannigan's boyfriend). He played a very Oz-like character in the *X-Files* episode 'Deep Throat'. Seth's a great actor and his (often understated) contribution to *Buffy* can't be praised highly enough. 'He can *own* a scene he has no lines in,' notes Joss Whedon. Danny Strong plays Juke Box Boy in *Pleasantville* and appeared in *Saved By the Bell: The New Class*.

Valley-Speak: Buffy: 'It's the *über*-suck.'

Cordelia on her Swedish exchange student: 'Isn't he lunchable?'

Logic, Let Me Introduce You to This Window: When Buffy opens Ampata's trunk the head of the mummified corpse is on the right. Later when she opens the trunk for a second time, it's moved to the left. With Rodney Munson attending how could Buffy and Sheila (see **15**, 'School Hard') be the two 'worst students in school'? (With Snyder you get the feeling it's all about appearances.) Xander and Ampata sit on the benches with Xander's bag lying on the seat in front of them. When the bodyguard attacks them the bag is knocked off and lands on a footrest. When Xander gets up and runs off with Ampata, the bag has returned to its original position. Ampata tells Buffy that she doesn't have any lipstick. However, she applied some in the school restroom. In the museum Giles is about to reassemble the final piece of the seal when Ampata grabs it from him. In the next shot the seal appears whole, just before Ampata smashes it. Given that Cordelia has a book showing (presumably) all of the exchange students it's a surprise that nobody questions Ampata's credentials. How well could Xander drive so soon after almost having his life force sucked out of him? Given that Xander can drive in this episode why does he need Cordelia to give him a lift in **21**, 'What's My Line?' Part 1?

Quote/Unquote: Buffy's sarcastic impression of Giles: 'I'm so stuffy, give me a scone.'

What impresses Oz in a girl involves 'a feather boa and theme from *Summer Place*'.

Xander on Sunnydale bus depot: 'What better way to welcome somebody to our country than the stench of urine?' And: 'We're in the Crime Club, which is kind of like the Chess Club. Only with Crime. And no Chess.'

Notes: 'I can translate salivating boy talk.' Nobody ever sets out to make a deliberately bad hour of television, but sometimes nothing goes according to plan. This is one such instance. 'Inca Mummy Girl' is a dreadfully uneven story which lacks explanations, a focus and a degree of rationality. The direction, on the other hand, is terrific so at least this hollow tale of unrequited love and betrayal isn't a complete loss. But it's ugly and depressing stuff.

Xander claims his dad tried to give him to some Armenians. He can drive and knows approximately four words of

Spanish ('*dorritos*', 'Chihuahua' and '*Ay carumba*'). Buffy refers to how upset she was at the prophecy of her death in **12**, 'Prophecy Girl'. During the dance at the Bronze, a 'WP' sticker is seen representing the band Widespread Panic (these stickers crop up in several episodes, so it's fair to assume somebody on the production team is a fan). This episode was one of the stories novelised by Keith RA DeCandido in the Pocket Books anthology *The Xander Years [Vol. 1]* published in February 1999.

Soundtrack: The Dingoes Ate My Baby songs, 'Shadows' and 'Fate', are by Four Star Mary.

17
Reptile Boy

US Transmission Date: 13 Oct. 1997
UK Transmission Date: 25 Apr. 1998 (Sky),
6 May 1999 (BBC2)

Writer: David Greenwalt
Director: David Greenwalt
Cast: Greg Vaughan (Richard), Todd Babcock (Tom),
Jordana Spiro (Callie), Robin Atkin-Downes (Machida),
Christopher Dahlberg (Tackle), Jason Posey (Linebacker),
Coby Bell (Young Man)

Buffy discovers a bracelet in the graveyard. She accepts Cordelia's invitation to a fraternity house party, much to Xander and Willow's surprise. While Buffy and Cordelia attend the party Willow discovers that the bracelet belonged to a missing student called Callie. When confronted by Giles and Angel, Willow tells them where Buffy is. Xander gatecrashes the party but is humiliated and thrown out. Buffy is drugged and passes out, waking chained up next to Cordelia and Callie in the basement. They discover that the fraternity is a cult who worship a snake-demon called Machida, to whom the girls are to be offered as sacrifices. Giles, Angel and

Xander invade the ceremony just as Buffy frees herself and kills Machida.

Dudes and Babes: Buffy says her dreams about Angel contain 'surround sound'. You and just about every other female on the planet, girl. Plus frat party! Babes!

Authority Sucks!: Giles's chastising Buffy ('And don't think sitting there pouting is going to get to me because it won't') is worthy of Joyce. Or Snyder.

A Little Learning is a Dangerous Thing: Willow explains the plot of the Hindi movie she, Xander and Buffy are watching on Channel 59: 'She's sad because her lover gave her twelve gold coins, but then the wizard cut open the bag of salt and now the dancing minions have nowhere to put their big maypole fish thing . . .'

It's a Designer Label!: A nice collection of miniskirts – Cordelia's blue one we've seen before; Buffy's green effort also looks familiar; but Willow's dark-purple skirt is a beaut. Cordelia states that Buffy shouldn't wear black, silk, chiffon or Spandex to the frat party as these are Cordelia's trademarks. She also tells Buffy not to 'do that thing with your hair'.

References: Herman's Hermits 'There's a Kind of Hush', Nancy Sinatra's 'These Boots Are Made for Walkin'', *The Incredible Hulk, Godzilla* and the *Superman* comics ('You could go on to live among rich and powerful men . . . In Bizarro World').

Bitch!: Cordelia tries being friendly. 'Buffy, it's like we're sisters. With *really different hair*.'

Awesome!: Buffy taking on the entire frat coven *and* the snake-demon while Xander, Angel and Giles muck about upstairs with the varsity footballers. Stylish!

'You May Remember Me From Such TV Series As . . .': Robin Atkin-Downes, hiding inside the snake costume, is best known as the poetry-spouting telepath Byron in *Babylon 5*.

Valley-Speak: Tom: 'And you are?' Buffy: '. . . *So* not interested.'

Cigarettes and Alcohol: Buffy and Cordelia both drink in this episode. The implication is that it's the first time Buffy has ever had alcohol (though after a summer of partying mentioned in **13**, 'When She Was Bad', you've got to wonder what sort of parties she gets invited to).

Logic, Let Me Introduce You to This Window: The student lounge seems to have the quickest Coke machine in the world. Willow buys a can of Coca-Cola Classic, which is delivered almost before the coins have left her hand. What kind of glass was that balcony door made of? Callie just runs through it. Greg Vaughan's name is misspelled as 'Vaughn' in the opening credits. Willow asks a question that most of us have been *dying* for *someone* to articulate for years. If Angel casts no reflection then how does he (and other vampires) shave? Sadly, she doesn't get an answer. Why does Buffy wear black to the party when Cordelia specifically asked her not to? Or perhaps we shouldn't need to ask!

Motors: Cordelia's car is a red Chrysler Sebring convertible with the licence plate 'Queen C'.

Quote/Unquote: Angel: 'This isn't some fairy tale. When I kiss you, you don't wake up from a deep sleep and live happily ever after.' Buffy: 'When you kiss me, I want to die.'

Willow's rant at Giles and Angel: 'She's sixteen going on forty. And *you* . . . You're going to live for ever – you don't have time for a cup of coffee?'

Xander's beating up the frat boy who made him dance in women's clothes: 'And *that's* for the last sixteen and a half years.'

Notes: 'Party's over, jerkwater.' Two substandard episodes in a row. A pity, really, as a lot of the ideas in this one are very good and Greenwalt's script is well structured. But . . . it's just so *obvious*. And the acting of a lot of the nonregulars is really poor.

The local paper is called the *Sunnydale Press*.

Soundtrack: 'Wolves' by Shawn Clement and Sean Murray, 'Bring Me On' by Act of Faith, and 'She' by Louie Says.

18

Halloween

US Transmission Date: 27 Oct. 1997
UK Transmission Date: 2 May 1998 (Sky)

Writer: Carl Ellsworth
Director: Bruce Seth Green
Cast: Abigail Gershman (Girl)

Halloween, a traditionally quiet time in the supernatural community, is interrupted by the opening of a new costume store owned by a warlock, Ethan Rayne. Forced by Snyder into accompanying groups of children on their trick-or-treating, Buffy, Xander and Willow find themselves in a clothes-created nightmare as Rayne's spell transforms people into the reality of their costumes. While the children turn into monsters and ghouls, Xander becomes a soldier, Willow emerges from her body as an intangible ghost and Buffy becomes a helpless noblewoman. Willow leaves Xander and Buffy with the unaffected Cordelia to get Giles's help. Angel arrives, but is confused by the transformations and frightens Buffy, who runs from the house and hides in a warehouse, pursued by Spike, who is about to kill Buffy when Giles forces his 'old mate' Ethan to reverse the spell. Later, Buffy and Angel finally spend some time together and share a kiss. Giles finds a note on the counter of Ethan's shop saying 'Be seeing you'.

Dudes and Babes: Buffy and Angel kissing at the climax. Aaah. Buffy tells Giles that Ms Calendar thinks he is 'a babe' and 'a hunk of burning . . . something'. Giles wants to know 'of what?' Of course, it's a lie to allow Willow to steal the Watcher Diaries, but Giles doesn't seem too displeased by it. Plus Cordelia in her pussycat costume.

Authority Sucks!: Snyder 'volunteers' Xander, Buffy and Willow for Halloween chaperone patrol duty. 'Just bring them back in one piece and I won't expel you.'

A Quiet Night In?: The subversion of the idea that Halloween is a festival for the undead by having them all 'stay home' that night and let the children get on with it!

It's a Designer Label!: Xander likes his women in Spandex but 'completely renounces it' when he sees Buffy in the eighteenth-century dress. It's certainly preferable to the chequered flares she wears to school, which are a crime against humanity. Willow's 'hooker' look is effective but she's right: it isn't her (though again it gets Oz's attention).

References: Name checks for the Care Bears, *Xena: Warrior Princess* (a compliment *Xena* recently returned referring to 'Buffus the Bachae Slayer'), Catwoman (from *Batman*), an oblique reference to US sitcoms clichés ('Hi honey, I'm home') and a misquote from *The Godfather*. 'Be seeing you' echoes the catchphrase of *The Prisoner*.

Bitch!: Cordelia on Buffy after a fight: '*Love* that hair. It screams "street urchin".'

Awesome!: The black-and-white camcorder footage of Buffy's fight with the vampire in the pumpkin patch. Giles's beating up of Ethan is very effective, but the best bit of the episode is Giles's reaction to Willow walking through the wall – pure comedy (and *what* was that he almost said?).

Surprise!: Giles's entire conversation with Ethan ('Hello, Ripper!') despite being nothing more than innuendo just screams 'back-story alert . . .'

'You May Remember Me From Such Films and TV Series As . . .': Robin Sachs (Rayne) was in one of this author's favourite films, Hammer's notoriously sexy *Vampire Circus*. *Babylon 5* fans will recognise him from his appearances as Hedronn. He also appeared as the Silver Surfer in *The Fantastic Four*.

Valley-Speak: Cordelia to Angel: 'Is the Bronze *so* not happening?'

Logic, Let Me Introduce You to This Window: When Buffy slams Larry against the drinks machine, a Diet Dr Pepper falls out. However, this was not a choice according to the selection buttons (see **55**, 'Graduation Day' Part 1). While reviewing the video of Buffy's fight Spike orders the vampire with the remote control to rewind. At this point both Buffy and the vampire are standing and fighting. However, after the tape is 'rewound', Buffy has the vampire on the ground and is raising the wooden sign for the death blow. Perhaps he hit 'fast forward' by mistake. Vampires cast no reflection in a mirror (see **11**, 'Out of Sight, Out of Mind'), so how do they appear on video tape, which uses mirrors as part of the focusing/viewfinding mechanism (see **46**, 'Helpless')? After Giles tells Willow to leave when he confronts Ethan, you can see Willow bump a curtain and hear her close the door despite her supposedly being an intangible ghost. If the editing during the sequence in the warehouse is done in real-time, then why does Giles hold the sculpture over his head for so long?

I Just *Love* Your Accent: Aside from the episode featuring two fine British actors, the van that Oz drives has its steering wheel on the right, which suggests it's also British.

Quote/Unquote: Xander: 'A black eye heals, but cowardice has an unlimited shelf life.'

Spike on the mayhem Ethan has caused: 'This is just . . . neat!'

Cordelia's reaction to Willow telling her that she isn't a cat, she's in high school and that they are her friends, well sort of . . .: 'That's nice Willow. And you went mental *when* . . .?'

Notes: 'This could be a situation.' One of the best of the season, showing that *Buffy* had come out of the lethargy of the previous episodes with a vengeance. A story about perception with a cool subplot in which the clothes, literally, maketh the man (or The Slayer). Plus an icy-cold yet very funny performance from

Robin Sachs. Willow gets to do all the groovy detection stuff, Xander becomes macho and Buffy faints a lot. What more could one ask for?

This episode answers the question of whether or not Cordelia knew about Angel's vampirism. Amusingly, she appears not to have known. Giles says he has many relaxing hobbies including cross-referencing. The dark hints about his past would be explored further in **20**, 'The Dark Age'. Cordelia is still dating Dingoes Ate My Baby's singer, Devon (see **16**, 'Inca Mummy Girl'), although a break-up may be on the cards given her conversation with Oz. Angel was eighteen in 1775 which (just) fits in with his being 241 in 1997 (but see **33**, 'Becoming' Part 1). This episode was novelised as part of *The Angel Chronicles Vol. 2* by Richie Tankersley for Pocket Books, published in January 1999.

Soundtrack: 'Shy' by Epperley and 'How She Died' by Treble Charger.

Head On . . .: One of the great things about interviews with Tony Head are his insights into Giles's view of Buffy and her friends, as he told *DreamWatch*'s Paul Simpson: 'I think Giles likes Buffy, but she annoys him. The mere fact that she doesn't want the job that he's offering her – she frustrates him. She represents everything he doesn't understand. Ultimately he becomes extremely fond of her. People have said, what is it? A father/daughter relationship? And it's not quite. There's nothing like it on TV. It's difficult to pigeonhole. He becomes extremely fond of her and gets into all sorts of terrible trouble because of it . . . Xander is a complete anathema to him. A great annoyance because he never seems to take anything seriously. Cordelia is . . . Who knows where she's coming from? Willow he respects greatly, but it's all a confusion to him. He's never really sure of anybody or anything. The only thing he is sure about is what he's supposed to do.'

19

Lie to Me

US Transmission Date: 3 Nov. 1997
UK Transmission Date: 9 May 1998 (Sky)

Writer: Joss Whedon
Director: Joss Whedon
Cast: Jason Behr (Billy Fordham), Jarrad Paul (Marvin),
Will Rothhaar (James)

Billy 'Ford' Fordham, Buffy's boyfriend at Hemery, arrives
in Sunnydale. At the Bronze, Buffy introduces Angel to Ford
but the situation is awkward. Outside, Buffy hears a scuffle
and sends Ford back while she confronts a vampire. She
makes up a story explaining her actions, but Ford simply says
that he knows she is The Slayer. After Buffy goes home, Ford
returns to a club full of groupies who dream of joining the
undead. Angel asks Willow to find out what she can about
Ford. She discovers that he never registered at Sunnydale
High, confirming Angel's suspicions. Buffy and Ford
encounter two vampires. Ford tackles the female, but instead
of staking her he lets her go. At the library the female vampire whom Ford supposedly killed attacks Buffy and Giles to
steal a book. Ford meets Spike and offers him The Slayer in
exchange for immortality. Buffy goes to the club and while
they wait for Spike to arrive she tries to reason with Ford,
who reveals he has incurable brain cancer. Spike and his
cohorts arrive and begin to feed. Buffy grabs Drusilla and tells
Spike to let the clubbers go. Later, Buffy returns and finds
Ford's body. Buffy and Giles attend Ford's grave and discuss
the complexities of life. Ford rises from the dead and Buffy
kills him.

Dudes and Babes: The idea of a goth club full of vampire wor-
shippers would be *so* cool if only Ford's friends weren't such a
bunch of dweebs. Especially Marvin in that cape. Willow, on
why Angel was in her room: 'Ours is a forbidden love!'

A Little Learning is a Dangerous Thing: Cordelia says she can relate to Marie Antoinette (the executed wife of King Louis XVI of France). Unfortunately she gets 'oppressed' and 'depressed' mixed up.

It's a Designer Label!: Willow's high-collared blouse in the Bronze. Giles claims not to have any clothes other than those he wears to school (which, judging by the stripy tie he takes to his date with Jenny, seems to be true). And what about Xander's red Adidas top and Ford's orange shirt? Chanterelle's low-cut red dress is a definite highlight.

References: The film that Ford is so fascinated by is a 1973 TV-movie adaptation of *Dracula* starring Jack Palance. Buffy notes that when Ford ignored her in fifth grade she sat around in her room for months 'listening to that Divinyls song "I Touch Myself".' Before adding, 'Of course I had no idea what it was about.' For anybody who *doesn't* know, it was about masturbation and was a worldwide hit in 1991. Joss Whedon seems to be a fan of the Doors judging by frequent references to 'The End' ('This is the end') and a misquote from 'Five to One' ('No one gets out of here alive').

Awesome!: The pre-title sequence, Angel and Drusilla in the playground, is about as sinister as *Buffy* has ever got. I'm sure we've *all* got people we'd like to shout 'lying scumbag' at, as Buffy does to Ford, so *that's* a satisfying moment.

Don't Give Up The Day Job: The make-up supervisor, Todd McIntosh, has a cameo in the club as the man dressed as a vampire standing in a coffin who says 'Hi' to Xander.

Valley-Speak: Buffy: 'Willow, do we have to be in total share mode?'

Logic, Let Me Introduce You to This Window: Before they leave for the club, Spike gives specific orders to all the vampires to make The Slayer their first priority. When they enter, however, they attack everybody *but* The Slayer. When Buffy fights in the alley behind the Bronze as Ford watches, pay attention to the length of her hair. From behind it seems much longer than Buffy's normal shoulder-length (it's very obviously Sarah's stunt double Sophia Crawford). Yet again we don't get to see Willow's parents, though we do hear her mom's voice. It's also worth asking exactly *when* (and *how*) Ford worked out Buffy is The Slayer? Remember, when he first tells her he knows, he hasn't met Spike at that point. It's midnight when Giles phones Britain where, he says, it's 5 a.m. However, the West Coast of the USA is *eight* hours behind UK time.

Quote/Unquote: Xander upon learning that the vampires are known as 'the lonely ones': 'We usually call them "the nasty, pointy, bitey ones".'

Drusilla on Angel's infatuation with Buffy: 'Your heart *stinks* of her.'

Buffy on the stupidity of the club teenagers: 'Spike and all of his friends are going to be pigging out at the All You Can Eat Moron Bar.'

Notes: 'I know you're The Slayer.' This one potters along for a while seemingly concerned with jealousy, before becoming an essay on betrayal and obsession (the juxtaposition of what Angel did in the past to Drusilla, with Billy's attempted manipulation of Buffy, is nicely realised). Highlights include Angel entering Willow's house for the first time.

Ford was Buffy's fifth-grade crush (though he was a year older). Something embarrassing seems to have happened to Buffy during the swimsuit section of her ninth-grade beauty contest. Willow has upgraded from a desktop computer to a laptop sometime between **8**, 'I Robot . . . You Jane', and this episode. Angel was obsessed by Drusilla when she was still human. He sent her insane by killing everyone she loved and tortured her before following her to a convent, where she sought refuge and sired her (see **33**, 'Becoming' Part 1). Angel is said to have cold hands, which fits in with the idea first presented in **12**, 'Prophecy Girl', that his body is basically dead (see **26**, 'Innocence', **55**, 'Graduation Day', Part 1). Giles thought Drusilla had been killed by a mob in Prague (see **15**, 'School Hard'). Jenny takes Giles to a Monster Truck rally, at which he seems to have a *really* bad time. Drusilla's mother used to sing her to sleep. Coffee is said to

make Willow 'jumpy' (something she shares with Angel –
see **54**, 'The Prom').

Soundtrack: On first US transmission, a voice-over stated,
'Tonight's presentation of *Buffy* included music from Sisters
of Mercy' (the song 'Never Land'), and a caption featured the
cover of the band's *Flood* LP. This credit (to become something of a regular feature in the third season) was shown
between the final scene and the preview for the next episode.
However, owing to copyright problems, all subsequent broad-
casts (including those in the UK) have removed 'Never Land'
and replaced it with a song called 'Blood of a Stranger' by
Shawn Clement and Sean Murray. Also featured are 'Lois,
On the Brink' by Willoughby and 'Reptile' by Creaming
Jesus.

20
The Dark Age

US Transmission Date: 10 Nov. 1997
UK Transmission Date: 16 May 1998 (Sky)

Writer: Dean Batali, Rob Des Hotel
Director: Bruce Seth Green
Cast: Stuart McLean (Philip Henry), Wendy Way (Deirdre),
Michael Earl Reid (Custodian), Daniel Henry Murray
(Creepy Cult Guy), Carlease Burke (Detective Winslow),
Tony Sears (Morgue Attendant), John Bellucci (Man)

Giles identifies a body found at the school as Philip, an old
friend from London. He is asked about the tattoo on Philip's
arm, but denies any knowledge. Buffy prevents a vampire
attack on the hospital blood supplies with Angel's help, but is
surprised that Giles didn't turn up as planned. At his apartment, she finds him drinking. After she leaves, Giles rolls up
his sleeve, revealing an identical tattoo. Buffy finds Ethan
Rayne, who tells her about the Mark of Eyghon that both he
and Giles wear. Buffy locks the resurrected Philip in the book

cage while Giles argues with Ethan, but they are disrupted by
Philip breaking open the doors. He dissolves into a liquid
puddle, which touches Jenny's unconscious body, transforming her into Eyghon. Buffy stops her from killing Giles, who
explains that in their youth he and his friends conjured up the
demon Eyghon, who is trying to kill everyone who wears his
mark. Ethan knocks Buffy out and tattoos her, burning off his
own tattoo with acid. Eyghon enters Angel's body but is
destroyed by the demon within.

Dudes and Babes: Giles and Jenny's kiss. ('I trust I gave
good squirm?') Is it any wonder Tony Head has such a following among the ladies? Xander believes that he could live
without the thought of Giles and orgies in the same sentence.

A Little Learning is a Dangerous Thing: Willow informs
Xander that hot lava is used to kill a heretic, not a demon.

It's a Designer Label!: Buffy's green training vest, Giles's
blue jim-jams and Willow's fluffy green jumper. Rather
cruelly, Buffy speculates that Giles's nappies were tweed.

References: A bizarre array include *Hamlet* ('The rest is
silence'), *E.R*, *Lost Weekend*, *The Sound of Music*, Frank
Sinatra's 'I've Got You Under My Skin' and Bill Withers's
'Lean on Me'. 'Be seeing you' crops up again (see **18**,
'Halloween').

'Anywhere But Here . . .': A game anyone can play: Buffy
wants to be on a beach having her feet massaged by Gavin
Rossdale (singer with the British grunge band Bush).
Willow's contribution is a dinner date in Florence with the
actor John Cusack. Xander implies that both have recently
changed their fantasies, though his remains the large-chested
actress Amy Yip 'at the Waterslide Park'.

Bitch!: Xander's moment of Premier League sarcasm: 'A
bonus day at class, plus Cordelia? Mix in a little rectal
surgery and it's *my best day ever*.'
   Cordelia: 'Do you know what you need, Xander, besides a
year's supply of acne cream? A brain.'

Awesome!: Angel and Buffy taking on three vampires in the hospital car park. Willow's anger at Xander and Cordy bitching (and their reactions to it). Giles's nightmares (the first one, especially). Cordelia tripping up Ethan.

Surprise!: The photograph of a much younger (and rockier) Rupert. '*That* is Giles?'

Never Mind the Warlocks!: Tony Head, interviewed on the BBC's *Fully Booked*, confirmed that the photo of Giles playing bass was actually his head superimposed on the body of Sid Vicious!

Valley-Speak: Cordelia: 'It's *totally* bogus.'

Cigarettes and Alcohol: A clearly drunk Giles answers the door to Buffy.

Logic, Let Me Introduce You to This Window: Cordelia says the police were asking Giles about a homicide. However, she entered the library after that was mentioned. After Giles learns of Deirdre's death and hangs up the phone, he removes his spectacles and puts them on the desk some inches away from his notebook. In the next shot, the glasses are on top of the notebook. After Philip bursts from his cage, Buffy lunges at him. When the camera angle switches, Buffy's kicking leg switches with it.

Quote/Unquote: Giles: 'I know music. Music has notes. This is noise.'

Buffy: 'Have I ever let you down?' Giles: 'Do you want me to answer that, or shall I just glare?'

Eyghon: 'You're like a woman, Ripper. You cry at every funeral.'

Notes: 'So, you're back?' A direct sequel to **18**, 'Halloween' (containing a plethora of continuity references), whose only disappointment is that the viewer expects the revelations about Giles's past to be bigger than a university dropout experimenting with Bad Magik (as opposed to white magic). Clever ending, though, and some great stunts (Jenny jumping out of the window).

   This was the first episode since **12**, 'Prophecy Girl', to
earn the TV-14 rating (the subject matter is pretty dark, but
the violence is no worse than normal). Buffy thinks Giles
counts tardiness as a deadly sin. Notice the look Willow
shoots at Xander when he asks, 'When are we gonna need
computers for real life?' Xander tells Cordelia, 'Twelve years
of you and I'm snappin',' which implies they've known each
other since kindergarten (in the prologue to *The Xander
Years*, Keith RA DeCandido provides a lovely cameo of the
five-year-old Xander dumping a bowl of ice cream on the
five-year-old Cordelia's head). Xander's Uncle Rory was a
'stodgy taxidermist' by day, while by night it was 'booze,
whores and fur flying' (see **47**, 'The Zeppo'). Giles studied
history at Oxford. When he was twenty-one, he dropped out
and lived in London. He played bass in a band (see **40**, 'Band
Candy') and fell in with a 'bad crowd' of occultists who
included Ethan, Philip Henry, Deirdre Page, Thomas Sutton
and Randall (whom Eyghon killed). Giles's approximate age
(mid-forties) and his reference to the Bay City Rollers should
place this in the mid-1970s. But weren't the Rollers a bit
'tame' for such badass mothers as Giles and his gang? Black
Sabbath or Led Zeppelin would seem more their gig. Of
course, he may simply be being flippant to Buffy.

Soundtrack: The music Buffy uses for her callisthenics: the
riff sounds a lot like the KLF's 1991 hit '3 AM Eternal'; however, it's a common sample and it could be almost anything.

21
What's My Line? Part 1

US Transmission Date: 17 Nov. 1997
UK Transmission Date: 23 May 1998 (Sky)

Writers: Howard Gordon, Marti Noxon
Director: David Solomon
Cast: Kelly Connell (Norman Pfister), Michael Rothhaar
(Suitman), PB Hutton (Mrs Kalish)

Buffy interrupts two vampires robbing a mausoleum of artefacts. Frustrated with Buffy's thwarting of his schemes, Spike summons the Order of Taraka, a society of deadly assassins, to deal with The Slayer. Several strangers arrive in Sunnydale, including a girl who stowed away in an aircraft cargo hold. That night, Buffy skates on the empty ice rink while waiting for Angel to meet her. A one-eyed man attacks her, but Angel helps Buffy to kill the assassin. Giles tells Buffy that the Order will not stop until they complete their mission. Distraught, Buffy goes to Angel's apartment. Angel asks his usual informant, Willy, for information but is attacked by the mysterious girl. She traps Angel in a cage, soon to be flooded with sunlight, and tells him that she is going after his girlfriend. Buffy wakes as an axe swings towards her. She asks whom she is fighting, and is told, 'I am Kendra, the Vampire Slayer.'

Dudes and Babes: Kendra the, seemingly Caribbean, *second* Slayer. Initial impressions: *Phwoar!*

Authority Sucks!: Although Snyder's hardly seen, his shadow hangs heavy over the episode. His 'hoop of the week' for Buffy to jump through is the Career Fair. And he tells Xander, 'Whatever comes out of your mouth is a meaningless waste of breath.'

A Little Learning is a Dangerous Thing: Willow discovers that both 'slayed' and 'slew' are acceptable as the past tense of 'slay'.

It's a Designer Label!: Cordy and Buffy both have extremely cute black miniskirts. Check out Kendra's red satin pants.

References: The title is from a legendary 1950s TV show in which members of the public mimed their jobs for a team of celebrities to guess their occupation. (That was the British version at least. The US game show of the same name was apparently quite different.) There are dialogue allusions to *The Simpsons* ('Have a cow!'), *Highlander* ('There can be only one'), *My Fair Lady* ('By George, I think he's got it') and *Scooby Doo, Where Are You?* (this is the first occasion where Buffy's friends, in this case Xander, refer to themselves as 'the Scooby Gang'). Plus another biblical reference, this time to King Solomon.

Bitch!: Cordelia: 'I aspire to help my fellow man. Check. As long as he's not smelly, dirty or something gross.' Cordelia asks if she's 'mass transportation' and Xander replies, 'That's what a lot of the guys say but it's just locker-room talk.'

Awesome!: The location filming of Buffy and Giles in the graveyard during daylight hours. Kendra's fight with Buffy, and the triple cliffhanger.

Surprise!: The last six words of the episode. Give me a '*what*?'

'You May Remember Me From Such Films As . . .': Eric Saiet (Dalton) was Shermerite in *Ferris Bueller's Day Off* and has a small role in *Godzilla*.

Don't Give Up The Day Job: Howard Gordon was previously writer and co-producer on *The X-Files* (co-writing the episode 'Synchrony' with David Greenwalt).

Valley-Speak: Buffy: 'Note to self: Religion – freaky.'
Willow: 'Goody. Research party.'

Logic, Let Me Introduce You to This Window: When the bus carrying the first bounty hunter arrives, look at the steps. The flooring is white and a WATCH YOUR STEP sign is stuck to the side of each step. However, when the hunter steps down the flooring is now red and the signs have disappeared. In the sequence where Pfister's right arm is generated the cuff of his shirt sleeve is three or four inches above his elbow. However, subsequently the sleeve ends at elbow level. During the 'chick fight', Kendra slams Buffy on to Angel's table, causing its legs to break and the table to collapse. In the next shot, we see a dazed Buffy lying on the remains of the broken table. However, for the remainder of the fight the debris is nowhere to be seen. How does Kendra know where Angel's apartment is? It's possible that she followed him from the ice rink, but why didn't she attack him then? (It could be reconnaissance, of course.) How does Dalton manage to carry the cross of du Lac? Surely (like all crosses) it should be *deadly* (or at least very unhealthy) to a vampire. Angel's reflection is briefly seen in the frame of a picture in Buffy's bedroom.

Quote/Unquote: Willow wakes up in a panic: 'Don't warn the tadpoles.'

Giles tells Buffy she'd be amazed at how 'numbingly pompous and long-winded' some of the Watcher Diaries are. Buffy: 'Colour me stunned.'

Notes: 'She's a bloody thorn in my bloody side.' What a *great* episode this is, full of super dialogue, terrific action sequences and a sense of impending horror.

Buffy owns a stuffed pig called Mr Gordo. When she was younger, she wanted to be an ice skater (her heroine was Dorothy Hamill, the 1976 Olympic figure-skating champion). Willow suffers from fear of frogs (see **30**, 'Killed By Death'). Angel is supplied his blood (pig's, seemingly) by Willy the Snitch (see **54**, 'The Prom'). Geographical note: Sunnydale is on Route 17. This episode was novelised as part of *The Angel Chronicles Vol. 2* by Richie Tankersley for Pocket Books, published in January 1999.

Soundtrack: 'Spring' from Vivaldi's *The Four Seasons*.

22
What's My Line? Part 2

US Transmission Date: 24 Nov. 1997
UK Transmission Date: 30 May 1998 (Sky)

Writer: Marti Noxon
Director: David Semel
Cast: Kelly Connell (Norman Pfister),
Spice Williams (Patrice)

Giles realises that Kendra must have been called when Buffy briefly died. Kendra informs the others about her encounter with Angel. They go to Willy's bar but Angel has been taken by Spike, who needs him as part of a ceremony to restore Drusilla's strength. Xander and Cordelia discover the perfume salesman is not human and take refuge in the basement. They argue, then passionately kiss, before escaping. There is an attempt on Buffy's life by the third assassin, dressed as a policewoman, during which Oz saves Willow and is shot in the arm. Buffy and Kendra force Willy to lead them to Spike. Kendra refuses to go with Buffy and reports back to Giles. At the church, Buffy discovers that she has walked into a trap. Kendra arrives and attacks the assassins who are holding Buffy. Giles and Willow take on a couple of vampires, while Xander tricks Pfister into becoming stuck in liquid adhesive and he and Cordelia stomp the worms to death. Spike takes Drusilla but Buffy knocks him out and everyone flees the burning church. However, Spike and Drusilla are far from dead.

It's a Designer Label!: Cordy's wet dress. Kendra's best shirt is her *only* shirt, and she's naturally a bit peeved when it gets torn in a fight.

References: Disneyland is mentioned, along with John Wayne, Kate Douglas Wiggin's novel *Rebecca of Sunnybrooke Farm*, *Mighty Morphin Power Rangers* and the bratpack actress Molly Ringwald (*Pretty in Pink*, *The Breakfast Club*), and there's a sarcastic reference to Chevy Chase. Plus a misquote from the Beatles, 'I Am the Walrus' ('I am the bug man, coo coo ca choo').

Bitch!: Buffy's Sigourney Weaver moment: '*Nobody* messes with my boyfriend.'

Awesome!: Every scene featuring Xander and Cordelia (particularly when he turns the hose on her). Plus the huge fight in the burning church.

Surprise!: Xander and Cordy in the basement. 'Coward!' 'Moron!' 'I hate you!' Dramatic music. *The kiss*. Now *who* guessed *that* was going to happen?

Valley-Speak: Cordy; 'We *so* need to get out of here.'

Buffy tells Kendra about Angel: 'Trust me on this one – he's on the home team now.'

Willow notes that Oz is experiencing 'computer-nerd solidarity.'

Xander discovers that Angel sired Drusilla: 'Man, that guy got some *major* neck in his day.'

Cordelia: 'I know what it means, dork-head.'

Logic, Let Me Introduce You to This Window: As with the previous episode, how is Spike able to hold the cross without getting burned? Cordelia pulls a worm from her hair and drops it on to a book marked 'Biology', which Xander then slams shut. In later shots, it's a different book. Spike says that the full moon is required for the ritual. Giles reports the ritual must take place on the night of the *new* moon. You can't have both on the same night, so one of them must be wrong. If Kendra was sent to her Watcher at an early age, long before she was called to be The Slayer, then how many potential Slayers exist at any one time? In **M1** Merrick suggests that Watchers are given only one Slayer and that it's up to them as to when they tell the girl of her destiny and begin training – although Merrick talking of getting a new Slayer if Buffy dies and Giles asking Gwendolyn in **41**, 'Revelations', if she's had a Slayer before seems to refute this. The suggestion from this episode, plus **37**, 'Faith, Hope and Trick', is that there are always dozens of would-be Slayers awaiting the call. Joss Whedon has noted: 'There is only one active Slayer at a time (except now cuz of the *wacky* circumstances). Inactive, I don't know. The Watchers pinpoint the potentials if they can. In some cultures (like Kendra's) they can announce their presence and whisk the girl off. In some, they can't. And sometimes they can't pinpoint the girl until she is called, which is what happened with Buffy.'

I Just *Love* Your Accent: The only episode to feature the word 'flummoxed'. Xander asks, 'Who sponsored Career Day today? The British Soccer Fan Association?' This shows that he knows as much about the complexities of a serious social phenomenon as he does about everything else.

Quote/Unquote: Willy: 'I swear on my mother's grave . . . Should something fatal ever happen to her, God forbid.'

Notes: 'You've been a very bad daddy.' The series' first attempt at a two-part storyline just about manages to make the grade, though the episode sags in the middle and it needs the Xander/Cordelia subplot to beef it up.

Kendra's Watcher is called Sam Zebuto. Giles has never met him but knows him by reputation (and seemingly speaks to him on the telephone during this episode). There are continuity references to Buffy's 'death' in **12**, 'Prophecy Girl', as well as the She-Mantis from **4**, 'Teacher's Pet'. There *is* a Slayer handbook (which Giles has never thought it necessary that Buffy read, directly contradicting what he said in **5**, 'Never Kill a Boy on the First Date'). There are 43 churches in Sunnydale. Drusilla and Spike have previously lived in Paris. Drusilla's mother (whom Angel killed, along with most of the rest of her family) ate raw lemons. Oz eats Animal Crackers. Despite being something of a computer expert and brilliant at tests, he doesn't want a career, instead describing his ambition as being able to play 'E flat diminished ninth' ('a *man's* chord'). That's actually a fancy name for a pretty bog-standard chord, telling us something about Oz's confidence in his own ability (see **47**, 'The Zeppo', **52**, 'Earshot'). This episode was novelised as part of *The Angel Chronicles Vol. 2* by Richie Tankersley for Pocket Books, published in January 1999.

23
Ted

US Transmission Date: 8 Dec. 1997
UK Transmission Date: 6 Jun. 1998 (Sky)

Writers: David Greenwalt, Joss Whedon
Director: Bruce Seth Green
Cast: John Ritter (Ted Buchanan),
Ken Thorley (Neal),
Jeff Pruitt (Vampire #1), Jeff Langton (Vampire #2)

Buffy finds her mother kissing a man. Joyce introduces Ted, who makes an impression on Xander and Willow, but not Buffy. While playing mini-golf Ted takes exception to Buffy's sullenness and threatens her, but regains his pleasant personality when Xander, Willow and Joyce join them. Buffy tells her mother about Ted's threat but Joyce doesn't believe her. After patrol, Buffy finds Ted in her room reading her diary. Buffy attempts to get it back but he throws her against the wall. Enraged, Buffy sends him tumbling down the stairs, killing him. Xander, Willow and Cordelia discover a drug in the cookies that Ted baked. At Ted's home, they find the bodies of his previous four wives in a cupboard. Ted appears again in Buffy's room. Buffy stabs Ted with a nail file, revealing wires and circuits. The android Ted knocks Buffy unconscious and confronts Joyce. She believes his lies at first, but then grows suspicious. Buffy regains consciousness and smashes a frying pan over Ted's robotic skull.

Dudes and Babes: Xander and Cordelia's utterly strange relationship continues to develop, if that's the right word. Xander asks Cordy if she'd like to accompany him to the utility cupboard to make out. Cordelia asks if *that's* all he ever thinks about (it is: see **52**, 'Earshot'). Then she adds, 'OK'. Jenny refers to Giles's 'puppy-dog eyes' and Xander talks about Buffy playing games of 'the naughty stewardess'.

Authority Sucks!: Another walk along the tightrope of child abuse (see **3**, 'The Witch').

A Little Learning is a Dangerous Thing: 'How was school today, Buffy? Did you learn anything?' There's very little in the way of classroom scenes, though news of Ted's death seems to have made it to school before Buffy did.

Mom's Sticky Buns: Buffy: 'Seeing my mother Frenching a guy is definitely a ticket to therapy-land.' The secret of Ted's great mini-pizzas is, after baking, to fry them in herbs and olive oil in a cast-iron skillet. Joyce asks Buffy if she wants any sticky buns, which is a bit of innuendo crying out for a suitable reply.

Denial, Thy Name is Joyce: Even by her own standards some sort of award is due to Mrs Summers for even *thinking* about believing Ted's story of *not* having died.

It's a Designer Label!: *What* is that on Willow's head? It looks like a tea cosy. 'Hey, Cordy, nice outfit,' says Xander. That's a brazen lie. The yellow miniskirt is particularly unfortunate.

References: Xander ('Somebody was raised in a culture-free environment'), Willow and Buffy have a pointless discussion about the 70s pop stars Captain and Tennille ('Love Will Keep Us Together'). There's a discussion on the psychology of Sigmund Freud (1856–1939). Both *Psycho* and *The Terminator* seem to be influences (the heroine cheating at golf may be a subtle *Goldfinger* reference) and *Thelma and Louise*, *Licence to Kill* and *Superman* all get name-checked along with John Stanley's legendary Saturday-night horror-movie slot *Creature Features*, which ran for several years on KTVU in Oakland, California. There's an allusion to *The Stepford Wives*. 'Good morning, sunshine' is a misquote from *Hair*.

Awesome!: A terrified Giles holding up a cross . . . to Jenny ('I get that reaction from men all the time'). Plus Buffy kicking the daylights out of the vampire ('You don't normally beat them into quite such a bloody pulp') and Buffy and Ted's fight.

Surprise!: 'You killed him.' Not as surprising as Ted's return from the dead minutes later.

The Drugs Don't Work: Or, in this case, *do*. Willow identifies the drug Ted uses in his cookies as demotoran, which shares properties with ecstasy, the street name for MDMA (methylenedioxymethamphetamine), the powerful hallucinatory stimulant popularised by rave culture in the early 90s.

'You May Remember Me From Such Films and TV Series As . . .': John Ritter was the star of the sitcom *Three's Company* (the American version of *Man About the House*). He also had the leading role in the two *Problem Child* movies and *Stay Tuned*. Ken Thorley was the Bolian barber Mr Mott in *Star Trek: The Next Generation*.

Valley-Speak: Xander: 'You *rock*!'

Logic, Let Me Introduce You to This Window: When Buffy climbs into her room her nightstand is in darkness. However, in close shots it's well illuminated. After Buffy punches Ted, he drops her diary and, as Ted hits Buffy, it can be seen on the floor. However, when Ted picks Buffy up the diary has vanished. Xander opens Ted's cupboard door with his left hand while holding a torch in his right, down by his side. As the door opens, the shot cuts to a different angle and the torch is by his head. Where is the miniature golf course? At the end of **13**, 'When She Was Bad', Willow says that there's no such course in Sunnydale. Silly explanations about 'layers of tweed' aside, how did Giles not only survive a point-blank hit in the back with a crossbow bolt, but also have the strength to pull it out *and* stab the vampire with it? Without fainting? And what was Willow looking *at* under the microscope when examining Ted's cookies? Crumbs? Analysing a foodstuff for its chemical make-up requires lots of complicated tests, but magnifying it wouldn't seem to be one of them.

Quote/Unquote: Giles: 'I believe the subtext here is rapidly becoming the text.'

Xander on his triumphant discovery that Buffy is having 'parental issues': 'Freud would have said the exact same thing. Except he might not have done that little dance.'

Giles, after Cordelia mentions his summoning of Eyghon in a conversation about how difficult it is to face the responsibility for someone's death: '*Do* let's bring that up as often as possible.'

Stepford Dad: There are two schools of thought on this episode. One is that it's almost the definitive *Buffy*-as-teenage-horror tale in a series in which hyena-kids, vampires and witches are *de rigueur* as opposed to real life where we have bullies and stepfathers. The implication is that Joss Whedon uses the clichés of the horror genre to represent the terrors of being a teenager (Joyce's new boyfriend is a violent robot because, to a teenage girl, that's exactly how a prospective stepfather appears). Put simply, in *Buffy the Vampire Slayer* the obsessions and fears of teenagers are made flesh. All valid. But there is another, more logical, critical analysis on 'Ted', which is nowhere near as positive. What ruins the episode for many is that this is not a 'Buffy-Universe story': it's straight SF. This is the *only* episode in the series in which there is *no* supernatural element whatsoever. There's no magic or demons at work – instead we are asked to believe (in a series that, for instance, takes its technology pretty seriously) that in the 1950s (with the components of the era) a convincing android/replicant could be made. Even Moloch in **8**, 'I Robot . . . You Jane', utilising the peak of research technology, could only come up with something like *Robocop*.

Notes: 'I'm not wired that way.' A disturbingly uneven episode. 'Ted' contains one of *the* great performances in *Buffy*: John Ritter's chilling portrayal of a psychotic control freak on the verge of screwing up two people's lives. Unfortunately, *Buffy*'s *raison d'être* required some form of 'demonisation' of the central character and a huge opportunity to explore an important, relevant issue is lost. He's a robot – it's no longer scary, so you can come out from behind the sofa and laugh at the risible final scenes. Otherwise, 'Ted' contains everything you'd expect from *Buffy*'s best writers: pithy dialogue, intelligent characterisation and superb timing. It's a pity that it couldn't have contained more *feeling*.

There are continuity references to the previous episode (Angel's absence for most of the episode is touched upon). According to Jenny it's been three weeks since the events of **20**, 'The Dark Age' (she says she is still having trouble sleeping). Buffy says she doesn't bruise easily, which suggests that Slayers have abnormally high recuperative powers (see **30**, 'Killed By Death', **56**, 'Graduation Day' Part 2).

24
Bad Eggs

US Transmission Date: 12 Jan. 1998
UK Transmission Date: 13 Jun. 1998 (Sky)

Writer: Marti Noxon
Director: David Greenwalt
Cast: James Parks (Tector Gorch),
Rick Zieff (Mr Whitmore), Brie McCaddin (Mall Girl),
Eric Whitmore (Night Watchman)

Buffy encounters cowboy vampires, Lyle Gorch, and his idiot brother Tector. Mr Whitmore gives eggs to his students for a parenting assignment. When Buffy goes to sleep a tentacle slithers from her egg and attaches itself to her face. Xander reveals he boiled his egg to prevent it from breaking. When Buffy notices her egg shaking, a purple insect-like creature bursts out and Buffy stabs it with a pair of scissors. At school, Buffy and Xander are knocked unconscious by Cordelia and Willow. A parade of students march robot-like to the basement. Joyce arrives looking for Buffy. Giles places one of the creatures on her back, and they join the others in their effort to dig up Mother Bezoar, a pre-prehistoric parasite. While searching for a weapon, a recovered Buffy is faced with Lyle and Tector. They fight and both Tector and Buffy are pulled into the parasite creature, but seconds later Buffy emerges, having killed it. Giles invents a story involving a gas leak to prevent awkward questions.

Dudes and Babes: The opening shot of the legs of the mall girl suggests more than we actually get. Tector says that Sunnydale doesn't have a decent whore in the city limits, which doesn't fit in with what we know about the place.

A Little Learning is a Dangerous Thing: Mr Whitmore's sex-education class descends into farce. 'That was a rhetorical question, Mr Harris, not a poll.'

Mom's Apple Pie: 'I swear sometimes I don't know what goes on in your head.' The nadir of Joyce and Buffy's relationship with Buffy getting about four levels of punishment as the episode progresses. (When Joyce told Buffy in **15**, 'School Hard', that it would be 'at least a week and a half' before her pride in her daughter wore off, it seems she wasn't exaggerating. 'Bad Eggs' takes place in a weird parallel universe where the close relationship established in **15**, 'School Hard', never happened and where Joyce still thinks her daughter is an irresponsible tearaway.) Buffy says, 'Did I ask for back-seat parenting?' and notes that she doesn't want to be a single parent (even a surrogate one to an egg) like her mother.

It's a Designer Label!: The dress that Buffy wanted made her look 'like a streetwalker' according to Joyce. Cordy has a (rather cute) bear bag (she claims she started the nationwide craze for bags shaped like animals). See also Cordelia's little grey skirt and her leather slit miniskirt.

References: Lyle and Tector Gorch were the names of the brothers played by Ben Johnson and Warren Oates in *The Wild Bunch*, a film that also includes a character called 'Angel' (see **2**, 'The Harvest'). 'Bad Eggs' includes dialogue and textual references to *Die Hard* ('Yippie kai-aye'), the Beatles' 'Dig a Pony' ('All I want is you'), *Batman* ('Think about the future'), *Dial M For Murder* (the scissors scene) and William Castle's *The Tingler*.

Bitch!: Xander, kissing Cordelia: 'This would work a lot better for me if you didn't talk.'

Don't Give Up The Day Job: Both James Parks (a carpenter on *Reality Bites*) and Rick Zieff (the casting assistant on *Breakdown*) have film-industry jobs other than acting.

Valley-Speak: A tired Buffy: 'I just feel all funky.' And: 'My egg. It went postal on me.'

Logic, Let Me Introduce You to This Window: The opening scenes are set during the day, therefore how is Lyle not a small pile of ash on the floor? In the arcade, the girl with Lyle plays the pinball machine. In the initial shot, her handbag is hanging from her right wrist. However, in the next shot the straps are further up her arm. During Buffy's fight with Lyle in the arcade, both of them collide with the same pinball machine that the girl was playing earlier and the machine is now turned off. How does the shell of Buffy's egg repair itself? Watch closely in the scene in the library where Buffy puts her egg on the desk close to a chain. The respective positions of the chain and the egg change from shot to shot about four times. It's so obvious that one almost suspects it's been done deliberately to provide books like this with something to talk about! The 'walking around zombified' cliché enables Giles to converse with some intricacy with Joyce and allows Cordelia to knock Buffy out with a single blow, but also renders its slaves incapable of attacking a concrete floor in anything more than a 'slo-mo slave action'. Isn't it lucky that a pre-prehistoric creature lays eggs *exactly* like hen's eggs? After she loses consciousness, the parasite falls from Willow's back. However, when everyone else collapses no parasites can be seen dropping from their backs.

Quote/Unquote: Giles on Xander boiling his egg: 'I suppose there is a sort of Machiavellian ingenuity to your transgression.' Xander: 'I resent that . . . Or, possibly, thank you.'

Joyce on children: 'They're such a . . . Oh, I don't want to say burden, but . . . Actually, I kind of *do* want to say burden.'

Notes: 'Long story.' *And* a tall one. This is such a lopsided episode that it's surprising it doesn't collapse under its own weight. The main focus is the subplot about the parasitic eggs, while the two hick vampires are merely there to top-and-tail the episode (the Gorches serve absolutely no purpose – they're too stupid to be a threat to anyone). 'Bad Eggs' also seems to think it's being really funny in places where it clearly isn't. That the episode has to resort to devices such as Xander's pratfall when he and Buffy enter the cave is an indication of just how desperate a production this is.

Buffy had a giga-pet, but she sat on it and it broke. Xander implies Cordelia has bad breath. Cordelia says she has 'a friend' ('not me') who once had sex in a car at the top of a

hill and accidentally kicked off the handbrake. Angel cannot
have children. Before they became vampires, Lyle and Tector
massacred a Mexican village in 1886. The mall used at the
beginning of this episode is the Sherman Oaks Galleria north
of Los Angeles. After Willow enters the science lab and
stands next to the dead hatchling, on the blackboard behind
her is written POSTING BOARD. This was an acknowledgment
(by Jeff Pruitt) to all the regulars on the BtVS posting board.
When Joyce enters the library, keep your eyes on the sign in
the middle of shot. Under SUNNYDALE HS LIBRARY, it says,
WEBSITE COMING and BVS BRATS TALK, which seems to be
another in-joke for the series' many Internet fans.

25
Surprise

US Transmission Date: 19 Jan. 1998
UK Transmission Date: 20 Jun. 1998 (Sky)

Writer: Marti Noxon
Director: Michael Lange
Cast: Brian Thompson (the Judge),
Vincent Schiavelli (Uncle Enyos)

Buffy has a nightmare in which Drusilla kills Angel. Jenny is
visited by her Uncle Enyos, who tells her that Angel's fear is
weakening. Jenny reveals Angel's involvement with Buffy to
Enyos, who demands that she keep them apart. Because of
his injuries, Spike is confined to a wheelchair while Drusilla
(now much stronger) takes delivery of mysterious boxes. A
surprise birthday party is arranged for Buffy, but it is ruined
by a fight with some vampires. Angel realises that the vampires are collecting body parts of the Judge, an ancient demon
who (when assembled) can destroy humanity. Drusilla
throws a party in celebration of the coming of the Judge.
Buffy and Angel gatecrash and then escape. Angel finally
professes his love for Buffy and they consummate their
relationship. Angel gets out of bed in agony.

Dreaming (As Blondie Once Said) is Free: Buffy's nightmare: like all good dreams, it's got a rock-and-roll soundtrack; Willow speaks French accompanied by a small monkey; crockery smashes; and, in a moment dripping with Freudian symbolism, Angel is staked by Drusilla. Sexy. Buffy also mentions a dream she had in which she and Giles opened an office warehouse in Las Vegas, which sounds like a good series in itself.

Dudes and Babes: Oz says he's 'groupie free' these days which, I feel, frankly isn't nearly rock-and-roll enough (see **55**, 'Graduation Day' Part 1). Xander tells Buffy he feels 'a pre-birthday spanking coming on'. Drusilla's dancing is certainly provocative.

It's a Designer Label!: Drusilla's red party dress, Buffy's short black skirt, green pants and cool white jacket, Giles's stripy tie, plus another tea cosy on the head for Willow. There's a lovely close-up of Oz's Fender Stratocaster.

References: Xander mentions the diner chain Denny's. There are references to *Dead Poets Society* ('Seize the day') and 'Jack and the Beanstalk' ('grind his bones to make your bread'). 'Discretion is the better part of valour' is a misquote from *Henry IV*, Part 1.

Bitch!: Giles: 'A true creature of evil can survive the process. No one human ever has.' Xander: 'What's the problem? We send Cordy to fight this guy, and go for pizza!'

Awesome!: The reassembly of the Judge, followed by Dalton's rather messy death ('do it again!'). Buffy crashing into her own surprise party and killing a vampire with a drumstick. Plus Alyson Hannigan's charming performance in the scene where Willow and Oz ask each other out on a date.

'You May Remember Me From Such Films and TV Series As . . .': For Brian Thompson, see **1**, 'Welcome to the Hellmouth'. Vincent Schiavelli will also be well known to *X-Files* fans for his sympathetic performance as Lanny in 'Humbug'. His film appearances include *Ghost*, *One Flew Over the Cuckoo's Nest* and *Tomorrow Never Dies*.

Valley-Speak: Buffy to Willow: 'You can't spend the rest of your life waiting for Xander to wake up and smell the hottie.'

Xander to Giles: 'Are you ready to get down, you funky party weasel?'

Logic, Let Me Introduce You to This Window: When Buffy approaches Willow's table in her dream, the monkey is facing Buffy. In the next shot it's facing Willow, then it turns around to face Buffy as Willow waves (maybe it's just following the action). Why would Angel take the time to get dressed before running outside if he was in extreme pain? How do the boxes containing the body parts of the Judge fit together? When the panels open, inside is one big chamber, whereas it should be at least six little ones. The gypsy-curse subplot is indescribably dumb. The punishment for Angelus is to give him a soul. Fine. But to take it away again if he gets happy, turning him *back* into Angelus, the vicious creature that has killed thousands . . .? This whole thing shrieks 'plot device' and never really makes sense.

I Just *Love* Your Accent: Xander asks Giles: 'Are all you Brits such drama queens?'

Quote/Unquote: Enyos: 'Vengeance demands that his pain be eternal.'

Spike, on Dalton: 'He's a wanker, but he's the only one we've got with half a brain.'

Notes: 'The time for watching is past.' *This* is teen drama? An astonishingly sensual, erotic episode. 'Surprise' is about as far removed from traditional horror clichés as it's possible to get. Buffy takes her first, faltering steps into the adult world of passion. And the *real* horrors to come. Grown-up television.

Buffy loses her virginity (would it be too indelicate to ask whether the thought that she's committed what amounts to necrophilia occurred to anybody in Broadcast Standards and Practices?). Willow speaks to the monkey in French, saying, '*L'hippo a piqué ton pantalon*', which means 'The hippo stole your trousers', a reference to Oz's joke at the end of **22**,

'What's My Line?' Part 2, that all of the monkeys (who are French) in boxes of Animal Crackers have pants and the hippos are jealous. Angel refers to the Irish as 'my people' when giving Buffy the Claddagh ring. Jenny's real name is Janna. She is a Kalderash Romany gypsy and has been sent to America by her clan specifically to watch Angel, whom they cursed over eighty years ago. In addition to Prague and Paris, Spike and Drusilla also spent time in Vienna and Spain.

Soundtrack: 'Transylvanian Concubine' by Rasputina and 'Anything' by Shawn Clement and Sean Murray, featuring vocals by Care Howe.

26
Innocence

US Transmission Date: 20 Jan. 1998
UK Transmission Date: 27 Jun. 1998 (Sky)

Writer: Joss Whedon
Director: Joss Whedon
Cast: Brian Thompson (the Judge), Ryan Francis (Soldier), Vincent Schiavelli (Uncle Enyos), Carla Madden (Woman), Parry Shen (Student)

Angel reverts to his old self, Angelus, and visits Spike and Drusilla. The Judge attempts to disintegrate him, but there is no humanity left to kill. Drusilla tells Angelus they plan to bring forth Armageddon, but he asks for one night to punish The Slayer. Buffy goes to her lover's apartment but finds him cruel and dismissive. Angelus turns up at school, intending to kill those close to Buffy, starting with Willow. He is prevented by Xander and Jenny. Xander forms a plan to steal an army rocket launcher to defeat the Judge and with the help of Willow, Oz and Cordelia he succeeds. Buffy and Giles discover Jenny's dark secret and that the curse cannot be re-invoked. Putting Xander's plan into action, they follow the Judge, Angelus and Drusilla to a shopping mall, where Buffy uses the weapon to destroy the Judge. Giles drives Buffy home and assures her that she has not lost any of his respect.

Dudes and Babes: The semipornographic flashback to Buffy and Angel . . . ahem, 'getting it on' is, of course, all done in the best possible taste. Soft focus, unruffled sheets (without stains) and no sweating. Just like sex *isn't*.

Mom's Apple Pie: Mrs Summers doesn't notice that Buffy arrives home in different clothes from the ones she had on when she left the previous day. Very observant, Joyce. Her birthday muffin for Buffy is both affectionate and stupidly pointless.

It's a Designer Label!: 'Wear something trashy . . . er . . .' Xander's palm-tree shirt, Cordelia's extremely short tartan skirt and Buffy's white socks all fit the bill here.

References: The shot of the Judge zapping everyone in the mall appears to be a homage to the climactic scene in *Raiders of the Lost Ark*. The movie theatre where Buffy and Angelus fight is lined with posters for Warner Bros' animated feature film *Quest for Camelot*. At the end of the episode, Buffy and Joyce are watching *Stowaway* (starring Shirley Temple). There are references to the software giants IBM ('Big Blue') and the Smurfs.

Bitch!: Willow, on Xander and Cordelia's 'weird' attraction to each other: 'Weird? It's against all laws of God and man.'

Awesome!: The scene where Angelus threatens Willow in front of Jenny and Xander. The slow-motion killing of the Judge as Angelus and Dru are thrown away from the explosion (yes, *just* like that scene in *Die Hard*). Buffy fighting Angelus, and kicking his goolies.

Surprise!: The moment when we discover, along with Dru, Spike and the Judge, that Angel is Angelus again. 'Yeah baby, I'm back.'

'You May Remember Me From Such Films As . . .': Ryan Francis played the young Peter in Spielberg's *Hook*.

Valley-Speak: Xander: 'Now, I'm having a wiggins.'

Cigarettes and Alcohol: Angelus gives 'blowing off' a whole new meaning. (See **Logic, Let Me Introduce You to This Window**).

Logic, Let Me Introduce You to This Window: When Angel ran outside in **25**, 'Surprise', it was raining heavily. At the beginning of this episode, however, the rain has stopped. When Buffy cries herself to sleep and dreams about her intimate night with Angel, she is wearing silver nail polish. But, in **25**, 'Surprise', Buffy wasn't wearing any. The episode's time frame is completely up the spout. Buffy runs home distressed, as Xander tells Cordelia to meet him at Willow's house in half an hour. Willow, meanwhile, is supposed to bring Oz and his van. The scene then shifts to Buffy's bedroom, where she weeps and falls asleep. Buffy wakes up the next day and goes to school to force the truth out of Jenny. The following scene depicts Xander and Cordy stealing the rocket launcher, events that happened the night before. Presumably Giles managed to keep Buffy's attack on Jenny from Snyder, otherwise she'd be suspended on the spot. (One of the students even asks, 'Shall I get the principal?') How many vans does Oz have? In **18**, 'Halloween', he drove a zebra-striped van with a steering wheel on the right. Here he drives a dark-coloured left-hand-drive van. In **12**, 'Prophecy Girl', Angel confirmed he had 'no breath', so how does Angelus exhale all that smoke after feeding on the cigarette-smoking prostitute? In **34**, 'Becoming' Part 2, we find out vampires in general, and Spike in particular, are at pains *not* to see the end of the world, so what's the deal with the bringing on of Armageddon here?

Quote/Unquote: Drusilla: 'Psst . . . We're gonna destroy the world. Wanna come?'

Willow, angry at discovering Xander and Cordelia kissing: 'I *knew* it. Well, knew it in the sense of not having the slightest idea, but I *knew* there was something I didn't know.'

Spike to Angelus: 'I know you haven't been in the game for a while, mate, but we *do* still kill people. Sort of our *raison d'être*, you know?'

   Cordelia sums up the plot: 'This is *great*. There's an unkill-
able demon in town, Angel's joined his team, The Slayer's a
basket case, I'd say we've hit bottom.' Xander: 'I have a
plan.' Cordelia: 'Oh no, here's a lower place.'
   Cordelia asks Xander if looking at guns makes him want to
have sex: 'I'm seventeen. Looking at linoleum makes me
want to have sex.'

Notes: 'It's not justice we serve, it is vengeance.' Strangely,
this is nowhere near as effective as **25**, 'Surprise', despite
managing to tie up all the loose ends and containing some
very fine performances. Highlights include Alyson
Hannigan's uncanny ability to be angry and funny at the same
time (as in the sequence where she can't think of a nasty
word to call Giles and the others). I think what holds the
episode down is the unnecessary subplot about the rocket
launcher that pushes the viewer away from the important
stuff. And there's that odd, downbeat ending with Joyce and
Buffy, which deserved better direction.
   Buffy says she beat up Willy the Snitch to get information
about Angel (see **21/22**, 'What's My Line?'). There are references to Xander's military expertise in **18**, 'Halloween'. He
says he can still put together an M16 rifle in 57 seconds.
Xander is the treasurer of the 'We Hate Cordelia Club', of
which Willow is also a founder member.

27
Phases

US Transmission Date: 27 Jan. 1998
UK Transmission Date: 4 Jul. 1998 (Sky)

Writers: Rob Des Hotel, Dean Batali
Director: Bruce Seth Green
Cast: Camila Griggs (Gym Teacher),
Jack Conley (Cain),
Megahn Perry (Theresa Klusmeyer),
Keith Campbell (Werewolf)

Xander and Cordelia make out in her car. Without warning, they are attacked by a werewolf. Giles is excited, having never encountered a lycanthrope before. One of Buffy's classmates, Theresa, walks home alone and meets Angelus. Buffy and Giles investigate the woods and discover a very unpleasant werewolf hunter named Cain. They drive to the Bronze, arriving as teens flee from the werewolf inside, but it escapes before Buffy can capture it. Buffy and Giles hear on the radio that Theresa has been found dead. As the sun rises, the werewolf slowly transforms back into its human form. Oz. Willow invites Oz to help her do some research, but he refuses and runs off. Before he can lock himself up, Willow calls at his home. He tries to warn her of the danger, but it is too late and he is transformed. A lengthy chase begins, climaxing in Willow shooting Oz with a tranquilliser. The next day, Oz tells Willow that he'll be fine as long as he locks himself up around the full moon every month. To his surprise, Willow is still interested in continuing their relationship.

Dudes and Babes: As relationships become clearer (Oz and Willow, Xander and Cordy), poor Buffy is left to trail around with Giles for most of the episode. Theresa's cute, but something about her just screams 'Angelus bait'.

A Little Learning is a Dangerous Thing: Willow is helping Cordelia with her history homework (or possibly doing it for her).

It's a Designer Label!: Willow's got another of those tea-cosy bobble-hats, not to mention a smiley-face backpack and a pair of sickly yellow overalls. Oz's New York City Yoga T-shirt, Theresa's red 'burial' miniskirt(!), Buffy's miniskirt (also red).

References: Calvin Klein's Obsession aftershave, and Robbie the Robot from *Forbidden Planet*. 'Phases' contains numerous visual and dialogue references to classic werewolf films of the past including *The Wolf Man*, *Curse of the Werewolf*, *Dr Terror's House of Horror*, *The Beast Must Die*, *The Howling* and *An American Werewolf in London*. There's a reference to the exercise device the Thigh Master.

Bitch!: Willow says she had never got a 'miaow' before, but she's certainly awarded one for 'What's his [Xander's] number? Oh yeah, 1-800-I'm-dating-a-skanky-ho.'

Awesome!: Xander accidentally 'outing' Larry is funny, but also touching. Oz's telephone conversation with his aunt concerning his cousin ('. . . and *how long* has that been going on?') is hilarious, as is his reassuring Willow that bunnies can 'really take care of themselves'.

Surprise!: Who the werewolf changes into. Hands up who was surprised by *that*?

The Drugs Don't Work: Phenobarbitone is a powerful barbiturate used to relieve anxiety and treat insomnia, so it's a perfect tranquilliser.

'You May Remember Me From Such Films As . . .': Jack Conley often gets meaty detective-type roles in films like *Payback*, *Mercury Rising*, *L.A. Confidential* and *Get Shorty*.

Don't Give Up The Day Job: Keith Campbell is mainly known as a stunt man. His credits include *Mission: Impossible*, *Blade*, *Face/Off*, *Batman Forever*, *Stargate*, *Forrest Gump*, *The Last Action Hero* and *Patriot Games*.

Valley-Speak: Willow: 'I want smoochies.'
   Cordelia: 'Or it could be a crock.'
   Oz: 'That's fairly freaksome.'

Logic, Let Me Introduce You to This Window: Two men push Giles's car along as it arrives in front of the Bronze. Keen-eyed viewers can spot the tops of their heads through the rear window. While Buffy is trapped in the net her flashlight is off, but it's on again when the net lowers to the ground. After everyone evacuates the Bronze, Buffy runs inside putting her backpack on. She bumps someone on the way in and one of the straps falls off her left shoulder. As she walks inside, the camera angle switches and the strap has returned to its former position. After Buffy senses the werewolf's movement, she slides off the left strap and walks up the stairs and parts a curtain. The angle switches again, and now the backpack is in her right hand. During the chase through the woods, Willow trips. As she gets up notice the stains on her overalls. When she gets to the library, they're spotless. In the library scene, for several shots Giles is not wearing glasses but in others he is. After knocking the gun out of Buffy's hands, the werewolf shoves her backwards but she falls face first over Giles. What are Oz and Larry, two seniors, doing in a self-defence class full of juniors? If Oz didn't realise he was a werewolf until the morning after the full moon, then where did he wake up the morning after 'the night before the full moon'? Shouldn't the bullet Cain makes be too hot to handle seconds after having been molten silver? Buffy says a werewolf is human 'twenty-eight days each month'; it should be twenty-five days each lunar month. Sarah Michelle Gellar mispronounces '*Führer*' as 'Fourier'.

I Just *Love* Your Accent: Giles, on Cain: 'Pillock!'

Cruelty to Animals: Cain: 'First they tell me I can't hunt an elephant for its ivory. Now I've got to deal with People for the Ethical Treatment of Werewolves.'

Quote/Unquote: Larry: 'I would love to get some of that Buffy and Willow action, if you know what I mean.' Oz: 'That's great, Larry. You've really mastered the single entendre.'

Cordelia: 'We came here to do the thing I can never tell my father about because he still thinks I'm a good girl.'

Buffy asks Xander if he's sure he was attacked by a werewolf: 'Six feet tall, claws, a big old snout in the middle of his face, like a wolf? Yeah, I'm sticking with my first guess.'

Giles: 'You hunt werewolves for sport?' Cain: 'No, I'm in it purely for the money.'

Notes: 'Good doggy, now play dead.' A really fun episode, taking all of the best bits of recent (and ancient) werewolf texts and playing with them in an amusingly postmodern way. Lovely direction more than makes up for the terrible werewolf make-up (which in itself adds to the kitschy, sub-*Howling* homage that the episode is built around). Stellar performances from Seth Green and Alyson Hannigan.

Giles's delight on discovering a werewolf case ('It's one of the classics; yes, I'm sure my books and I are in for a fascinating afternoon') makes Buffy remark, 'He needs to get a pet.' Oz notes that the cheerleading statue has eyes that follow him around the room, referring to 3, 'The Witch'. He doesn't smoke. He took Willow to the movies last night, and, although he's forgotten the movie itself, he did enjoy the popcorn. He was bitten by his cousin, Jordy, whose parents are called Maureen and Ken. There are references to Xander becoming doglike in 6, 'The Pack', and to his allegedly being unable to remember those events, and a very funny PMS reference – Willow noting 'three days out of the month, *I'm* not much fun to be around either.' Cordelia has dated lots of guys in bands before. On patrol, Buffy sees Brittany Podell making out with Owen Stadeel, who is supposed to be going with Barrett Williams. Buffy's locker has a Velvet Chain (see 5, 'Never Kill a Boy on the First Date') sticker on it.

Soundtrack: 'Blind for Now' by Lotion.

Did You Know?: Joss Whedon gave Seth Green a copy of the script for 'Phases' to persuade the actor to accept an offer to become a regular: 'It had all this metaphorical stuff and gave strong shades to the character,' says Seth. 'I said "Yeah, I want to be part of this"!'

28
Bewitched, Bothered and Bewildered

US Transmission Date: 10 Feb. 1998
UK Transmission Date: 11 Jul. 1998 (Sky)

Writer: Marti Noxon
Director: James A Contner
Cast: Lorna Scott (Miss Beakman),
Jennie Chester (Kate),
Kristen Winnicki (Cordette),
Tamara Braun (Frenzied Girl),
Scott Hamm (Jock)

Harmony and her friends mock Cordelia for dating Xander. Giles warns Buffy that Angelus has a long history of committing horrid acts on Valentine's Day. Buffy receives a box of roses and a card with the word 'soon' on it. At the Bronze, Xander gives Cordelia a gift. After admiring the necklace, Cordelia breaks up with him. Xander is furious and it only gets worse for him the next day as everyone in school seems to know what happened. Xander tells Amy that he knows she's practising her mother's art of witchcraft. Xander blackmails Amy into casting a love spell on Cordelia, so that he can then dump *her*. Much to Xander's dismay, the spell has no effect on Cordy. However, every other female in Sunnydale seems attracted to him. Xander must now spend his time running away from all of the women in his life (including Buffy, Willow, Jenny, Harmony and Drusilla) while Giles and Amy try to reverse the spell. And also reverse a spell that's turned Buffy into a rat. While a mob of girls battle each other, Xander and Cordelia arrive at Buffy's house. Joyce starts seducing Xander, so he and Cordelia barricade themselves in the basement. Giles and Amy perform the reversal spells – first on Buffy, transforming her back to her (naked) human self, and then on Xander. Next day Harmony mocks Xander, but Cordelia comes to his defence, telling her (former) friends that she will date whom she wants to. However lame.

Dudes and Babes: In an episode all about the shallowness of relationships based purely on physical attraction, let's nail this one right away. Does anybody else wish there hadn't been a convenient object for Buffy to hide behind when she suffers from 'a slight case of nudity'? Glad to know I'm not alone. A pig-out and a vid-fest are said to be the time-honoured tradition of the loveless. Which sounds about right.

A Little Learning is a Dangerous Thing: Or *no* learning in Amy's case, since she uses her 'mojo' to con Miss Beakman into believing she handed in a test paper.

Mom's Apple Pie: Joyce coming on to Xander is a bit strong, even given the implications concerning what a little raver she used to be (see **12**, 'Prophecy Girl', **40**, 'Band Candy').

Denial, Thy Name is Joyce: How on *earth* could Joyce fall for Cordelia's utterly lame 'scavenger-hunt' excuse in reply to the obvious question, 'What are you twenty girls and one boy doing in my basement and why am I holding a carving knife?' Since everybody seems to have retained their memories of these events (note Buffy's 'sudden-need-for-cheese' confession) it's reasonable to assume that Joyce has also, and that she's just (as Buffy suggests) 'repressing' after 'hitting on one of my friends'.

It's a Designer Label!: Buffy's big red coat and black gloves and Xander's overcoat (it can get pretty cold in California once the sun goes down in February). Harmony's gang have some *horrible* clothes, including the blonde girl with the fat bottom wearing a very unflattering navy-blue miniskirt, a scarlet PVC coat and a lime-green blouse. Buffy's light-blue (sheep-motif) vest and leopardskin slit miniskirt and Cordelia's red Valentine dress are better. And Xander's 'nice shirt' is, actually, rather good. Cordelia admires his clothes and he admits he allowed Buffy to dress him. As John Travolta circa 1977, seemingly. Is Oz's hair going to remain the same colour two episodes running?

References: The title derives from lyrics in Rodgers and Hart's 'Bewildered' (the most famous version is by Frank Sinatra). Xander's reference to a 'parallel universe' takes us into a whole SF subgenre. Elvis gets name-checked. Oz's guitar is inscribed 'Sweet J', a possible reference to Lou Reed's Velvet Underground song 'Sweet Jane'. (It's also an *Austin Powers*' in joke.) The sequences of Joyce asking Xander to let her in and attacking the door with a carving knife may have been influenced by *The Shining*.

Bitch!: Xander, surprised that Cordelia hasn't been affected by the spell: 'Is this love? 'Coz maybe on you it doesn't look any different.'

Cordelia to Joyce: '. . . And keep your mom-age mitts off my boyfriend. *Former*.'

Awesome!: Cordelia's 'sheep' speech to Harmony. About time.

The Drugs Don't Work: Midol is an over-the-counter medicine frequently used in the US as a treatment for PMS. 'Roofie' is the street name for the 'date-rape' drug, Rohypnol.

Don't Give Up the Day Job: James A Contner's previous TV work includes *The Equalizer*, *Miami Vice*, *Lois and Clark: The New Adventures of Superman*, *The Flash*, *Dark Skies*, *The X-Files* and *Charmed*. Before that he was a camera operator and cinematographer on films such as *The Wiz*, *Superman* and *Times Square*.

Valley-Speak: Buffy: 'I'm glad you guys are getting along. Almost nearly.'
Harmony: 'A girl wants to look good for her geek.'
Guy in orange shirt: 'Dude, way to get dumped.'
Xander: 'I made her put the love whammy on Cordy.' And: 'Every woman in Sunnydale wants to make me her cuddle monkey.'

Logic, Let Me Introduce You to This Window: Xander nails three boards to the basement's doorframe. When Joyce's knife pokes through, sending Xander and Cordy running down the stairs, we see one of the boards runs all the way from the bottom left corner to the upper right. However, when Willow and the others open the door, the board is much higher. The timescale of the end of the episode is impossible. Xander saves Cordelia from the mob of girls early in the day, yet when they arrive at Buffy's house to hide it's evening.

Cruelty to Animals: Angel's past is littered with depraved displays of ultraviolence on Valentine's Day (including, on one occasion, nailing a puppy to something).

Quote/Unquote: Xander, after Cordelia has dropped her bombshell: 'Were you running low on dramatic irony?'
Xander, when Buffy suggests they should comfort each other: 'Would lap-dancing enter into that scenario at all? 'Coz I find that *very* comforting.'
Drusilla asks Xander how he feels about eternal life: 'We couldn't just start with the coffee?'

Notes: 'It's funny how you see someone every day, but not really *see* them.' I once reviewed this episode for a magazine and tried to give it twelve out of ten, but they wouldn't let me. Taking an old sitcom idea (loser-guy-becomes-babe-magnet-through-nefarious-skulduggery) and murdering it, this is *really funny*. Further comment is redundant.

Willow has been in Xander's bed before, but they were both (much) younger. We get our first decent look at Xander's room (it's got a HAZARDOUS WASTE sticker on the door). Among the Marvel and pop-art posters (including one for Widespread Panic, see **16**, 'Inca Mummy Girl'), it's nice to spot an acoustic guitar (so, maybe the daydream in **4**, 'Teacher's Pet' wasn't all fantasy, but see **47**, 'The Zeppo').

Two stickers for the band Lotion, who performed in **27**, 'Phases', are visible. The first is on the locker behind Giles when we first see him. The second is on the locker next to Cordelia's, best seen when Harmony slaps her. Chris Beck's incidental music is some of the best in the series, wonderfully fitting the tone of the episode. Sarah Michelle Gellar was missing for most of this episode as she was hosting *Saturday Night Live* that week. The story was novelised by Keith RA DeCandido as part of *The Xander Years*, published by Pocket Books in February 1999.

Soundtrack: Four Star Mary's 'Pain' is the song Dingoes Ate My Baby are miming to in the Bronze. Also 'Drift Away' by Naked and 'Got the Message' by the 70s funksters the Average White Band. *Niiice*.

Sky Nil: After this episode, Sky TV in the UK pulled *Buffy* from its 8 p.m. Saturday slot citing low viewing figures as a reason (it was replaced by *3rd Rock from the Sun*, which promptly drew *lower* ratings). It would be almost a year before the series was shown on Sky again, and then only after a long and often bitter campaign by fans.

29
Passion

US Transmission Date: 24 Feb. 1998
UK Transmission Date: 16 Jul. 1999 (Sky)

Writer: Ty King
Director: Michael E Gershman
Cast: Richard Assad (Shopkeeper),
Richard Hoyt Miller (Policeman)

Buffy wakes up to discover a drawing from Angelus on her pillow. She pleads with Giles for a way of stopping Angelus entering her home. She tells her mother that Angelus has been stalking her and that Joyce should never invite him in. Jenny, hoping to restore Angel's soul, purchases an Orb of Thesulah. The shopkeeper warns her that the spell's translation has been lost, but Jenny tells him that she's working on the text. With Jenny's help, Giles devises a spell to exclude Angelus from places he had previously been invited. Angelus asks Joyce to help him get Buffy back and mentions that they made love, but he is unable to enter the Summers' house as Willow and Buffy perform the spell. Jenny completes her programme, but Angelus knows what she is planning and kills her, leaving her body in Giles's bed. Giles attacks Angelus at the Factory and Buffy arrives in time to prevent Angelus from killing her Watcher, but Angelus escapes. Giles is furious at Buffy for interfering, but she tells him she won't allow him to kill himself. Willow takes over as substitute teacher and accidentally knocks a computer disk between the desk and a cabinet. It's the key to Angel's soul.

A Little Learning is a Dangerous Thing: Jenny asks Willow to take her computer class for her and after Jenny's death Snyder makes the same request.

Mom's Apple Pie: Joyce claims to have read 'all the parenting books' as she shares dinner with Buffy (roast chicken and vegetables). After Angelus tells Joyce that he and Buffy had sex, she and Buffy have the 'were you careful?' talk: Joyce regains a lot of plus points here with her sympathetic handling of the situation.

It's a Designer Label!: Willow's orange sweater, Buffy's grey pants and Xander's red shirt and checky strides.

References: The mass-murdering dictator Joseph Stalin (1879–1953), US book chain Barnes and Noble, *A Charlie Brown Christmas* and Russ Meyer's notorious biker sex-movie *Faster, Pussycat! Kill! Kill!* are all mentioned.

Ménage à Trois: Interviewed by *TV Guide*, David Boreanaz, James Marsters ('resembling an undecayed version of Billy Idol') and Juliet Landau described the Angel, Spike and Dru relationship in detail. Boreanaz: 'Angel has a very sarcastic side and he knows how to torment Spike. Everytime Spike pushes my buttons, I push his . . . He's all talk. It's like tennis and Drusilla is in the middle, watching.' Marsters: 'Angel was my mentor, [but] I'm grown up now and I don't need him anymore.' When the interviewer, Tim Appelo, described the relationship as 'the scariest romantic triangle since the *Archie* comics', Landau replied: 'In a funny way [Drusilla and Spike] have, like, a healthy relationship. I mean, we do go out and kill people, but we have a loving, giving relationship. But with Angel, it's almost like an incestuous, abusive relationship. That's why when I chained him to a bed and burned him with holy water, it was . . . a strange cross between sexuality and power.'

Bitch!: Cordelia: 'I'd do the same for you if you had a social life.'
Awesome!: Angelus killing Jenny against every dramatic convention that the viewer thinks they are party to, followed by the horribly voyeuristic sequence in which Angelus watches Buffy and Willow's reaction to the telephone call informing them of Jenny's death. Giles's murderous attack on Angelus and the moment when Buffy tells Giles that she won't let him kill himself because she can't do this alone. If you have tears, prepare to shed them.

Don't Give Up The Day Job: From the sublime to the ridiculous, the director Michael E Gersham's CV as a cameraman included *The Deer Hunter* and *The Golden Child*.

Logic, Let Me Introduce You to This Window: The object Willow is nailing to her wall is referred to as a crucifix. It isn't: it's a cross. How didn't Willow notice that her aquarium was empty as she poured fish food into it? Who put Jenny in Giles's apartment?

Cruelty to Animals: Willow on her dead fish: 'We hadn't really had time to bond yet.'

A Death in The Family: According to Alyson Hannigan 'Angel . . . had to kill somebody we loved – we were all warned about that. Actually I think it was supposed to be Oz that was killed, then they decided they'd keep Oz around and they killed Ms Calendar.' According to Robia LaMorte, '[The filming of] the confrontation in the classroom was one day in itself, that took probably four or five hours because of all the fire and explosions . . . On a separate day we did the rest . . . to the point of my death. A lot of running in high heels! The good thing about TV is, as soon as the camera goes to those tighter shots, put those sneakers on.'

Quote/Unquote: Giles: 'Yes, Xander, once again you've managed to boil a complex thought down to its simplest possible form.'

Angel's final words of wisdom: 'If we could live without passion, maybe we'd know some kind of peace. But we would be hollow. Empty rooms, shuttered and dank. Without passion, we'd be truly dead.'

Notes: 'Passion. It lies in all of us. Sleeping, waiting and though unwanted, unbidden, it will stir. Open its jaws and howl.' Not the masterpiece it's often made out to be, but containing a dramatic intensity that is occasionally overpowering. 'Passion' is another example of how adult a series *Buffy* can be.

Willow's parents would never let her have a puppy. Her father's name is Ira and the Rosenberg family are Jewish (as hinted in previous episodes). Once invited into a house, a vampire is always welcome (except if, as in this case, a reversal spell is performed). The sign on the front of the school says (in Latin) ENTER ALL YE WHO SEEK KNOWLEDGE, which Angelus claims is his invitation (but see **30**, 'Killed By Death', concerning vampires and public places). The places that Angelus can no longer visit include Buffy's house, Willow's house (which he entered in **19**, 'Lie to Me') and Cordelia's car (**14**, 'Some Assembly Required'). Joyce remembers Angel as 'the college boy' who was tutoring Buffy in history (see **7**, 'Angel').

In the scene where Buffy and Joyce are eating dinner, look over Joyce's shoulder at the picture. It's a publicity photo of Sarah Michelle Gellar that appeared in the August 1997 issue of *Entertainment Weekly*. During the graveyard scene, you can hear a choral voice accompanying the music. It belongs to Tony Head, who suggested to Christophe Beck that he sing.

Soundtrack: 'Never an Easy Way' by Morcheeba and Puccini's 'Acte 10 Soave Fanciulla' from *La Bohème*.

30
Killed By Death

US Transmission Date: 3 Mar. 1998
UK Transmission Date: 23 Jul. 1999 (Sky)

Writers: Rob Des Hotel, Dean Batali
Director: Deran Sarafian
Cast: Richard Herd (Dr Stanley Backer),
Willie Garson (Security Guard),
Andrew Ducote (Ryan), Juanita Jennings (Dr Wilkinson),
Robert Munic (Intern), Mimi Paley (Little Buffy),
Denise Johnson (Celia),
James Jude Courtney (Der Kindestod)

Buffy is in hospital with a nasty dose of flu. Overcome with fever, she sees a terrifying demonic figure stalking the halls and children are dying. A boy, Ryan, tells her that Death is coming for them and that he is invisible to adults. Angelus tries to visit Buffy, but Xander stops him. Buffy tells her friends about Death and they investigate. The prime suspect is one of the doctors, Backer, but Buffy sees him killed by an invisible force. Willow helps Buffy investigate Backer's office for clues, while Giles and Cordelia discover the legend of Der Kindestod, a demon who sucks the life from children. Buffy ingests some of the flu virus so that she will be able to see her enemy and (with Willow creating a diversion) she and Xander follow him to the basement where the children are hiding. They find Ryan pinned to the floor by Der Kindestod. Buffy kills the demon while Xander leads the children to safety.

Dudes and Babes: A sick Buffy in her fluffy bed socks is so cuddlesome, you want to hug her till she pops.

A Little Learning is a Dangerous Thing: Willow has done Buffy's homework for her. All she has to do is sign it and the ruse will be complete.

It's a Designer Label!: There's some horrible stuff on display here, including Buffy's white trainers, Willow's red tights and Cordy's green-lined parka. But Cordelia's short dark skirt and black bootees are heavenly.

References: Name checks for the actress Gwyneth Paltrow, 'Mr Potatohead', Humphrey Bogart, Death-as-a-chess-player in both Ingmar Bergman's *The Seventh Seal* and *Bill & Ted's Bogus Journey,* the DC comics' superheroine Power Girl and the Greek poet Homer. Angelus hums a snatch from Beethoven's ninth symphony ('Ode to Joy'). There are oblique references to Sherlock Holmes and *The Invisible Man* ('If I see a floating pipe and a smoking jacket, he's dropped'). Dare I mention how reminiscent of *Nightmare on Elm Street* the whole thing is?

Bitch!: Cordelia's inept sympathy for Buffy: 'We're all concerned about how *gross* you look.' As Giles notes, 'Cordelia, have you ever actually *heard* of tact?'

Plus Angelus: 'It must just eat you up that I got there first', to which Xander replies, 'You're going to die and I'm going to be there.'

'You May Remember Me From Such Films and TV Series As . . .': Richard Herd played James McCord in *All The President's Men*, Henry Skerridge in *Midnight in the Garden of Good and Evil*, and Commander John in *V*, though readers may remember his performance as 'Captain Galaxy', Moe Stein, in the 'Future Boy' episode of *Quantum Leap*. His other TV credits include *Starsky and Hutch*, *The A-Team* and *Hart to Hart*. Willie Garson, in addition to small parts in *There's Something About Mary*, *Mars Attack!*, *Groundhog Day* and *The Rock* and a recurring role (as Henry Coffield) in *NYPD Blue*, has made something of a career out of playing Lee Oswald, appearing in both the movie *Ruby* and the *Quantum Leap* episode 'Lee Harvey Oswald'. Denise Johnson is one of the voice artists on *A Bug's Life*.

Valley-Speak: Xander: 'I gotta get me a life.'

Buffy: 'I feel all oogy.' Xander: 'Increased ooginess. That's a danger signal.'

Cordelia's attempts to articulate what Der Kindestod does to children consists of several repetitions of 'Euw!'

Logic, Let Me Introduce You to This Window: When Buffy rants about killing vampires, Dr Wilkinson gives her a tranquilliser injection straight to her arm. The drug should have been administered intravenously. Before Buffy sees Der Kindestod, her bedside clock changes from 2.26 to 2.27. In the following shot, the clock reads 2.15. When Buffy looks into the children's ward for the first time, there is no blue BASEMENT ACCESS plaque on the exit door. Why is there an unlocked, clearly labelled door that leads from the children's ward straight to the hospital basement? Reports differ on the actual number, but there are certainly very few Krispy Kreme doughnut takeaways in Southern California, so Cordelia must have driven *miles* to get Xander his doughnut breakfast. It *must* be love.

I Just *Love* Your Accent: Giles visits Buffy in hospital carrying a brown paper bag. It couldn't contain *grapes* could it? It does. A ubiquitous gift for the invalid and a cultural stereotype that should be executed with extreme prejudice.

Quote/Unquote: Cordelia: 'I was using "watch her back" as a euphemism for "looking at her butt".'

Buffy, on how she intends to stop Der Kindestod: 'Thought I might try violence.'

Notes: 'Fear is for the weak.' Very well directed (the weirdly angled corridors for instance) and, despite the obvious Freddie Kruger riffs, for the most part a clear and simple story about the bogeyman. It gets a bit confusing towards the end, but the characterisation (particularly of Cordelia and Xander) is impressive. A piece of a much bigger jigsaw.

When Buffy was eight her cousin Celia (to whom she was close) died in hospital while Buffy was alone with her. It is subsequently revealed that the invisible Der Kindestod sucked the life from her. This presumably means either there is more than one Kindestod, or that Buffy is a victim of 'Jessica Fletcher's Syndrome', having *always* been a magnet for these kinds of deadly events. Or it's just a huge coincidence and an excuse for a contrived plot device. Your choice. There's an oblique reference to Buffy's amazing self-healing power as previously hinted (see **23**, 'Ted'). Joyce tells Giles how sorry she was to hear about Ms Calendar's death (see **29**, 'Passion'). Xander and Willow used to play 'doctor' (literally, since Willow had lots of medical textbooks and Xander never had the heart to tell her she was playing it wrong). Buffy claims never to have played the game. Cordelia's raised eyebrows at this suggest (a) she doesn't believe Buffy and (b) she herself has. Frequently. There's another reference to Willow's frog-phobia (see **21**, 'What's My Line?' Part 1). Buffy likes peanut-butter and jelly sandwiches without the crust, and drinks juice that is two parts orange to one part grapefruit. This episode explains how vampires can enter factories and school buildings. After Willow asks if Angelus can attack Buffy while she's in the hospital, Xander says, 'He can come in. It's a public building.'

31
I Only Have Eyes For You

US Transmission Date: 28 Apr. 1998
UK Transmission Date: 30 Jul. 1999 (Sky)

Writer: Marti Noxon
Director: James Whitmore
Cast: Meredith Salinger (Grace Newman),
Christopher Gorham (James Stanley),
John Hawkes (George), Miriam Flynn (Ms Frank),
Brian Poth (Fighting Boy),
Sarah Bibb (Fighting Girl), Ryan Taszreak (Ben),
Anna Coman-Hidy (50s Girl #1),
Vanessa Bodnar (50s Girl #2)

Buffy finds a boy and girl fighting in the school hallway. He
holds a gun and shouts, 'Don't walk away from me, bitch.'
Buffy stops the boy from shooting, but the couple are confused
about why they are arguing and where the gun came from. Or
went to, since it is nowhere to be seen. More weirdness occurs,
including a teacher writing the same words on a blackboard as
Buffy has a daydream about the school in the 50s. Xander is
attacked by a rotting arm in his locker. Willow looks up previous shooting victims at school and finds a case from 1955,
where a student (James) shot his teacher (Grace), then himself.
Buffy recognises their faces from her dream. In the cafeteria
all of the food turns into snakes. Willow plans to exorcise the
spirit with Buffy, Xander and Cordelia chanting from different
locations in the school at midnight. However, a swarm of
wasps invades the hallways. Giles, after initially thinking that
the troubled spirit is Jenny, believes James's soul is haunting
the school, seeking forgiveness from Grace, but this can never
happen, since, each time the scenario is re-enacted, Grace dies.
Buffy returns to school and meets Angelus and the pair are
possessed by the ghosts. Buffy (acting out James's role) 'kills'
Angelus. Buffy prepares to shoot herself, when Angelus stops

her, forgives her and they share a kiss before the souls depart, leaving Buffy and Angelus in an embrace. Angelus escapes, feeling violated. He takes Drusilla out to find blood. After they leave, Spike rises from his wheelchair.

Authority Sucks!: Snyder tells Buffy he intends to carefully look over the details of the gun incident until he can work out how it's all her fault. Unfortunately, he's interrupted mid-rant by a vegan chaining himself to the snack machine.

The Conspiracy Starts at Home Time: In one short exchange between Snyder and Bob, an entire back-story is created and the suspicions that viewers had from the scene featuring the same pair in **15**, 'School Hard' (about a conspiracy), is confirmed. We learn that Snyder was given his job by the City Council. Snyder refers to 'you people', which suggests that, whatever is taking place, it involves the Sunnydale PD (or perhaps he's talking in a wider context – see **33**, 'Becoming' Part 1) and the little flinch he gives when Bob suggests that he talk to the Mayor speaks volumes. But, when Snyder states 'we're on a Hellmouth', suddenly a lot of things become clear. They *know*.

A Little Learning is a Dangerous Thing: Buffy notes she 'pretty much repressed anything math-related' (nice to know repression runs in the family). Willow wants her students to read the chapters on 'information grouping' and 'binary coding'. Xander doesn't know the difference between a 'scapular' and a 'spatula'. There's an essay on the New Deal (before 1935 it concentrated on revitalising stricken businesses and agricultural communities). Also Giles's completely bonkers Fox Mulder-like leap to the wrong conclusion about the identity of the malevolent ghost.

School Dinners: Snakes in the spaghetti. If you have lunches, get ready to part with them.

It's a Designer Label!: A *big* round of applause for Cordelia's tight red sweater. Buffy's suede boots and impossibly short brown skirt (it's really a long vest, isn't it?) cop similar reactions. There's also the red and gold dress worn by the singer with Splendid. On the minus side, Willow's rainbow jumper and pale-green top.

References: Misquotes from *Julius Caesar* ('you came, you saw, you rejected') and *The Merchant of Venice* ('the quality of mercy is not Buffy'), plus references to OJ Simpson, the Nazi 'Final Solution', Ernest Hemingway, the Loch Ness monster, Alice Cooper's rebellion anthem 'School's Out' and *The Exorcist* ('I saw that movie – even the priest dies'). *Poltergeist* is mentioned and parts of the plot seem influenced by it (notably Cordelia's mirror sequence). 'You've got to roll with the punches' is a quote from Van Halen's 'Jump'. Snyder's line 'I'm no stranger to conspiracy: I saw *JFK*' is the series in microcosm. The characters of James and Grace share their names with those of the leading actors in Hitchcock's *Rear Window* (Stewart and Kelly respectively).

Awesome!: That incredibly touching scene between Giles and Willow at the start. And Buffy and Angelus playing out the James/Grace scenario.

'You May Remember Me From Such Films and TV Series As . . .': Christopher Gorham played Walt in *A Life Less Ordinary*. John Hawkes was Pete Bottoms in *From Dusk Till Dawn* and was terrific as the writer Phillip Padgett in the *X-Files* episode 'Milagro'. Miriam Flynn was the voice of Maa in *Babe*.

Don't Give Up The Day Job: Although the director James Whitmore's credits include *Melrose Place, Quantum Leap, The X-Files, Nowhere Man* and *The Pretender*, he is also an actor playing Bernie Terwilliger in *Hunter*.

Valley-Speak: Cordelia's incantation: 'I shall *totally* confront and expel all evil.'
    Xander: 'Oh yeah, baby, it's snakealicious in here.'
    Buffy: 'So, we have some bad *boo* on our hands.'
    Xander: 'I don't want to *poo-poo* your wiggins.'

Logic, Let Me Introduce You to This Window: After Buffy has re-entered the wasp-surrounded school, Giles and the others stand in front of the building. The shot of them staring at the wasps is the same one used earlier in the episode after they had escaped. Look closely and you'll be able to spot Buffy's legs. After Snyder leaves Buffy alone in his office, the 1955 yearbook falls from the bookshelf. When it hits the floor, you can see the cover flip open. As Buffy bends down the book is closed. 'I Only Have Eyes For You' by the Flamingos is used during the flashbacks to 1955. However, the song wasn't released until 1959. Why is Cordelia, who had her own diet in **4**, 'Teacher's Pet', eating spaghetti in the school cafeteria?

Quote/Unquote: Giles: 'You should never be cowed by authority. Except, of course, in this instance where I am clearly right and you are clearly wrong.'

Xander: ' "Something weird is going on"? Isn't that our school motto?'

Notes: 'Love is for ever.' Serious stuff, as Marti Noxon's combination of ghost story and pop-culture angst combines to produce an episode that flirts with saying something profound, but never quite delivers. The redemption theme is good and there's a great last scene, but, when you're dealing with something as horrific as teen suicide, you need more than gestures. Snyder's on top form, though, which covers a multitude of sins. Like **13**, 'When She Was Bad', this focuses on what an intolerant character Buffy can be (there are narrative links between Buffy ranting at her friends' stupidity here and her rows with Angel in the season opener).

Buffy says she's not seeing anybody, ever again. Willow gives Giles a rose-quartz stone that belonged to Jenny. It's been suggested that Willow should be unable to retrieve any of Jenny's computer files, as her PC was destroyed in **29**, 'Passion'. In the former episode, when Angelus threw the computer from her desk, the monitor smashed and burst into flames. The hard drive, however, fell on the ground away from the monitor. It's perfectly possible that it suffered no significant damage. Of course, there may have been backup disks. (Indeed, if *anyone* is going to keep backups it would be a computer teacher.) The original US broadcast was followed by a public-service announcement by Sarah Michelle Gellar on behalf of the American Association of Suicideology,

Soundtrack: Aside from the Flamingos' recording, 'Charge' by Splendid.

32
Go Fish

US Transmission Date: 5 May 1998
UK Transmission Date: 6 Aug. 1999 (Sky)

Writers: David Fury, Elin Hampton
Director: David Semel
Cast: Charles Cyphers (Coach Marin),
Jeremy Garrett (Cameron Walker),
Wentworth Miller (Gage Petronzi),
Conchata Ferrell (Nurse Greenliegh),
Shane West (Sean), Jake Patellis (Dodd McAlvy)

A victory party for the swim team sees everyone celebrating except Buffy. But, when two team members disappear, she and her friends become involved. Snyder encourages Willow to raise the (failing) grade of Gage, another swimmer. Giles believes that, since the two victims were the best swimmers in school, Gage is the next likely target. While keeping Gage under surveillance, Buffy saves him from an attack by Angelus. With a position open due to the deaths, Xander makes it on to the swim team. Buffy sees Gage tear away his own skin, emerging as a monster. Xander learns that steroids are passed to the team in the steam room, meaning that he has been exposed to the substance that transformed the others. Coach Marin tells Buffy about Russian experiments with fish DNA on their Olympic swimmers. He forces Buffy into the sewer so his boys can satisfy their 'other needs'. Xander struggles with Marin, as Buffy fends off the creatures, and the coach ends up in the sewer, with his boys.

Dudes and Babes: Xander in red Speedo swim wear ('I'm undercover', 'Not under much'). The double takes on the faces of Cordy, Buffy and Willow are wonderful. It must be said, Xander's far too well built to be a total geek – it *must* be his personality.

Authority Sucks: Xander on Snyder's manipulation of Willow to up Gage's grades: 'It's a slap in the face to every one of us that studied hard and worked long hours to *earn* our D's.'

A Little Learning is a Dangerous Thing: Since Willow is still in charge of the computer class, everybody's pie charts look like they're supposed to. Except Gage's. Xander seemingly doesn't know who wrote the Constitution. His take on history is little better ('the discus throwers got the best seats at all the crucifixions'). Cordelia's opinion on the 'all-men-are-created-equal thing': 'Propaganda spouted out by the ugly and less deserving.' And on Abraham Lincoln: 'Disgusting mole and stupid hat.'

It's a Designer Label!: Cordelia's miniskirts take much of the viewers' attention, but Buffy's stretchpants are practical *and* fun. She lets the side down, however, by sporting a pair of leather trousers in the sewer scenes – just the sort of thing to wear when chasing fish monsters. Willow's usual hippy-chick look is further emphasised by a pair of flared orange loon pants.

References: The title comes from Rose Troche's 1994 lesbian movie. Xander's favourite teams include the New York Yankees, Abbot and Costello, and *The A-Team*. Also referenced are Gertrude Edderley, the first woman to swim the English Channel, Twisted Sister, the 80s glam-metal band, *The Creature from the Black Lagoon* and the Brooke Shields film *Blue Lagoon*. Willow's line about the 'chocolatey goodness' of Oreo cookies may be an in-joke (Alyson Hannigan has done commercials for Oreo). There are dialogue and visual nods to *Jaws*. Xander misquotes from the Commodores' hit 'Three Times a Lady' and there's an oblique reference to Thomas Dolby's 'She Blinded Me With Science'. Magazines seen in the library include *Women's Sports and Fitness*, *Sports Illustrated*, *Vegetarian Times*, *National Geographic*, *PC World*, *Slam!*, *Smithsonian*, *Horseman*, *Skin Diver* and *Art News*.

Bitch!: Cordelia's suggestion after Xander asks what he can do to help the investigations: 'Go out into the parking lot and practise running like a man.'

Awesome!: Buffy taking on two monsters in the dressing room (nice use of a lacrosse stick) and Buffy and Angelus battling ('Why, Ms Summers, you're beautiful'). Cordelia's pride in Xander when he becomes the hero ('you were so courageous – and you looked really hot in those Speedos') is perfectly in character. Highlight of the episode is Willow's interrogation of Jonathan and her reaction to his 'confession' that he peed in the pool ('Euw!').

'You May Remember Me From Such Films and TV Series As . . .': Charles Cyphers was one of John Carpenter's repertory company appearing in *Assault on Precinct 13*, *Escape from New York*, *The Fog* and the first two *Halloween* movies. On TV he appeared in *The Dukes of Hazzard*, *Wonder Woman*, *Charlie's Angels* and *Starsky and Hutch*. Conchata Ferrell was Susan Bloom in *L.A. Law*, and was in *True Romance*, *Edward Scissorhands* and *Network*.

Valley-Speak: Xander: 'Last month he's the freak with jicama breath who waxes his back. He wins a few meets and suddenly inherits the cool gene?'

Gage: 'Aw, dude, what *is* that foulness?'

Buffy: 'There's just something about the smell of chlorine on a guy. Oh, baby.'

Logic, Let Me Introduce You to This Window: The first shot of the Bronze features a blank chalkboard. However, when Buffy observes Gage with Angelus, it has gained an advert: DJ 2NITE NO COVER. Coach Marin is concerned that the swim team will find out about the recent deaths. In the Bronze, Gage seems unaware of Cameron's death. When Buffy tells him of the killer, she doesn't mention Cameron by name. But Gage's question after Angelus's attack is, 'Was that the thing that killed Cameron?' In the final shot, we see three fish creatures in the ocean. Where's the fourth? Watch out for Buffy's *Wonder Woman*-style leap from the sewers to the trapdoor. Didn't know she could do that.

Quote/Unquote: Xander: 'It's officially nippy. So say my nips.'

Cordelia gets most of the best lines, including 'Xander, I know you take pride in being the voice of the common wuss.'

And, when believing that Xander had been turned into an aquatic monster: 'We can still date . . . Or not. I mean, I'd understand if you want to see other fish. I'll do everything I can to make your quality of life better, whether that means little bath toys or whatever.'

Buffy: 'I think we'd better find the rest of the swim team and lock them up before they get in touch with their inner halibut.'

Notes: 'Is steroid abuse usually linked with "Hey, I'm a fish"?' Another Xander-led episode, another comedy classic. Amid the hilarity of one of *Buffy*'s funniest episodes, however, is a cool essay on drug-enhanced performance and the ceaseless search for excellence and winners that the US school system seems hell-bent on.

The school board are having trouble finding a competent teacher this late in the term, so Willow is asked to continue subbing through finals (see **29**, 'Passion'). Although we had previously seen Sunnydale docks (**25**, 'Surprise'), this episode confirms that it is a coastal town with its own beach. Did the fish creatures eat Coach Marin, or did they have something else in mind? They leave at least half of Nurse Greenliegh intact and the coach specifically states that they've had their dinner and have 'other needs'. Xander's smirk when Buffy says 'those boys really loved their coach' suggests some horrible ideas.

Soundtrack: 'Mann's Chinese' by Naked, and 'If You'd Listen' by Nero's Rome.

33
Becoming Part 1

US Transmission Date: 12 May 1998
UK Transmission Date: 13 Aug. 1999 (Sky)

Writer: Joss Whedon
Director: Joss Whedon
Cast: Max Perlich (Whistler), Jack McGee (Doug Perren),
Richard Riehle (Buffy's First Watcher[6]),
Shannon Weller (Gypsy Woman), Zitto Kazann (Gypsy Man),
Ginger Williams (Girl), Nina Gervitz (Teacher)

Galway, 1753: Angel encounters Darla, who offers to show
him her world. Sunnydale, 1998: Giles is asked by the
museum to look at a stone artefact. London, 1860: Drusilla
enters a church, but the priest is already dead, killed by
Angelus, who tells her that she is the 'spawn of Satan'. Sunnydale, 1998: Buffy and Willow discover the disk on which
Jenny stored the spell to restore Angel's soul. Romania,
1898: The body of a gypsy girl lies on the ground, while a
curse of restoration is cast. Angelus is told that he will be
haunted by the souls of those he has killed. Sunnydale, 1998:
Angelus tells Spike about the demon Acathla, who possesses
the power to swallow the Earth into Hell. Kendra arrives,
having been sent by her Watcher because another dark force
is threatening Sunnydale. Manhattan, 1996: Angel, living as a
tramp, is approached by a demon, Whistler, who offers Angel
the chance to regain his dignity. Los Angeles, 1996: Whistler
shows Angel the Chosen One, observing Buffy's initial meeting with her first Watcher. Whistler says Buffy is just a child
and will need Angel's help. Sunnydale, 1998: Angelus fails to
revive Acathla. A girl vampire walks into an exam room, tells
Buffy that she must meet Angelus that night then bursts into
flames. Buffy finds Angelus at the cemetery and they fight,
but it is a trap to get The Slayer away from her friends. At the
library the vampires attack. Drusilla kills Kendra; Willow and

Xander are left unconscious, and Giles is taken away. Buffy arrives as a police officer orders her to freeze.

Dudes and Babes: This is the episode that gets all the girls banging on about how tragic (and therefore sexy) a figure Angel is. Mind you, the Irish accent could use a bit of work, David. *Begorrah*.

Authority Sucks!: Snyder on his students having relationships: 'These public displays of affection are not acceptable in my school. This isn't an orgy, people, it's a classroom.' He then asks Buffy to give him a reason to kick her out (see **34**, 'Becoming' Part 2).

A Little Learning is a Dangerous Thing: Willow is enjoying teaching and helps Buffy with some chemistry homework. 'When, in the real world, am I going to need chemistry. Or history. Or math. Or . . . the English language?' asks Buffy.

Mom's Apple Pie: A clever reversal of the 'Do you know what time it is?' scene from **M1**: Joyce catches Buffy coming in late from Slaying and has a blazing row with her.

School Dinners: Xander's re-enactment of Buffy's killing a vampire using two fish fingers is certainly worth seeing.

It's a Designer Label!: Watch out for Buffy's red dress and her brilliant trouser suit and ice-blue frock coat. Cordy's red sweater from **31**, 'I Only Have Eyes for You', puts in another appearance. On the minus side are Buffy's hooded top, her yellow coat and horrible pants in the LA 1996 sequences and Whistler's green shirt.

References: Allusions to *The Sword in the Stone* and other examples of Arthurian lore. Buffy calls Acathla 'Alfalfa' from *The Little Rascals*. The sequence in which Darla cuts her chest with her fingernail and makes Angel drink from it is yet another moment that seems to have been inspired by *Dracula, Prince of Darkness* (see **2**, 'The Harvest', **12**, 'Prophecy Girl').

Bitch!: After Cordelia is really nice to Willow, Xander notes: 'And almost sixty-five per cent of that was actual compliment. Is that a personal best?'

Cordy on Snyder: 'A tiny impotent Nazi with a bug up his butt the size of an emu.'

Xander: 'So, this spell might restore Angel's soul? Well, here's an interesting angle: who cares?'

I'd love to know what word it was that Willow calls Xander that causes Buffy to say, 'Do you kiss your mother with that mouth?'

Awesome!: The fight sequence in the library – five minutes of way-cool violence. And the moment when Angel's soul is cursed in a flash of pyrotechnics.

'You May Remember Me From Such Films and TV Series As . . .': Max Perlich was Johnny Hardin in *Maverick* and was a regular on *Homicide: Life On the Streets* (as James Brodie). Jack McGee is one of those actors who seem to be in *everything*: he's in *Backdraft, Lethal Weapon 2* and *Showgirls,* plays a sheriff in *Basic Instinct* and is the cop who sprays Val Kilmer with mace in *The Doors*. Richard Riehle had lots of film credits, including *Fear and Loathing in Las Vegas, Casino, The Fugitive* and *Fried Green Tomatoes at the Whistle Stop Café*. Zitto Kazann is in *Waterworld*.

Valley-Speak: Buffy: 'Ready to rock.'
Plus her *total* Valley-girl act in LA in 1996: 'Call me!'

Logic, Let Me Introduce You to This Window: In **14**, 'Some Assembly Required', Angel is 241 years old. Assuming that episode took place in 1997, he would have been born in 1755 or 1756. According to **18**, 'Halloween', Angel was eighteen years old in 1775 and still human, which ties in with this. However, here Angel is bitten by Darla in 1753, three years before he was born. It seems Buffy isn't the only character with a variety of birthdays. According to the flashbacks, Angel saw Buffy at least twice before they met in **1**, 'Welcome to the Hellmouth', despite his saying in the opening episode, 'I thought you'd be taller.'

Quote/Unquote: Drusilla: 'Met an old man. I didn't like him. He got stuck in my teeth.'

Willow says she has been researching the Black Arts – 'for fun'.

Spike: 'It's a big rock. Can't wait to tell my friends. They don't have a rock this big.'

Notes: 'So, what are we? Helpless puppets? No, the big moments are gonna come, you can't help that. It's what you do afterwards that counts.' 'Becoming' Part 1 explores the nature of destiny and does it *beautifully*. Sharing similarities with *Highlander* isn't the worst of crimes, as this poetic exercise in controlled storytelling delves into two centuries of Angel's past. However, Kendra's arbitrary death (well played as it is) is a real disappointment.

Giles has been using his Orb of Thesulah as a paperweight, which is a clever in-joke referring to what a Magik-Store guy told Jenny he had sold a couple of the Orbs for in **29**, 'Passion'. Xander says Buffy has killed five vampires over the previous three nights. Buffy's boyfriend when she first became The Slayer was called Tyler. Kendra calls the stake that she gives to Buffy 'Mr Pointy'. We see another copy of the *Sunnydale Press* (see **17**, 'Reptile Boy', **55**, 'Graduation Day' Part 1). The episode includes flashbacks to events first mentioned in **7**, 'Angel': Darla's 'siring' of Angel and his being cursed by the Romany people. The 1860 sequence shows that Drusilla was psychic before she became a vampire (she predicted a pit disaster). She refers to her mother in the present tense, which means these events must have taken place at the beginning of Angelus's relationship with her, since **19**, 'Lie to Me', makes clear he killed all of those close to her before finally killing her. Indeed, this could to be their first meeting (although Angelus is certainly taking a lot of risks to be close to Dru – entering a church, for example). Whistler's reference to Buffy as little more than a child seems to imply that The Slayer is normally older (but see **46**, 'Helpless'). The building used for Hemery High is a façade in the backlot of Universal Studios in North Hollywood. It was also used for the Hill Valley Clock Tower in the first two *Back to the Future* films. The Latin that Giles speaks during the restoration curse translates as 'that which was lost shall be found'.

34
Becoming Part 2

US Transmission Date: 19 May 1998
UK Transmission Date: 13 Aug. 1999 (Sky)

Writer: Joss Whedon
Director: Joss Whedon
Cast: Max Perlich (Whistler), Susan Leslie (First Cop),
Thomas G Waites (Second Cop)

Buffy is arrested for murder, but escapes and visits the hospital in disguise. Xander tells her that Willow is in a coma and Giles has disappeared. At Giles's apartment, Buffy meets Whistler, who tells her that Angel was destined to stop Acathla, not revive him. A patrol cop recognises Buffy but Spike helps her escape, explaining that he wants to stop Angelus. Buffy takes him back to her house, where a vampire attacks her mother. Buffy kills it and explains to Joyce that she is a Vampire Slayer. Joyce is angry at having been kept in the dark and tells Buffy that, if she leaves now, she shouldn't bother coming back. Giles refuses to divulge the information that Angelus needs, despite being tortured. Willow recovers and tells the others that she will try the curse again. Buffy returns to the library to retrieve Kendra's sword. Snyder finds her and gleefully expels her, calling someone to tell the Mayor the good news. Drusilla tricks Giles by making herself look like Jenny. Giles says Angelus's blood is the key to the awakening. Xander frees Giles as Buffy sword-fights Angelus, leaving Spike to hustle Drusilla away. Willow restores the curse on Angelus's soul just as Buffy is about to deliver the final blow. However, Acathla is awakening and Buffy must close the vortex and send Angel to Hell. Homeless and expelled, Buffy boards a bus and leaves Sunnydale.

Dudes and Babes: Buffy's claim to be the drummer in a rock band with Spike as the singer is such a wonderful image that we almost wish it were true.

Authority Sucks!: 'You stupid little troll, you have no *idea*.' But Snyder *does*, as Buffy discovers in the scene where he expels her.

Denial No More!: 'Mom, I'm a Vampire Slayer.' There's not much even Joyce can say to that, although 'Have you tried *not* being a Slayer' is an impressive comeback. Buffy rages at her mother's inability to see what's been staring her in the face for the last two years, asking how many times Joyce has washed blood out of Buffy's clothes (see **4**, 'Teacher's Pet').

It's a Designer Label!: Buffy's undercover hat is so funny, you'll fall on the floor and kick your legs in the air laughing. Xander's purple jumper crops up again. There's also Oz's yellow shirt and a pink one in the final scene. Cordelia's lemon dress is a highlight.

References: Snyder's 'Your point being?' echoes Homer Simpson's reply in *The Simpsons* episode 'Marge on the Lam', when asked if he is just holding on to the Coke cans that have got both his arms stuck in two drinks machines. 'A gay old time' is a reference to *The Flintstones*. 'Goodbye Piccadilly, farewell bloody Leicester Square' is a misquote from the World War One song 'It's a Long Way to Tipperary'.

Bitch!: Buffy to Snyder: 'You never got a single date in high school, did you?'

Awesome!: Willow's 'resolve'-face: a comedy classic. The lengthy Buffy–Angelus sword fight. Plus the delightful comedy scene of Joyce and Spike on the couch (see **42**, 'Lover's Walk').

'You May Remember Me From Such Films As . . .': Thomas G Waites appeared in two of this author's favourite movies, playing Windows in *The Thing* and Fox in *The Warriors*.

Valley-Speak: Buffy to Xander: 'That was equal parts protecting me and copping a feel?'

Logic, Let Me Introduce You to This Window: Why does Buffy invite Spike into her home? You'd think she would have learned something from the events of **29**, 'Passion'. When did Xander show Buffy the 'funky-looking mansion' on Crawford Street? Buffy couldn't have known that Drusilla was responsible for Kendra's death (Xander was unconscious before Drusilla entered the library), yet that's what she tells Spike. Principals cannot expel students without a school board hearing. If Spike is so anti-the-End-of-the-World then what was all that business with the Judge in **26**, 'Innocence'? During the final battle scene, Buffy's hair changes from loose to ponytailed several times. Spike drives out of the garage and turns the steering wheel hard to the left, keeping it in that position for several seconds (the car should, therefore, be going in circles). Angelus's sword-fighting double looks more like Xander than Angelus. Major logic flaw: the script implies that only Angel could have been able to open Acathla, even though it is supposed to be his destiny to stop this happening. Until Angel turned into Angelus, this story would never have happened.

I Just *Love* Your Accent: Spike says he likes dog racing and Manchester United (in that, he's typical – most of their supporters live *anywhere* but Manchester). Whistler says, 'Raiding an Englishman's fridge is like dating a nun: you're never going to get to the good stuff.'

Quote/Unquote: Buffy to Whistler: 'If you're gonna crack jokes, I'm gonna pull out your rib cage and wear it as a hat.'

Spike: 'I don't fancy spending the next month trying to get librarian out of the carpet.'

Go Straight to Hell: Angelus: 'You're going to Hell.' Buffy: 'Save me a seat.'

Notes: 'I've had a *really* bad day.' Initially more concerned with power politics and characterisation than plot. For twenty minutes the episode completely loses its focus, stuttering (despite the hospital scenes contrasted with the grotesque brutality of Angelus torturing Giles) before a magnificent recovery to its tragic conclusion.

Xander tells an unconscious Willow that she is his best friend and that he loves her. Significantly, the first word

Willow says on coming out of her coma is 'Oz'. The last time Angelus tortured someone the chainsaw hadn't been invented. Spike refers to Joyce hitting him with an axe in **15**, 'School Hard'. Snyder says the Sunnydale police are deeply stupid, which seems about right on the evidence we've seen (see **48**, 'Bad Girls'). The road sign at the end of the episode reads NOW LEAVING SUNNYDALE. COME BACK SOON!

Soundtrack: 'Full of Grace' by Sarah McLachlan. (On the same CD is a song called 'Angel'. Coincidence?) Christophe Beck's magnificent score won a deserved Emmy. The love theme 'Close Your Eyes', which accompanies the final Buffy–Angel scenes, is truly epic.

Something very strange is happening.

– 'Doppelgängland'

Third Season (1998–9)

**Mutant Enemy Inc./Kuzui Enterprises/Sandollar
Television/20th Century Fox**
Created by Joss Whedon
Producer: Gareth Davies
Executive Producers: Sandy Gallin, Gail Berman,
Fran Rubel Kuzui, Kaz Kuzui,
David Greenwalt, Joss Whedon
Co-Producers: Marti Noxon, David Solomon, Kelly Manners

Regular Cast:
Sarah Michelle Gellar (Buffy Summers)
Nicholas Brendon (Xander Harris)
Alyson Hannigan (Willow Rosenberg)
Charisma Carpenter (Cordelia Chase)
David Boreanaz (Angel/Angelus)
Anthony Stewart Head (Rupert Giles)
Mark Metcalf (the Master, 43)
Kristine Sutherland (Joyce Summers, 35–7, 40, 42, 44–6,
48–9, 51–5)
Mercedes McNab (Harmony, 43, 55–6)
Elizabeth Anne Allen (Amy Madison, 45)
Robia LaMorte (Jenny Calendar, 44)
Armin Shimerman (Principal Snyder, 36–7, 40, 45,
50, 53, 55–6)
James Marsters (Spike, 42)
Seth Green (Oz, 35–48, 50–6)
Jason Hall (Devon, 36, 39–41, 50)
Danny Strong (Jonathan, 36, 39, 43, 52, 54, 56)
Larry Bagby III (Larry, 35, 43, 52, 56)
Robin Sachs (Ethan Rayne, 40)
Julia Lee ('Chanterelle'/'Lily', 35)
Saverio Guerra (Willy, 44, 47)
James G MacDonald (Detective Stein, 49)
Jeremy Ratchford (Lyle Gorch, 39)
James Lurie (Mr Miller, 35[1], 55)
Fab Filippo (Scott Hope, 37–9)

Eliza Dushku (Faith, 37–9, 41, 44, 47–51, 53–6)
K Todd Freeman (Mr Trick, 37, 39–40, 48–9)
Harry Groener (Mayor Richard Wilkins III, 39–40, 42, 45,
48–51, 53–6)
Jack Plotnick (Deputy Mayor Allan Finch 39, 42, 48–9)
Emma Caufield (Anya, 43, 50, 54–5)
Alexis Denisof (Wesley Wyndham-Price, 48–56)
Ethan Erickson (Percy West 50, 52, 55–6)
Bonita Friedericy (Mrs Finkle 53,³ 54)

35

Anne

US Transmission Date: 29 Sep. 1998
UK Transmission Date: 20 Aug. 1999 (Sky)

Writer: Joss Whedon
Director: Joss Whedon
Cast: Carlos Jacott (Ken),
Mary-Pat Green (Blood Bank Doctor),
Chad Todhunter (Rickie), Michael Leopard (Roughneck),
Harley Zumbrum (Demon Guard),
Barbara Pilavin (Old Woman),
Harrison Young (Old Man), Alex Toma (Aaron),
Dell Yount (Truck Guy)

Willow, Xander and Oz try to carry on Buffy's work in her
absence, but they aren't very good at it. Buffy, meanwhile, is
renting an apartment in Los Angeles and working as a wait-
ress in a diner. There she meets 'Lily', whom she knew as
'Chanterelle' in Sunnydale. Lily tells Buffy that her boyfriend, Ricky, is missing. Buffy reluctantly agrees to help and
finds an old man dead in the street, whom she identifies as
Ricky from his unique tattoo. 'Lily' is ensnared by Ken, who
runs the Family Home, a refuge for homeless teenagers.
Clues lead Buffy to the home, where she finds Lily about to
be initiated. Lily, Buffy and Ken pass through a black pool

into an other-dimensional factory where hundreds of missing teenagers are working as slave labour with demonic guards. Ken says a day on Earth equates to a hundred years in this dimension. Buffy organises a rebellion among the slaves and helps them to freedom. Buffy gives her apartment and job (along with her 'name') to Lily and returns home.

Dreaming (As Blondie Once Said) is Free: Buffy and Angel on a beach at sunset with the classic line: 'I'll never leave you, not even if you kill me.'

Dudes and Babes: Willow: 'Come and get it, big boy.' 'Lily' (see **19**, 'Lie to Me') is *still* as wet as a slap in the face with a haddock and now has 'dead-boyfriend issues' to deal with.

Buffy's Peach Pie: Buffy tells 'Lily' that she can't guarantee that the peach pie at the diner actually contains peaches.

Denial, Thy Name is Joyce: Joyce says she doesn't blame herself for Buffy's leaving: she blames Giles (which is pretty hypocritical since it was she who threw Buffy out of the house).

It's a Designer Label!: The pink flowery dress Buffy wears in her dream is the same one she has in **36**, 'Dead Man's Party'. Cordelia wears a tasteful green skirt but Willow's at it again, with a short purple skirt and tea-cosy hat. (This is, incidentally, the only episode in which 'tea cosy' is mentioned – it's something Buffy says she's always wanted, even though she doesn't know what one is. She ought to have a look on her best friend's head.) There are some nice pants on display, including Cordelia's blue flares, the tight red pair worn by the lead singer of Belly Love and the hippychick cream hipsters worn by 'Lily'.

References: 'Duck and cover' was a 50s information campaign aimed largely at children on how to protect themselves in the event of a nuclear attack. Buffy beats up Ken, telling him it's her impression of Mahatma Gandhi (1869–1948) when he was 'really pissed off'.

Bitch!: Cordy notes that Xander has always been attracted to monsters (see **4**, 'Teacher's Pet') and refers, caustically, to the mummy-girl of **16**, 'Inca Mummy Girl'. Xander gets his own back with 'The vampire kills you, we watch, we rejoice.' Then there's a repeat of the kiss sequence from **22**, 'What's My Line?' Part 2 (with *that* music again).

Awesome!: The chase through the underworld chamber.

'You May Remember Me From Such Films As . . .': Harrison Young played the old Private Ryan in *Saving Private Ryan*.

Don't Give Up The Day Job: The stunt co-ordinator, Jeff Pruitt, has a cameo role as the Family Home doorman. He previously played a vampire in **23**, 'Ted'.

Logic, Let Me Introduce You to This Window: Willow's scream interrupts Xander and Cordelia's fight and we see Cordy run towards Willow with Xander behind her. In the following shot, Oz is running in the same direction while Xander and Cordy are standing still. For most of the episode Buffy wears a purple T-shirt under a black hooded sweatshirt. However, after she beats up the guards and tells the other runaways, 'Anyone who's not having fun here, follow me,' she's wearing a different top beneath her sweatshirt. For the rest of the episode the purple top is back. Buffy also wears (for the last half of the episode) a pair of white Nike shoes. During several scenes you can see a red Nike symbol. After Lily pushes Ken off the balcony, watch Buffy's shoes as she climbs up. Instead of Nikes they are light-grey deck shoes. How could Willow have not known that Oz didn't finish school? Larry was a senior last year, wasn't he? What were those slaves working on? A *huge* MacGuffin that's as yet unexplained.

Quote/Unquote: Ken: 'You've got guts. I'd like to slice you open and play with them.'

Notes: 'I'm Buffy the Vampire Slayer. And you are . . .?' Clever opening (particularly Oz's pathetic attempt at throwing a stake) but this is a disappointment. A downbeat story about the sick underbelly of LA, it tries hard to say something about society, but it's uninvolving stuff and after a while the viewer simply wants the episode finished and Buffy back in Sunnydale. It's a *long* forty minutes to sit through just to get to 'I'm Buffy the Vampire Slayer'!

Buffy's middle name is Anne. She has a fluffy toy duck in her rented apartment. Cordelia spent the summer in Mexico where, she says, they have cockroaches big enough to own property (see **13**, 'When She Was Bad'). Giles has a friend in Oakland who gives him a (false) lead on vampire activity.

Soundtrack: Belly Love perform 'Back to Freedom' in the Bronze.

Critique: The third season began with a glowing write-up in *TV Guide*: 'Can we tell you how great it is not to have to choose between *Buffy* and *Ally McBeal* anymore? Kicking off a hot Tuesday line-up (followed by the much anticipated *Felicity*), this smart-sexy-funny-scary original is at the top of its game.' The piece also included a few gems from Joss Whedon, including a comment that Angel has 'been in Hell, so he's going to be a little cranky'!

36
Dead Man's Party

US Transmission Date: 6 Oct. 1998
UK Transmission Date: 27 Aug. 1999 (Sky)

Writer: Marti Noxon
Director: James Whitmore Jnr
Cast: Nancy Lenehan (Pat),
Paul Morgan Stetler (Young Doctor),
Chris Garnant (Stoner #1)

A Nigerian mask that Joyce bought for her gallery proves to be an even bigger headache for Mrs Summers than organising a homecoming that will please her (still confused) daughter. First a cat that Buffy finds is raised from the dead, then an elaborate party with all of Buffy's friends and Oz's band is ruined by the arrival of gatecrashing zombies. Buffy, whose uncommunicative, sulky demeanour proves trying even to Xander and Willow, manages to fight the demon of the mask Ovu Mobani, the Evil Eye, which is inhabiting the body of Joyce's neighbour Pat. Killing the demon makes the zombies vanish and leaves Buffy alone with those closest to her, to come to her senses and start acting like herself again.

Dreaming (As Blondie Once Said) is Free: For the second episode running, Angel appears only in a dream sequence. And a very surreal one at that, set in a deserted school with weird music and Buffy in a very revealing top.

Authority Sucks!: Snyder's reply to Joyce saying that Buffy was cleared of all charges surrounding Kendra's death: 'While she may live up to the "not a murderer" requirement for enrolment, she *is* a troublemaker.' And he advises Buffy that 'Hot Dog on a Stick' are hiring. Joyce later describes Snyder as a 'nasty little horrid bigoted rodent-man'.

The Conspiracy Starts at Home Time: The Mayor is mentioned twice. When Joyce says she will take Buffy's expulsion up with him, Snyder says *that* will be an interesting meeting.

Mom's Apple Pie: Joyce believes that Buffy has 'no appreciation of primitive art' (this is a *bad* thing?). Buffy says she was starving until the four-course snack Joyce made her after dinner. The mom's-not-perfect scene is a tremendously effective one – and, for once, we're actually on Joyce's side.

It's a Designer Label!: Joyce's orange mom-pants. Giles wears a very tasteful three-piece suit in grey. Buffy's jogging pants are also good. On the minus side, Devon's brown shirt.

References: The fashion designer Tommy Hilfiger, the popular 70s children's toy the Weebles, *Rambo*, *The Bad Seed*, the UK techno group Shut Up and Dance, the newspaper *USA Today*, the sitcom *Mr Belvedere* (1985–90) and Jacquelyn Mitchard's novel *The Deep End of the Ocean*. The title comes from a song by Oingo Boingo. Various aspects of the story may have been influenced by *Night of the Living Dead* and *Mask*.

Awesome!: Buffy's fight on (and off) the roof with the demon, especially the garden-spade ending. (It'll be interesting to see how much of *that* survives the editor's scissors when the BBC broadcast this episode.)

'You May Remember Me From Such Films As . . .': Both Nancy Lenehan and Paul Morgan Stetler are in *Pleasantville*.

Valley-Speak: Oz's hilarious bit on the differences between a 'gathering', a 'shindig' and a 'hootenanny'.

Xander: 'It's great to have the Buffster back.'

Stoner on whose party it is: 'Heard it was for some chick that just got out of rehab.'

And (answering the telephone): 'Party Villa. Can I rock you?'

Logic, Let Me Introduce You to This Window: Buffy sets the table for six. However, Joyce invited seven (eight counting Pat). When Xander asks the group to vote on how Buffy's homecoming should be celebrated, Willow raises her right hand with a pencil in it. When the camera angle returns to Willow, her hand is still raised, but where's the pencil? When Buffy goes to her bedroom and starts to pack her bag, she leaves the door slightly open. After the commercial break, when Willow finds Buffy, the door is *fully* open. (Despite a *major* party taking place downstairs, these scenes have virtually no background noise.) When Buffy stakes the zombie to see if it is a vampire, the zombie raises its left arm in reaction to the attack. Next shot, the arm is still on the floor. During the scenes in Joyce's bedroom, the wallpaper pattern changes between shots after Buffy and Pat fall out of the window. Will Dingoes Ate My Baby ever do their guitarist another personal favour after *this*? And grabbing the principal like that could easily cost a librarian his job. (There *has* to be more to this scene than we see. Why does Giles believe he can get away with it? And why does Snyder give in?)

Quote/Unquote: Buffy: 'What about home schooling? It's not just for scary religious people any more.'

Giles: ' "Do you like my mask? Isn't it pretty? It raises the dead!" *Americans!*'

Xander: 'Generally speaking, when scary things get scared, not good.'

Notes: 'So, is this a typical day at the office?' A really long-winded way to get Buffy and her friends back together again, though it's much funnier than **35**, 'Anne', and, consequently, more interesting. At least the effects are very good.

Giles hot-wires his car (he says it's 'like riding a bloody bicycle', which suggests he's done some of this during his 'dark' past – see **45**, 'Gingerbread'). Willow isn't a fully fledged witch yet – that takes years (see **45**, 'Gingerbread', **50**, 'Doppelgängland'). Xander's call sign during the patrol is 'Night Hawk'. The Summerses have skis in their closet.

Soundtrack: Dingoes Ate My Baby mime to 'Never Mind' and 'Sway' by Four Star Mary.

37
Faith, Hope and Trick

US Transmission Date: 13 Oct. 1998
UK Transmission Date: 3 Sep. 1999 (Sky)

Writer: David Greenwalt
Director: James A Contner
Cast: Jeremy Roberts (Kakistos), John Ennis (Manager)

At Sunnydale's Happy Burger, two vampires search for The Slayer. Principal Snyder readmits Buffy to school, under orders from the board. Giles tells Buffy he needs to perform a binding spell on Acathla to keep the demon dormant and asks for details of Angel being sent to Hell. At the Bronze, Cordelia points out a couple on the dance floor. Buffy follows and discovers the boy is a vampire. What takes her by surprise is the girl's ability to deal with him, stopping only to greet Buffy and introduce herself as Faith, the new Slayer, called forth in response to Kendra's death. Faith tells Buffy that her Watcher is at an annual retreat, but Giles discovers that the Watcher is dead. Buffy and Faith are attacked by

Kakistos, Mr Trick and their acolytes. The Slayers defeat Kakistos. Unable to keep her secret any longer, Buffy tells Giles and Willow that Angel was cured before she killed him. Buffy revives plans for her weekend date with Scott Hope just as, unknown to her, Angel is returned from Hell.

Dudes and Babes: Faith, the new Slayer, is 'personable', according to a green-eyed Buffy. She says Slaying makes her 'hungry and horny' (Buffy agrees about the hungry part). Willow notes that Buffy does 'that thing with your mouth that boys like – no not *that* thing . . .' What on Earth is she talking about? Also debuting is Scott Hope, Buffy's 'nice normal non-boyfriend'. Angel appears naked in the final scene. Quite popular with the girls, this one . . .

Authority Sucks!: Joyce tells an outmanoeuvred Snyder 'what I believe my daughter is trying to say is "Nyah-nyah-nyah"!' Nice one, Mrs S.

A Little Learning is a Dangerous Thing: The preconditions of Buffy's becoming a schoolgirl again are that she take make-up tests on all of the classes she skipped last year; that she provide a letter of recommendation from a member of the faculty who 'isn't an English librarian'; and that she see the school psychologist (see **38**, 'Beauty and the Beasts'). She eventually passes all of these, although her initial reaction to the English test ('they give you a credit for speaking it, right?') makes us wonder how, exactly. (See **42**, 'Lover's Walk'.)

Mom's Apple Pie: Faith certainly seems to enjoy the fries Joyce serves for dinner.

It's a Designer Label!: Willow's fluffy light-blue sweater sums up her personality wonderfully well. Cordelia's vampy Raybans are worth watching the episode for alone. And there's Faith's impressive trouser wardrobe (tight multi-coloured hipsters in her first scene, crimson leathers later on). She says she sometimes sleeps naked, unlike Buffy, who's seen in a lime-green nightshirt. Oz's horrible dyed shirt puts in another appearance.

References: Martha Stewart (American home-and-garden guru) is mentioned (see U1). Mr Trick says that Sunnydale's death rate makes 'DC look like Mayberry' (a reference to *The Andy Griffiths Show*). The 70s disco kings KC & the Sunshine Band are name-checked and there are allusions to George Gershwin's 'Summertime' and *Single White Female*. Scott wants to take Buffy to a festival of films by the silent comedy genius Buster Keaton (what a fabulous chat-up line *that* is). Angel's climactic return is a tribute to *The Terminator* with him falling from the sky, naked, in a blaze of light.

Bitch!: Buffy and Faith get their claws out several times (chiefly over what little the latter knows about Angel). As usual, though, neither can hold a candle to Cordy, particularly her initial opinion of Faith: 'Does anyone believe that's her *actual* hair colour?'

Awesome!: Kakistos is a vampire so old that his hands have turned into cloven hooves. His protégé Mr Trick is a slippery jive-talking vampire who is interested in Sunnydale as a new location and wants to get vampiring on to the Internet. There are two *brilliant* fight sequences for Buffy and Faith to take on the vampires. The pre-titles at the Happy Burger ('*now* I'm hungry') is a classic.

'You May Remember Me From Such Films As . . .': A very young Eliza Dushku (Faith) played Dana Tasker in *True Lies*. K Todd Freeman (Mr Trick) was McCullers in *Grosse Point Blanke*.

Valley-Speak: Faith asks an annoyed Buffy: 'What are you getting so strung up about, B?'
    And: 'The Vamps, they better get their asses to *Def Con 1*.'

Not Exactly A Haven For The Bruthas: Let's have this one in full. Mr Trick: 'Admittedly, it's not a haven for the bruthas . . . Strictly the Caucasian Persuasion here in the 'Dale. But you just gotta stand up and salute that death rate.'

Logic, Let Me Introduce You to This Window: During the tour of Sunnydale High, Willow identifies one of the classrooms as the cafeteria. After Buffy tries to stake Kakistos the second time, she leaves the stake sticking out of his chest. When Faith drives the huge beam through Kakistos's chest, the smaller stake is gone.

Quote/Unquote: Buffy's idea of 'girly stuff' is: 'Date and shop and hang out and go to school and save the world from unspeakable demons.'

Xander's reaction to Faith's semierotic Slaying tale: 'Wow, they should film that and show it every Christmas.'

Buffy mispronounces Kakistos as 'Khaki Trousers'.

Mr Trick: 'There's a reason these vengeance crusades are out of style. The modern vampire, we see the big picture.'

Buffy's first rule of Slaying: 'Don't die.'

Notes: 'Gee, if doing violence to vampires upsets you, you're in the wrong line of work.' A great David Greenwalt script, with many fine moments (the 'uncoupling' scene, Buffy's silent exasperation at her friends' sudden desire to be with Faith while she has to study). A subtle game played by Giles to get Buffy to confront her own demons leads to a shocking conclusion. A little gem.

Buffy doesn't believe in two things: coincidence and leprechauns. Giles tells her the former *does* exist but, as far as he knows, the latter do not. In the final scenes Buffy is wearing a heart-shaped pendant instead of her usual crucifix. Willow says that when Giles is mad he makes a 'cluck, cluck' sound with his tongue. Giles likes kayaking. A Watcher retreat is held in the Cotswolds each year (Giles had never been invited). In a hilarious exchange, Buffy tells Faith that Oz is a werewolf. 'It's a long story.' 'I got bit,' says Oz. 'Obviously not *that* long,' notes Buffy (see **27**, 'Phases'). Faith grew up in South Boston. She had a female Watcher (the second time a female Watcher has been mentioned: see **5**, 'Never Kill a Boy on the First Date', **41** 'Revelations'). Faith tells a vampire, 'My dead mother hits harder than that' (see **51**, 'Enemies'). Whatever Kakistos did to Faith's Watcher before killing her, it wasn't pleasant. Interesting Fan Theory: was Kakistos Faith's Cruciamentum (see **46**, 'Helpless')? A Watcher test that 'went wrong', causing the death of Faith's Watcher, may help to explain (almost) all of Faith's subsequent actions.

Soundtrack: 'Going to Hell' by the Brian Jonestone Massacre, 'The Background' by Third Eye Blind, and 'Cure' and 'Blue Sun' by Darling Violetta.

38
Beauty and the Beasts [a.k.a. All Men Are Beasts]

US Transmission Date: 20 Oct. 1998
UK Transmission Date: 10 Sep. 1999 (Sky)

Writer: Marti Noxon
Director: James Whitmore Jnr
Cast: John Patrick White (Pete), Danielle Weeks (Debbie),
Phill Lewis (Mr Platt)

It's Oz's 'time of the month', but Xander sleeps during his watch and a brutal murder may mean that Oz escaped. Buffy meets her counsellor Mr Platt and discusses her relationship with Angel. At the morgue, Willow collects evidence that proves the victim was mauled by a savage animal. Buffy encounters someone running through the woods. To her horror, it is Angel. Chaining him up, Buffy is unable to tell her friends about her discovery. Buffy visits Mr Platt's office, ready to confess that she needs help, but finds him dead. Scott's friend Pete and his girlfriend Debbie are in a storage room. Pete transforms into a monstrous creature, and strikes Debbie. Oz notices Debbie's bruised eye, but she says she walked into a door. While Buffy and Willow confront Debbie, Pete goes to the library and finds Oz ready for transformation. Insane with jealousy, Pete attacks Oz just as it begins. A chase follows in which Oz is tranquillised and Pete kills Debbie. He attacks Buffy but she is saved by Angel, who has escaped his chains. He recognises Buffy before collapsing.

Dudes and Babes: Faith appears not to have been joking when telling Buffy that Slaying makes her 'horny'. Their discussion about boys and Faith's observation about 'a good, down-low tickle' is only half a notch above *filthy* (compare Buffy's handling of the phallic crystal in **46**, 'Helpless'). In an episode all about repressed male sexual aggression, it's interesting that the two most direct references to sex are both from girls. (Willow tells Xander she and Oz have done a 'half-monty', though tactfully she refuses to reveal which half.) Angel appearing almost naked and Faith dancing to her Walkman in the library are highlights.

It's a Designer Label!: Willow's nasty crimson and green jumper and Scott's yellow shirt vie for attention. Buffy's green top is great, but the last word goes to Willow's grey tights.

References: Willow seems to have an affinity for *Scooby Doo, Where Are You?* We've seen her wearing a *Scooby* T-shirt in an earlier episode and now we learn that she owns a *Scooby* lunchbox. References to Jack London's *The Call of the Wild*, *The Full Monty*, the board game Monopoly, Barbie and Ken dolls, *The Strange Case of Dr Jekyll and Mr Hyde*, *The Sound of Music*, *The English Patient* and the 1983 TV series *Manimal*.

Awesome!: Buffy and Angel scrapping in the dirt and Oz and Peter battling in the library. Plus Willow, Xander and Cordelia in the morgue examining the first victim's body. And Giles is shot in the back by one of his friends aiming for someone else *again* (see **23**, 'Ted').

'You May Remember Me From Such Films As . . .': Phill Lewis was Steve Jessup in *City Slickers* and Dennis in *Heathers*.

Valley-Speak: Pete: 'Check out Scotty liking the manic-depressive chick.'

Xander: 'This guy is pretty barf-worthy. Can't we be else-where?'

Logic, Let Me Introduce You to This Window: When Oz transforms, he doesn't remove his clothes. During the trans-formation, there's no indication that Oz's clothes are ripping apart, but when we see Wolf-Oz his clothes are gone. When

Cordelia says, 'Now I'm gonna be stuck with serious thoughts all day,' a close shot of Xander reveals the strap of his bag is covering the right side of his collar. In the next shot, it's under his collar. Why is everybody sitting around in the library, waiting for Buffy to come in, at 5.25 p.m.?

Quote/Unquote: Mr Platt: 'Lots of people lose themselves in love, it's no shame. They write songs about it.'

Oz: 'You know that thing where you bail in the middle of an upsetting conversation? I have to do that.'

Notes: 'Pete's not like other guys, is he, Debbie?' The issue of domestic violence is dealt with in much the same way as parental abuse is in **23**, 'Ted' – by avoiding and demonising it. The episode is disturbingly misanthropic, for example, Faith's 'all men are beasts' speech, which I'm very uncomfortable with for all sorts of reasons, not least that the writer has the same character talking about 'down-low tickles' moments later. Not only that, but the way to stop male violence towards women seems, from the resolution, to be female violence back at them. That's one solution, but it becomes even more suspect when Buffy (who has taken out far more dangerous opponents than Pete) suddenly requires Angel to rescue her. There's an unpleasant and aggressive side to the points the episode makes. Too well written to be easily dismissed, but far too wrapped up in a handbag full of hate to be likable.

Giles says he has dreams that he saved Jenny (see **29**, 'Passion'). He notes there is no record of anyone returning from the demon dimension, adding that time runs a very different course there. Buffy says, 'I know' (see **35**, 'Anne'). Sunnydale High has a marching jazz band in which Debbie and Jeff, the first victim, played.

Soundtrack: The delightfully named 'Teenage Hate Machine' by Marc Ferrari.

Joss Whedon's (Ironic) Comments: 'Someone mentioned that the show has developed a feminist subtext. Well, I never! I just wanted to show a quiet, obedient girl learning to attract men through cosmetics and physical weakness. (Probably a mistake to cast the off-puttingly plain Miss Gellar, in that case.) But sometimes we can't control our creations. Forgive me.'

39
Homecoming

US Transmission Date: 3 Nov. 1998
UK Transmission Date: 17 Sep. 1999 (Sky)

Writer: David Greenwalt
Director: David Greenwalt
Cast: Ian Abercrombie (Old Man), Billy Maddox (Frawley),
Joseph Daube (Hans Gruenshtahler),
Jermyn Daube (Frederick Gruenshtahler),
Lee Everett (Candy Gorch), Tori McPetrie (Michelle Blake),
Jennifer Hetrick (Ms Mason), Chad Stahelski (Kulak)

While Cordelia plans her campaign for Homecoming Queen and Buffy breaks up with Scott, Mr Trick assembles a team of specialists to take part in Slayerfest '98 and rid him of Buffy and Faith. Buffy is furious that she missed the yearbook photo session because of Cordelia's thoughtlessness and runs against her friend for Queen, putting Xander, Willow and Oz in very awkward positions. They get Buffy and Cordelia together in a limo and tell them to work out their problems. Unfortunately the car is hijacked by Trick's men and Buffy and Cordelia take refuge in a cabin. Disposing of some of their enemies, they return to school and defeat the rest just in time to attend the Homecoming Queen announcement. And discover they have both lost. Mr Trick arrives at City Hall, where Mayor Wilkins introduces himself.

Babes and Babes (Bring Your Own Subtext): Buffy tells Angel about Scott ('a nice solid guy – he makes me happy'), at which point Scott breaks up with Buffy and attends the Homecoming with another girl. Trick refers to Buffy's 'nubile flesh', which proves what we already suspected: he's a vampire with

taste. Xander notes that Buffy and Faith 'are in the library getting all sweaty', which *presumably* means they're training.
Throw in Oz's reference to Buffy and Cordelia mud-wrestling
and you have a slash-fiction fan's delight. In response to a
question about a lesbian relationship between Slayers, Joss
Whedon commented, 'I just read the piece on Buffy and Faith .
. . and by God, I think she's right! I can't believe I never saw it!
(Actually, despite my facetious tone, it's a pretty damn convincing argument. But then, I think that's part of the attraction
of the Buffyverse. It lends itself to polymorphously perverse
subtext. It encourages it. I personally find romance in every
relationship (with exceptions), I love all the characters, so I say
Bring Your Own Subtext!)'

The Conspiracy Starts at Home Time: We finally meet the
dirt-obsessed Mayor Wilkins. He reveals that he's aware Mr
Trick is a vampire and he wants his help in eliminating the
'rebellious element' from Sunnydale. Wilkins says he's been
Mayor for 'quite some time' and that this is 'an important
year' (see **48**, 'Bad Girls', **49**, 'Consequences', **51**, 'Enemies',
53, 'Choices' and **55/56**, 'Graduation Day').

It's a Designer Label!: Buffy's gym shorts. Willow asks
Xander if he remembers 'that eighth-grade cotillion and you
had that clip-on?' It's worth noting that *everyone* looks great
in their Homecoming clothes (Xander in a tux, Willow's long
black dress, Buffy's and Cordy's dresses). Watch out for
Trick's crimson crushed-velvet jacket and orange tie. Candy
Gorch's pink feather boa and purple satin pants are equally
desperate.

References: Oz's line 'as Willow goes, so goes my nation'
refers to a famous quote about General Motors. Cordelia says
she's been doing 'the Vulcan Death-Grip' since she was four.
Of course, as all Trekkies know, the Vulcan Death-Grip
doesn't exist. Mr Trick makes an ironic comment about the
American frontiersman Daniel Boone (1735–1820). The flying ace Amelia Earhart (1898–1937) and the author Maya
Angelou (born 1928) are name-checked alongside an allusion
to the English evangelist John Wesley (1703–91).

Bitch!: Faith's revenge on Scott over his break-up with Buffy, telling him, in front of his date, that the doctor says the itching, swelling and burning should clear up, 'but we have to keep using the ointment'. 'And speaking of big heads, if I had a watermelon as big as Cordelia's, I'd be rich.' Buffy's strategy board lists the strengths and weaknesses of her opponents: Cordelia's strengths are: 'Popular with boys', 'Makes friends easily', 'Expensive clothes' and 'Perfect teeth'; while her weaknesses include: 'Manipulative', 'Two-faced', 'Fake smile', 'Bad in sports', 'Superficial', 'No sense of humour' and 'Xander!' (Does anybody else think the exclamation mark here makes this incredibly mean?) Michelle's entries include (strengths): 'Popular', 'Nice', 'Friendly', 'Good cook' and 'Athletic'; (weaknesses): 'Bad skin', 'Wears polyester', 'PB Crazy', 'Dandruff' and 'Too much make-up.' Holly's entries are difficult to see but one strength is her 'debating skills'. Cordelia's opinion of 'I laughingly use the phrase "competition" ' is: 'Holly Charlston: nice girl, braindead, doesn't have a prayer. Michelle Blake: open to all mankind, especially those with a letterman's jacket and a car. She could give me a run.' Once Buffy joins the race, it gets nasty: 'Crazy freak!', 'Vapid whore!', 'Do you have parents?', 'Yes, two of them, unlike some people!' Et cetera, Et cetera.

Awesome!: One of the series' *great* moments as Buffy battles the yellow-skinned demon. Cordelia begins to hit him with a cooking spatula. 'Cor, the gun!' shouts Buffy. Cordelia picks up the gun and fires wildly. 'Cordelia,' says Buffy, in resignation, 'the spatula!' 'Homecoming' also contains fine characterisation as Willow and Xander help each other dress, remember old times, speculate on the future, dance and kiss. Wonderful stuff. But it's Buffy and Cordelia's episode with the scenes in the cabin, Cordy facing down Lyle Gorch and the disgusted looks on their faces at the end all highlights.

'You May Remember Me From Such Films and TV Series As . . .': German-born Harry Groener (Wilkins) played Tam Elburn in the *Star Trek: The Next Generation* episode 'Tin Man'. He also appeared in *Amistad* and *Dance With Me*, the US version of *Dear John* (playing Ralph Drang) and *Mad*

About You (as Brockwell). Jack Plotnick (Deputy Mayor) was Edmond Kay in *Gods and Monsters* and had a recurring role as Barrett in *Ellen*. Ian Abercrombie was Justin Pitt in *Seinfeld*. Jennifer Hetrick played Jean Luc Picard's girlfriend Vash in *Star Trek: The Next Generation* and *Deep Space 9* and Walter Skinner's wife in *The X-Files*. She was also Corrine Hammond in *L.A. Law*.

Don't Give Up The Day Job: Chad Stahelski, in addition to being David Boreanaz's stunt double, had also worked on such films as *The Matrix, 8mm* and *Alien: Resurrection*.

Logic, Let Me Introduce You to This Window: After Buffy and Faith finish their training session Faith lays the punching pads on the table. In the next shot, Faith is still holding them. When we first see Mr Trick and The Slayerfest participants, notice the rifle being held at chest level in Frawley's hands. As Mr Trick walks past him, the camera angle switches and we see Frawley bringing the rifle up into the position that he was already holding it in.

Quote/Unquote: Mr Trick: 'We all have the desire to win. Whether we're human, vampire . . . Whatever the hell you are, my brother. You got a spiny-looking head thing, I never seen that before.'
   Willow: 'I'm not a friend, I'm a rabid dog who should be shot. But there are forces at work here. Dark, incomprehensible forces.'
   Xander: 'How do you get from "chick fight" to "our fault"?' Willow: 'Because we felt so guilty about "The Fluke", we overcompensated helping Cordelia and we spun the whole group dynamic out of orbit and we're just a big meteor shower heading for Earth . . .'
   Giles: 'We have to find Buffy. Something terrible's happened. Just kidding. Thought I'd give you a scare.'
   Cordelia: 'Listen up, needle-brain. Buffy and I have taken out four of your cronies, not to mention your girlfriend.' Lyle: 'Wife!' Cordelia: 'Whatever!'

Notes: 'You've awakened the Prom Queen within.' What an astonishing piece of work. *Buffy*-as-sitcom taking such an *obvious* idea (two friends fight over who will be Homecoming Queen) and throwing in a bunch of misfit monsters for them to kill. This is what we all probably imagine American teenage life is like. If we've done enough acid. One of two outstanding back-to-back jewels that highlight everything that is *great* about this series. Another twelve out of ten.

Buffy refers to **36**, 'Dead Man's Party', saying that lots of people came to her 'Welcome Home' party. Willow helpfully adds, 'They were killed by zombies.' Ms Moran was Buffy's favourite teacher in her class called 'Contemporary American Heroes'. Unfortunately, she doesn't remember Buffy at all. At Hemery, Buffy was 'Prom Princess', 'Fiesta Queen' and on the Cheerleading Squad (see **M1**, **3**, 'The Witch').

Soundtrack: 'Fell into the Loneliness' by Lori Carson, 'Jodie Foster' by the Pinehurst Kids, 'How' by Lisa Loeb, 'Fire Escape' by Fastball and 'She Knows' by Four Star Mary (the song that Oz supposedly wrote for Willow).

40
Band Candy

US Transmission Date: 10 Nov. 1998
UK Transmission Date: 24 Sep. 1999 (Sky)

Writer: Jane Espenson
Director: Michael Lange
Cast: Peg Stewart (Ms Barton)

The Mayor asks Mr Trick to help him collect a tribute to a demon and Trick subcontracts the sale of cursed chocolate to Ethan Rayne. Snyder makes the students sell the chocolate to raise money for the school band. Buffy sells her bars to Joyce and Giles and is surprised when Giles doesn't show up for school. She finds him at his home with Joyce, apparently working out a schedule to make it easier for Buffy to spend time with both of them. At the Bronze, Buffy and Willow notice the vast number of adults present acting like rowdy teenagers. Buffy realises that there is something wrong with the candy. At the factory, she discovers her mother and Giles making out. Inside, Buffy finds Ethan, whose job was to divert the adults from the main objective, paying tribute to the demon Lurconis, who eats babies. In the sewers Buffy finds the babies along with Mr Trick and the Mayor. While Buffy fights the vampires, Giles and Joyce move the babies out of harm's way. Lurconis, a huge serpentine creature, emerges. Buffy detaches a gas pipe and creates a blowtorch to defeat the demon.

Dreaming (As Blondie Once Said) is Free: One that we don't get to see. Buffy being chased by 'an improperly filled-in answer bubble screaming, "None of the above".'

Dudes and Babes: Joyce: 'So, why do they call you Ripper?' Giles: 'Wouldn't you like to know?' Oz imagines Giles was a 'pretty together' teen. Buffy corrects him: 'Giles at sixteen? Less "Together-Guy", more "Bad-Magic-Hates-the-World-Ticking-Time-Bomb-Guy".' When Joyce gives Buffy her pair of handcuffs, Buffy orders her to '*Never* tell me.' In 52, 'Earshot', we find out what interaction occurred between Giles and Joyce. There are more gratuitous bare-torso shots of David Boreanaz and two plump miniskirted cheerleaders who walk behind Giles and Buffy in the final scene.

Authority Sucks!: 'Everybody expects me to do everything around here because I'm the principal. It's not fair.' Snyder says he got a commendation for being principal from the Mayor, who shook his hand twice. (Knowing what we subsequently do about Mayor Wilkins, it's to be hoped that Snyder wore gloves.) But he still ends up getting the kids to clean the graffiti off the lockers. Some things never change.

The Conspiracy Starts at Home Time: The Mayor tells Mr Trick, 'I made certain deals to get where I am today. This demon requires its tribute,' adding, 'That's what separates me from other politicians. I keep my campaign promises.' We see that his cupboard is full of skulls.

A Little Learning is a Dangerous Thing: Willow says that Oz is the highest-scoring person (on SATs) never to graduate.

It's unclear whether she's talking about just Sunnydale High or the whole country. Xander is against a system that 'discriminates against the uninformed'. Cordelia, on the other hand, is looking forward to the SATs, noting that she usually does well on standardised tests (see **42**, 'Lover's Walk'). Buffy says, 'We can study at the Bronze. A little dancing, a little cross-multiplying.'

Mom's Apple Pie: Buffy tells Joyce she's a good mom, but not the best, because she won't let her daughter drive. While they eat Chinese food (with chopsticks) there is a lengthy discussion on responsibility ('I don't need this much Active Parenting'). Once the cursed chocolate kicks in, we have something of a paradox.

Denial, Thy Names are Joyce and Rupert: Buffy: 'At least I got to the two of you before you actually did something.' Joyce: 'Right.' Giles: 'Indeed.' (Liars! See **52**, 'Earshot'.)

It's a Designer Label!: 'Mom started borrowing my clothes. There should be an age limit on lycra pants,' notes Cordelia. One could say the same about Joyce and that miniskirt. On the plus side there's Buffy's red top and grey jogging pants, her green skirt, Willow's light-blue miniskirt and Cordy's tartan skirt. Minus points for Oz's yellow T-shirt, Willow's fluffy red jumper and orange trainers and Trick's purple shirt.

References: Cordy's dad takes copies of *Esquire* magazine and locks himself in the bathroom. There are references to MTV's *The Real World*, Charles Dickens's *A Christmas Carol* ('The Ghost of Christmas Past'), Willy Loman from Arthur Miller's play, *Death of a Salesman*, the TV show *Nightline,* the 70s soft-rockers Seals & Crofts, *The Rocky Horror Picture Show* ('Let's do the time warp again'), the singer Billy Joel, the US sitcom *Welcome Back Kotter* (and the character Vinnie Barbarino played by John Travolta), the country-and-western singer Juice Newton, the actor Burt Reynolds, a misquote from *The Wild Ones* ('I just gotta see what you got') and Bow Wow Wow's 'I Want Candy'. 'Kiss Rocks!' refers to the American glam metal band. 'Louie

Louie', a hit for the Kingsmen in 1963 and a classic song of teenage rebellion, is performed a cappella by lots of old guys. 'Now for the bonus question – and believe me when I say that a wrong answer *will* cost you all your points' is a general parody of game shows.

Bitch!: Giles and Joyce are at it this week: 'Oh, for God's sake, let your mum have a sodding candy bar.' And 'You wanna slay stuff and I'm not allowed to do anything about it. Well, this is what I wanna do, so get off my back.' Respectively.

Awesome!: Buffy hitting Giles with the ball, blindfolded, and her double take when spotting her mother and Giles kissing ('Go away, we're busy'). Top marks for the characterisation of Giles, Joyce and Snyder as teenagers with Tony Head's incredible cockney wide-boy act ('Ooo, copper's got a g*un*!') *just* outdoing Armin Shimerman's equally valid interpretation of Snyder as a cowardly nerd who desperately wants to be part of the cool kids' scene ('I am *so* stoked'). Joyce, meanwhile, becomes what we always suspected she was – a totally uncool, overtalkative (rather sly) wannabe who's hanging around with the coolest guy in town. The disgusted look on Giles's face when she asks if he likes Seals & Crofts is proof of that. (Kristine Sutherland's view of this is interesting: 'I found particularly painful the scene where we're listening to the music in Tony's apartment and I thought Joss captured it perfectly. He's really ignoring me, he's completely into the music and I'm trying to figure out, as the girl, how to connect with him. It brought up a lot of those horribly painful adolescent feelings . . .')

Best moment of this remarkable episode: The '*Yes!*' from Giles, punching the air as Buffy hits Ethan.

Valley-Speak: Giles: 'Let's not "freak out".'

Buffy: 'Voilà! Driveyness!' and 'You guys are just wigging me out.'

Sex and Drugs and Rock and Roll and Cigarettes and Alcohol: Giles smokes and drinks red wine with Joyce while listening to Cream's 'Tales of Brave Ulysses'. ('Man, I got to get a band together,' he says as Eric Clapton's guitar solo starts and he adds, 'Listen to this bit.') 'You've got good albums,' notes Joyce. *Love* to know what else is in his collection (bet it's not the Bay City Rollers either – see **20**, 'The Dark Age').

'Whoa, Summers. You Drive Like a Spaz!': Snyder's comments are echoed by Buffy: 'Look at that dent the size of New Brunswick. I did that.' Joyce: 'Oh my God. What was I thinking when I bought that geek machine?' Later Joyce notes, 'Buffy assures me that it happened battling evil, so I'm letting her pay for it on the installment plan.'

Logic, Let Me Introduce You to This Window: When Buffy drives her mom's jeep, a pair of headlights can be seen behind Buffy and Willow. The car appears to be no more than a few feet behind the jeep. When Buffy makes the right turn, however, the car following them is some distance away. When Buffy bends down to switch on the radio, you can still see the headlights through the jeep's rear window, but seconds later there's no sign of them. Although the boxes of band candy say 'Milkbar', Giles says that Buffy persuaded him to buy twenty 'Cocoariffic' bars. Why do all of the spell-affected adults, regardless of their age, speak and act as though their teenage years were during the 70s?

I Just *Love* Your Accent: Joyce says it must be very cool being from England. Giles's reply is, 'Not particularly!'

Quote/Unquote: Giles on the SATs: 'It's a rite of passage.' Buffy: 'Is it too late to join a tribe where they just pierce something or cut something off?'

Ms Barton: 'Willow. That's a tree . . . Are there any nachos in here, little tree?'

Mr Trick: 'That's the reason I love this country. You make a good product and the people will come to you. Of course, a lot of them are gonna die, but that's the other reason I love this country.'

Giles on Buffy's interrogation technique: 'You're *my* Slayer. Go knock his teeth down his throat.' And, to Snyder: 'You filthy little *ponce*. Are you afraid of a little demon?'

Buffy on Trick's parting shot: 'They never just leave. Always gotta say something.'

Notes: 'And *don't* do that.' It was going to take a work of *genius* to best **39**, 'Homecoming'. Here, then, ladies and gentlemen, is 'Band Candy'; a work of *genius*! Again, the central idea is not new (adults acting like children, to the chagrin of the *real* children), but there's a cleverness to the presentation here that charms the viewer while they are rolling on the floor laughing. My favourite episode. Thirteen out of ten.

Buffy says Giles is allergic to being late. Cordelia refers to her life before Xander as 'BX'. Snyder claims to have taken tae kwon do 'at the Y'. Scott Hope is mentioned by Angel (Buffy hasn't told him that she and Scott have broken up – see **39**, 'Homecoming').

Soundtrack: Aside from the Cream classic, 'Blasé' by Mad Cow, 'Violent' by Four Star Mary and 'Slip Jimmy' by Every Bit of Nothing.

Did You Know?: In Mike Hodges' 1987 film *A Prayer for the Dying*, Tony Head played a cockney thug named Rupert. For his legion of female fans, it's a movie worth checking out as he removes most of his kit.

41

Revelations

US Transmission Date: 17 Nov. 1998
UK Transmission Date: 1 Oct. 1999 (Sky)

Writer: Douglas Petrie
Director: James A Contner
Cast: Serena Scott Thomas (Gwendolyn Post),
Kate Rodger (Paramedic)

Faith's new Watcher, Gwendolyn Post (Mrs), sets the group a task, the recovery of the Glove of Myhnegon. Gwendolyn has little respect for Giles and his frustration grows as he is unable to find any information on the demon Lagos, also searching for the Glove. Xander sees Angel, and follows him back to the mansion, where he observes Buffy and Angel kissing. Buffy is quizzed about Angel by her friends, Giles feeling she has betrayed him. Faith finds an angry Xander at the Bronze playing pool and decides to kill Angel with Xander's help. Giles tells Gwendolyn he has recovered the Glove and she smashes a statue over his head. Xander tells Buffy that Faith is already on her way to the mansion, convinced that Angel must die. Faith sees her new Watcher about to be killed by Angel and attacks him but is stopped by Buffy. Gwendolyn finds the Glove and gains the ability to fire bolts of lightning. Buffy picks up a shard of glass and severs the Glove from Gwendolyn, leaving Faith feeling betrayed.

Dudes and Babes: Gwendolyn is a typically Hitchcock-style villainess. Faith refers to Buffy's liaison with Angel, asking what it was like 'boinking the undead' (see **25**, 'Surprise'). Faith lists some of her ex-boyfriends as 'Ronnie (deadbeat); Steve (klepto); Kenny (drunk)'. She says her motto now is 'get some, get gone' (see **47**, 'The Zeppo', **48**, 'Bad Girls').

A Little Learning is a Dangerous Thing: Books that the library *doesn't* possess include Hulme's *Paranormal Encyclopaedia* and *The Labyrinth Maps of Malta* (which *is* on order). Giles *does* have a copy of Sir Robert Kane's *Twilight Compendium*.

It's a Designer Label!: Oz's gold-lamé waistcoat is extremely rock-and-roll. So is Buffy's pink Bronze dress, though her 'bomb' ski cap isn't. Faith's crimson leathers appear again.

References: Name checks for *Mary Poppins* and *Marathon Man*.

Bitch!: Gwendolyn: 'Faith, a word of advice. You're an idiot.'

Awesome!: An exercise in 'synchronised Slaying': about ten minutes is taken up with one fight or another including Faith and Angel battling and the Buffy–Faith fight. Plus the effects as Gwendolyn is killed. Angel and Buffy's t'ai-chi-style exercises are impressive, but the best bit of the episode is the series of facial expressions Willow gives as Buffy fights the demon.

The Drugs Don't Work: 'Cold turkey', mentioned in this episode, is a euphemism for heroin withdrawal without the aid of a secondary drug, and is now used as a general term for quitting any form of addiction.

Valley-Speak: Cordelia: 'Why are you guys so hyper?'
    Buffy refers to the Glove as 'the magic-mitten-thingy'.

Logic, Let Me Introduce You to This Window: While a frustrated Giles instructs Xander to find whatever information he can on Lagos, Willow stands on the upper level of the library, inches from one of the knobs on the railing. As Xander ascends the stairs the camera angle switches. From here, Willow is standing some distance from where she was in the previous shot. In the scene at Willow's locker, she hoists her backpack on to her right shoulder, then starts to close the locker door with her right hand. In the reverse-angle shot, Willow's right hand is on her shoulder strap while she closes the locker with her left. Why is Faith's door unlocked in the last scene when Buffy enters?

I Just *Love* Your Accent: Giles gets all flustered when Gwendolyn arrives. (Buffy says, 'Interesting lady. Can I kill her?') Gwendolyn says there is talk within the Council that Giles has become a bit 'too American'. 'Him?' asks Buffy. (This is later revealed to be a lie, along with much else Gwendolyn says.) She notes at one point that she is 'completely knackered' training with Faith, who refers to her as 'Mary Poppins'. Gwen also uses lots of supposedly British expressions like 'everything's gone to Hell in a hand basket' and shares Giles's obsession with tea. *Must* be British, then. Xander believes Giles needs a qualified surgeon to remove the British flag from his butt.

Notes: 'Keeping secrets is a lot of work.' A case of 'after the Lord Mayor's Show'. There's little *wrong* with 'Revelations' – indeed it's a Tasmanian devil of an episode, a whirlwind of manic violence. Perhaps it's the missing subtlety that lets it down, although the final scenes and Faith's growing cynicism at the world signal the way her character will develop.
    Giles indicates that a Watcher may have more than one

Slayer, which contradicts what we thought we knew about the Watcher–Slayer relationship (see **21/22**, 'What's My Line?'). There are twelve cemeteries in Sunnydale. Xander notes Buffy has been 'killing zombies and torching sewer monsters' – references to **36**, 'Dead Man's Party', and **40**, 'Band Candy', respectively. Gwendolyn was kicked out of the Watcher's Council for 'misuse of Dark Power'.

Soundtrack: 'Run' is the Four Star Mary song that Dingoes Ate My Baby mime to. Also 'West Of Here' by Lotion and 'Silver Dollar' by Lolly.

42
Lover's Walk

US Transmission Date: 24 Nov. 1998
UK Transmission Date: 7 Oct. 1999 (Sky)

Writer: David Vebber
Director: David Semel
Cast: Marc Burnham (Lenny), Suzanne Krull (Clerk)

Spike is back, having split with Drusilla. Desperate to win her back, he kidnaps Willow and Xander and threatens to kill them unless Willow performs a love spell. Buffy arrives home to find Spike telling his sob story to her mom, while a horrified Angel is unable to enter the house. Spike tells them what he's done with Willow and Xander, and they reluctantly agree to help him get what he needs and then get out of Sunnydale. Realising that their situation seems hopeless, Xander and Willow kiss, unaware that Oz and Cordelia have just arrived to rescue them. As Cordelia runs upstairs, she falls and is impaled on a steel rod. Spike, Buffy and Angel fight a large group of vampires. Spike is reawakened by the battle and decides to forget about the love spell and win Drusilla back by good old-fashioned torture. Cordelia survives but will not forgive Xander's betrayal.

Dudes and Babes: Spike's arrival mirrors the opening scene of **15**, 'School Hard' (his car crashing into the WELCOME TO SUNNYDALE sign). Everyone has a bad time, relationship-wise, in this episode but it's hard not to feel for poor Xander. That final scene with Cordy is heartbreaking.

The Conspiracy Starts at Home Time: The Mayor practising his putting says he would sell his soul for 'a decent short game' before adding, 'It's a bit late for that now.' He was aware of Spike's activities last year (and approved) but says this year is different and agrees with the deputy's suggestion to ask Mr Trick to send a 'welcome committee'.

A Little Learning is a Dangerous Thing: Willow's SAT score for English verbal of 740 (which she is disappointed with) is more than all of Xander's scores added up (since the maximum score in one subject is 800, this suggests that Xander's likely occupation once he finishes school will include the words 'Do you want fries with that?'). Buffy's combined score, 1,430, surprises not only everybody else but also herself. Cordelia also seems to have done very well (as she predicted she would in **40**, 'Band Candy').

Mom's Apple Pie: Spike's talk with Joyce over a cup of hot chocolate is hilarious – he asks if she has any of those 'little marshmallow things'. She tells Buffy, 'You belong at a good old-fashioned college with keg parties and boys, not here with Hellmouths and vampires.' So, replace Slaying with alcohol and sex? Interesting . . .

It's a Designer Label!: The horrible stuff first – Willow's red pants, Xander's purple shirt and Willow's stripy miniskirt. Buffy's green vest-type T-shirt and tight training pants make up for these. Willow's fluffy pink sweater appears (see **50**, 'Doppelgängland').

References: The title comes from an Elvis Costello song on his 1981 'Trust' LP. There are references to 'Cletus the Slack-Jawed Yokel' (from *The Simpsons*), *The Exorcist* and *Scanners* ('Her head span around and exploded') and *Weird Science*. The novel Angel's reading is *La Nausée* by the French existentialist philosopher Jean-Paul Sartre (1905–80).

Bitch!: Spike on Drusilla after she gave him the we-can-be-friends nonsense: 'She just left, she didn't even care enough to cut off my head, or set me on fire. Is that too much to ask? Some little sign that she cared.'

Buffy, to Spike: 'I violently dislike you.'

Awesome!: Spike at The Magik Shoppe, asking for a leprosy curse to make Angel's 'parts fall off'! The brilliant action sequence of Buffy, Angel and Spike taking on dozens of vampires. Plus the excellently timed funeral-site gag.

Cigarettes and Alcohol: Spike spends half the episode wasted on Jack Daniel's.

Logic, Let Me Introduce You to This Window: While Spike holds the broken bottle up to Willow's face, the position of her hair changes from shot to shot. Something similar happens to Spike's red shirt when he's pinned to the kitchen table by Buffy and Angel. Why did Joyce leave the back door unlocked? With all her concerns over her daughter's occupation (and after the events of **29**, 'Passion', and **36**, 'Dead Man's Party') you'd think she'd be more protective of the sanctity of her own home.

I Just *Love* Your Accent: With Spike around the insults get rather 'football-terrace', telling Buffy to 'shut your gob' and referring to Angel as 'your great pouf'.

Quote/Unquote: Cordelia: 'What if they were kidnapped by Colombian drug barons? They could be cutting off Xander's ear right now? Or other parts.'

Spike on Buffy and Angel: 'You'll be in love till it kills you both. You'll fight and you'll shag and you'll hate each other till it makes you quake, but you'll never be friends. Love isn't brains, children, it's blood. Blood screaming inside you to work its will. I may be love's bitch, but at least I'm man enough to admit it.'

Notes: 'Love's a funny thing.' Yet another classic – a confident, articulate, amusing vehicle for a production at the peak of its creativity. Very little happens, but it's a pivotal reaffirming link to the past while pointing a way forward. It's *great* to see Spike back (his scenes with Joyce being a particular joy).

Xander wanted to be a fireman in sixth grade. Cordelia has pictures of Xander and herself (and some group shots) inside her locker. She says they were taken on the pier. Oz can smell Willow when she's nearby (Cordy speculates it's 'some residual werewolf thing'). Spike says he used to bring Dru rats in bed along with the morning paper. After leaving Sunnydale, they went to Brazil but she never forgave him for his pact with Buffy. She flirted frequently, including a tryst with a 'Chaos Demon' (whom Spike describes as 'all slime and antlers, they're disgusting'). The US broadcast was followed by an advert for the phone service '1-800-Collect', featuring Sarah Michelle Gellar and David Boreanaz in character with a prize of a walk-on part in an upcoming *Buffy* episode (see **54**, 'The Prom').

Soundtrack: Contrary to fan-myth the version of 'My Way' at the end is *not* by Sid Vicious, but rather is a sound-alike cover by Gary Oldman from the soundtrack of *Sid and Nancy*.

The Comic: In another continuity-knitting exercise, April 1999 saw Dark Horse's one-shot comic *Spike and Dru: Paint the Town Red*, co-written by James Marsters and Christopher Golden, which takes place between **34**, 'Becoming' Part 2, and **42**, 'Lover's Walk', with the couple living (and killing) in Turkey.

43

The Wish

US Transmission Date: 8 Dec. 1998
UK Transmission Date: 8 Oct. 1999 (Sky)

Writer: Marti Noxon
Director: David Greenwalt
Cast: Nicole Bilderback (Cordette #1),
Nathan Anderson (John Lee),
Mariah O'Brien (Nancy), Gary Imhoff (Teacher),
Robert Covarrubias (Caretaker)

When a new girl, Anya, asks Cordelia if she wishes things were different, Cordy wishes Buffy had never come to Sunnydale, since that was when all of her problems started. In the blinking of an eye, Cordy finds herself in the world she wished for: a terrifying grey place of tiny classes, horrible clothes and rampant vampire activity; a world where Xander and Willow are still together, even in death; where the Master lives and is about to unleash the ultimate terror on mankind. Giles and his 'white hats' try to fight forces against which their weapons are useless, in a world made by Anyanka the 'Patron Saint of Scorned Women' and Cordelia's wish. Buffy arrives but she dies at the hands of the Master just as Giles smashes Anyanka's amulet and puts the world to rights.

It's a Wonderful What?!: Lots of shows have done 'what if?' treatments, *Moonlighting*'s 'It's a Wonderful Job' being a good example. The 'dark' versions of the regulars may have been suggested by the 'Mirror Universe' in *Star Trek*. (The characterisation of Evil-Willow owes much to the mirror Major Kira in *Deep Space 9*.)

Dudes and Babes: Willow in leather, licking Angel. *Oh yes!*

It's a Designer Label!: Cordelia has a Prada bag, which Anya recognises (Cordy says most people in Sunnydale can't tell the difference between Prada and Payless – a discount shoe chain). She asks if Anya's amulet is a Gucci. There's a reference to *W* ('the fashion magazine for the discerning woman').

References: Buffy calls Giles 'Jeeves', referring to the butler in PG Wodehouse's Jeeves and Wooster novels. 'What's done is done' is a line from *Macbeth*, while there are allusions to Smokey Robinson and the Miracles' 'Tears of a Clown', Sam and Dave's 'Soul Man', Aldous Huxley's *Brave New World*, *Superman* comics ('Bizarroland') and *Star Trek* ('Your logic doesn't resemble our Earth logic').

Bitch!: Harmony suggests Cordy date Jonathan: 'He won't cheat on you. At least for a week.'

Awesome!: What's the deal with the octopus-headed demon in the opening scene? The sequence in which Willow and Xander kill Cordelia (while Giles can only watch) is one of the most disturbing in the series, while the later slow-motion deaths of Xander, Willow and Buffy are extraordinary.

Surprise!: The end of act one, Anya revealed as a demon. 'Done!'

Valley-Speak: Buffy: 'You're acting a little schizo.' And: 'Slaying's a rough gig.'
   Xander: 'Slap my hand, soul man.'

Logic, Let Me Introduce You to This Window: The last cut that Cordelia makes to Xander's photograph is around chin level. However, when we see it burning the photo includes Xander's chest.

Quote/Unquote: Cordelia: 'Buffy changes it. It was better, I mean the clothes alone. The people were happy. Mostly.'
   Buffy: 'We fight, we die. Wishing doesn't change that.'
   Buffy: 'This is a "get-in-my-pants thing"? You guys in Sunnydale talk like I'm the Second Coming.'
   Anya: 'You trusting fool. How do you know the other world is any better than this?' Giles: 'Because it *has* to be.'

Those Prosthetics?: Alyson Hannigan confirmed: 'They're quite comfortable . . . They're squishy. It was fun to be evil for a week, but if you had to do it week in and week out your face would fall off with all that glue.'

Notes: 'Don't you kind of wish . . .?' Fan-fiction-in-the-area. Such an *obvious* idea, so well done. The characterisation is magnificent with Tony Head's anguished, out-of-his-league Giles just topping Sarah Michelle Gellar's portrayal of a scarred Buffy who never experienced Giles's influence and as a result is hardened and cynical (like Faith), living only for Slaying. Plus the little things like the cloves of garlic on the school lockers. Amazing stuff.
   There's a reference to Cordelia being bitten by a snake in **31**, 'I Only Have Eyes for You', to Angel having previously seen Buffy in 1996 in **33**, 'Becoming' Part 1, plus references

to Amy (see **3**, 'The Witch', **28**, 'Bewitched, Bothered and Bewildered', **45**, 'Gingerbread'). In the world in which Buffy never came to Sunnydale, Willow and Xander were turned into vampires and the Harvest happened. Giles runs a motley band of vampire hunters called 'the white hats' (who include Oz and Larry). He speaks to Buffy's Watcher (is it Merrick?), who tells him she is currently in Cleveland. Giles refers to Sunnydale as '*a* Hellmouth', which indicates there is more than one. Nancy notes that vampires are attracted by bright colours.

Soundtrack: 'Tired of Being Alone' by the Spies, 'Dedicated to Pain' by Plastic and 'Never Noticed' by Gingersol.

44
Amends [a.k.a. A Buffy Christmas]

US Transmission Date: 15 Dec. 1998
UK Transmission Date: 14 Oct. 1999 (Sky)

Writer: Joss Whedon
Director: Joss Whedon
Cast: Shane Barach (Daniel),
Edward Edwards (Male Ghost),
Cornelia Hayes O'Herlihy (Margaret),
Mark Kriski (Weatherman),
Tom Michael Bailey (Tree Seller Guy)

Christmas is coming, but for Angel (reliving, in his dreams, the numerous murders he has committed) it isn't a time of festive cheer. Angel visits Giles for help but is distracted by the 'ghost' of Jenny Calendar in the apartment. Buffy confides in Giles that she shared Angel's dream. Jenny tells Angel that he is losing his soul again and killing Buffy is the only act that will bring him peace. Giles links these manifestations to the Harbingers, a group of priests who can summon the First, a name given to Absolute Evil. Angel contemplates suicide but is saved by a combination of Buffy's persuasion and a freak snow storm.

Dreaming (As Blondie Once Said) is Free: Buffy's line about making 'guest spots' in Angel's dreams may be a reference to the *Angel* spin-off. His dreams (shared with Buffy) contain an interesting balance of historical fact (the murders of Daniel and Margaret), surrealist nightmares (the scary monks, Buffy appearing at the Victorian dinner party) and erotic stimulation of the moist variety (*that* night with Buffy – see **25**, 'Surprise').

Dudes and Babes: Nice hair-and-moustache combination in the 1838 sequences but Boreanaz's Irish accent is still woefully naff (see **33**, 'Becoming' Part 1). Margaret's description of Angel before Darla got to him is of a 'drunken, whoring layabout' who was a disappointment to his parents and whose only success in life was to die before he got syphilis.

Mom's Apple Pie: Christmas in the Summers household seems nice and relaxed, despite Buffy suggesting, 'You're still number one with the guilt trip, Mom.'

Denial, Thy Name is Joyce: Watch Joyce's reaction to Buffy's suggestion that they invite Giles around to Christmas dinner.

It's a Designer Label!: Xander's trampy red sweatshirt is a definite black mark on the episode, but on the plus side we have Buffy's blue shirt and white overcoat, Willow's slinky red dress and Faith's extremely short miniskirt.

References: A cheesy version of 'Joy to the World' is heard when Buffy and Joyce visit the tree farm. There's an oblique reference to David Bowie's 'Scary Monsters (And Super Creeps)'. Giles quotes from the Crystals' 'He's a Rebel'.

Bitch!: Cordy will spend Christmas skiing in Aspen, she gleefully tells her former friends.

Awesome!: Two great sequences – Giles inviting Angel into his home at the point of a crossbow and Oz and Willow deciding *not* to have sex.

'You May Remember Me From Such Films and TV Series As . . .': Cornelia Hayes O'Herlihy played the teenage

Princess Margaret in *Gods and Monsters*. Before moving to America, she appeared in a couple of episodes of *Newman and Baddiel in Pieces*.

Don't Give Up The Day Job: Although Mark Kriski often plays news reporters (he's in both of the *Speed* movies) he's a *real* weatherman for KTLA Morning News in Los Angeles.

Valley-Speak: Buffy: 'These are the guys working the mojo on Angel?'

Faith decides to spend Christmas with the Summerses: 'Looked like that whole party thing was gonna be a bit of a drag.'

Logic, Let Me Introduce You to This Window: The snow-drift seems to be the quickest in meteorological history. (Is it supposed to be magical and/or at the intervention of some higher power? If so, then we're getting frighteningly close to *Quantum Leap* territory. See **Joss Whedon's Comments**.)

I Just *Love* Your Accent: Buffy reads an ancient text about a child being born of a man and a goat, a child who had two heads, the first of which 'shall speak only in riddles'. 'No wonder you like this stuff,' she tells Giles. 'It's like reading the *Sun*' – a reference to the British tabloid. I always had Giles figured for a *Times* man.

Quote/Unquote: Angel asks 'Jenny' what she wants: 'I wanna die in bed surrounded by fat grandchildren, but I guess *that's* off the menu.'

Xander: 'That's the Christmas spirit.' Willow: 'Hello? Still Jewish. Hanukkah spirit, I believe that was.'

'Jenny': 'I'm not a demon, little girl, I'm something you can't even conceive . . . I am the thing the darkness fears.'

Notes: 'I think we're losing him.' Redemption is the theme of this variant on *A Christmas Carol*. In places the ideas are better than the execution. As with **35**, 'Anne', the episode deals with potentially massive subjects that then get pushed into the background. This is, theoretically, the most dangerous enemy that Buffy has ever encountered, but there's no real ending. The good stuff on offer is mostly in the way of characterisation.

Angel says vampires aren't 'big on Christmas'. Is it the commercialisation they object to, or just the Christianity? Xander always sleeps out of doors on Christmas Eve (he says it's so that he can look at the stars and feel the 'nature vibe', though in reality Cordelia reveals it's so he can avoid his family's drunken fights). What drink is chilling in the ice bucket on Willow's coffee table? It looks like a two-litre bottle of either Sprite or 7-Up. Two (seemingly fictitious) films are playing at the Sunnydale cinema. *Abilene* (rated PG), and one that begins *Pray For* . . . The two books Giles gives Xander and Buffy for research purposes are *The Black Chronicles* and *The Diary of Lucius Temple*.

Soundtrack: Willow's attempt to seduce Oz is accompanied by 'Can't Get Enough of Your Love, Babe' by the Walrus of Lurv himself, Barry White.

Joss Whedon's Comments: On the BtVS posting board shortly after the episode's broadcast, Whedon noted: 'The snow was not evil! The snow was good. It was "hope". Was the snow a cheap *Deus Ex Machina*? Well, obviously I don't think so or I would avoid the question . . . I know some people here thought it was corny, but I didn't just pull it out of a hat. The whole episode was leading to that, it was the point, not just a way to end it . . . Was it God? Well, I'm an atheist, but it's hard to ignore the idea of a "Christmas miracle" here (though "Pray" on the marquee was an unintentional coincidence). The Christian mythos has a powerful fascination to me and it bleeds into my storytelling. Redemption, hope, purpose, Santa, all these are important to me, whether I believe in an afterlife or some universal structure or not. I certainly don't mind a strictly Christian interpretation being placed on this episode by those who believe that – I just hope it's not limited to that.'

45

Gingerbread

US Transmission Date: 12 Jan. 1999

Teleplay: Jane Espenson
Story: Thania St John, Jane Espenson
Director: James Whitmore Jnr
Cast: Jordan Baker (Sheila Rosenberg),
Lindsay Taylor (Little Girl),
Shawn Pyfrom (Little Boy), Blake Swendson (Michael),
Grant Garrison (Roy),
Roger Morrissey (Demon), Daniel Tamm (MOOster)

The discovery of two children's bodies by Joyce Summers has a profound effect on life in Sunnydale. Apparently the work of occultists, it leads to a witch hunt within the town from which no one is immune. Willow, Amy and eventually Buffy are targeted while Giles's books are confiscated, leaving him to rely on the Internet. Oz sends a message to Willow, who discovers that these same children have been repeatedly murdered every fifty years back to their origins in the 'Hansel and Gretel' fairy tale. Buffy, Willow and Amy are tied to stakes in City Hall to be burned alive. Giles and Cordelia stop the ceremony and reveal the children to be a hideous demon. Buffy impales the demon with the stake she is tied to.

Authority Sucks!: Snyder's glee at being given the power to search the lockers: 'This is a glorious day for principals everywhere. No pathetic whining about students' rights. Just a long row of lockers and a man with a key.'

Mom's Milk of Human Bigotry: Joyce's 'bonding visit' to see what Buffy does (complete with thermos flask and sandwiches) goes disastrously wrong and she finds herself in her worst nightmare. She says that for too long she's been too afraid to speak out and that silence is 'the town's disease'. Her setting up of Mothers Opposed to the Occult ('Nice acronym, Mom') turns Sunnydale into Salem. Oh well, we all make mistakes.

Denial, Thy Names are Joyce and Rupert: The awkward scene between them is really funny. ('It's been a while'; 'Not since . . . a while'.)

Denial, Thy Name is Sheila Rosenberg: Willow's mom is an academic, the co-author of a recent paper on 'The Rise of Mysticism Among Adolescents'. The implication (from her not noticing her daughter's five-month-old haircut and the last long chat they had being about a children's TV show) is that she and Willow do not talk much. She believes Willow's claim to be a witch is delusional and 'a cry for discipline', though she later says, 'It seems I've been rather closed-minded.' At the end of the episode Willow tells Buffy that her mother is doing 'that selective-memory thing your mom used to be so good at'. Sheila *does* remember that Willow is dating a musician and Oz must attend the Rosenbergs' for dinner next week.

It's a Designer Label!: Buffy's blue frock coat and pink jumper. Cordelia's hairspray is imported and costs $45.

References: *My Friend Flicka,* the pre-school TV show, *Mr Roger's Neighbourhood* and the puppet King Friday (1968–date) and *Apocalypse Now* ('I love the smell of desperate librarian in the morning') are referenced, along with the Salem witch trials. Xander says, 'Oh, man, it's Nazi Germany and I've got *Playboy*s in my locker,' and refers to 'Jack and the Beanstalk'. The writer of the article Willow finds is 'Howard Fine', the name of two of the Three Stooges.

Bitch!: Cordelia: 'Everyone knows that witches killed those kids and Amy is a witch. And Michael is whatever a boy witch is, plus being the poster child for "yuck". If you're going to hang with them, expect badness 'coz that's what you get when you hang with freaks and losers. Believe me, I know. That was a pointed comment about me hanging with you guys.'

Giles refers to Snyder as 'that twisted little homunculus'.

Awesome!: The shocking pre-title sequence (Joyce's horrified cry of 'it's Mr Sanderson from the bank' would be comical in other circumstances). The Giles, Xander, Oz and Buffy scenes in the library – an example of a minimalist setting helping with the development of a storyline. And Oz's and Xander's incompetent attempts to save Buffy and Willow.

It's *That* Idea Again: Willow's mother calls Buffy 'Bunny' (see U1).

Don't Give Up The Day Job: Grant Garrison also has a flourishing career as a carpenter and art labourer on films like *Dreammaster: The Erotic Invader* and *Cyberella: Forbidden Passions*. Roger Morrisey is another tech guy moonlighting as an actor. He was a grip on *Access Denied* and *Silent Lies*.

Valley-Speak: Buffy on her mother: 'She's completely wigging.'

Logic, Let Me Introduce You to This Window: During the locker search, a cop is looking through a coin purse behind Snyder. Some time later the same cop is looking through the same purse (maybe Snyder was right about how stupid the Sunnydale police are). For the final scene with Buffy and Willow in the bedroom, we first see an establishing shot which reveals it's night and the lighting is appropriate for this. However, the rest of the scene looks like it takes place in the middle of the day. Where did those pictures of Hans and Greta Strauss come from? It's pretty strange that the residents of Sunnydale are holding a witch burning indoors. A more politically correct name for Joyce's group would have been '*Parents* Opposed to the Occult', but that would have made the acronym even more unfortunate.

I Just *Love* Your Accent: Giles: 'There is a fringe theory, held by a few folklorists, that some regional stories have actual, very literal antecedents.' Buffy: 'And in some language that's English?' Giles believes the murders may be the work of European wiccan covens.

Quote/Unquote: Joyce: 'Good, honey! Kill him!'
Buffy: 'We need those books.' Giles: 'Believe me, I tried to

tell that to the nice man with the big gun.'

Snyder: 'Just how is *Blood Rites and Sacrifices* appropriate material for a public school library? Chess Club branching out?' (As with a lot of questions asked in this episode, you've got to wonder why somebody hasn't asked it before.)

Buffy, on MOO: 'Who came up with that lame name?' Snyder: 'That would be the founder. I believe you call her "Mom".'

Willow: 'I'm a witch. I can make pencils float. And I can summon the four elements. OK, two, but four soon. And I'm dating a musician . . . I worship Beelzebub. I do his biddings. Do you see any goats around? No, because I sacrificed them . . . Prince of Night, I summon you. Come fill me with your black, naughty evil.'

Buffy: 'I'm like that kid in the story, the boy that stuck his finger in the duck.' Angel: 'Dyke. It's another word for dam.' Buffy: 'OK, that story makes a lot more sense now.'

Willow: 'Another step and you will all feel my power.' Buffy: 'What're you gonna do, float a pencil at them?'

Notes: 'How many of us have lost someone who just disappeared? Or got skinned?' There's a *lot* of anger in this episode. Its *probable* targets are those people who use sudden violent incidents to pursue an agenda of censorship. How ironic it was that just months afterwards they'd be out in force again, with *Buffy* on their hit list. It really was disturbing watching this episode mere days after the Littleton High School massacre where news programmes were full of similarly hysterical reactions from people in search of anyone to blame. The anger in 'witch hunt' stories is often blind, but I'll give any episode that rages against being judgemental in such a refreshingly honest manner ten out of ten for effort.

Slayers are not supposed to kill people (see **23**, 'Ted', **48**, 'Bad Girls'), though Buffy's horrified 'someone with a *soul* did this?' suggests breaking that rule is on her mind. It's Buffy's birthday next week (see **46**, 'Helpless'). Cordelia asks Giles how many times he's been knocked out and (as with Buffy constantly allowing herself to get distracted by diversionary tactics) he does, indeed, seem to fall for that one rather a lot (see **39**, 'Homecoming'). He has the ability to pick locks with a hairpin (Cordelia notes, 'You really *were* the little youthful offender, weren't you?' – see **36**, 'Dead Man's Party', **40**, 'Band Candy'). Amy performs the same spell as she did on Buffy in **28**, 'Bewitched, Bothered and Bewildered', with similar results, turning *herself* into a rat. Buffy and Willow are still trying to reverse the spell at the end of the episode (see **46**, 'Helpless'). Giles has somehow found his way into the 'Frisky Watchers' Chat Room'.

Should The Bible Be Banned?: Buffy: 'Maybe next time that the world is getting sucked into Hell, I won't be able to stop it because the anti-Hell-sucking book isn't on the Approved Reading List.' It was inevitable that this episode would happen sooner or later. The Christian Right in America have never quite known what to make of *Buffy* – the plethora of wiccan elements was an immediate cause for concern, but essentially it was about teenage good fighting evil so they couldn't complain on that score without dragging *The Hardy Boys* and *Nancy Drew* into the equation and, despite our never quite knowing if it took place in a Christian universe or not, *Buffy* seemed to achieve 'moral acceptability'. That was until the magic 's' word ('sex') started cropping up. When Buffy slept with Angel in **25**, 'Surprise', it was open target practice on the series for anybody with access to the Old Testament and a computer, and the Net was swamped with warning articles emanating from the Bible Belt (real 'Watch *Buffy the Vampire Slayer* and be damned for eternity' stuff). Whether 'Gingerbread' was a reaction to this (albeit brief) wave of hysteria is unknown (certainly the episode has been used by fans to rub in the face of any religious objector ever since). Interestingly, however, there is little criticism of religion in either the series in general or 'Gingerbread' itself (that would be commercial suicide in a TV industry still dominated by advertising and network nervousness of offending *anyone*). Instead, what 'Gingerbread' *does* question, vocally and angrily, is a more disturbing saga. In America, many schools and public libraries ban certain books. The website http://www.cs.cmu.edu/People/spok/most-banned.html lists the fifty most commonly suppressed, including works by William Shakespeare, John Steinbeck, JD Salinger, Mark Twain, Roald Dahl, Maya Angelou, William Golding, Kurt Vonnegut, Alice Walker and Margaret Atwood. It's sad that a nation that promotes freedom of speech has within it elements that seek to limit this on their own people. (Joyce's line 'MOO just wants to weed out the offensive material' seems chillingly realistic.) Readers can find more information at http://www.ala.org/bbooks/, which is the American Library Association's webpage.

46

Helpless

US Transmission Date: 19 Jan. 1999

Writer: David Fury
Director: James A Contner
Cast: Jeff Kober (Zackary Kralik),
Harris Yulin (Quentin Travers), Dominic Keating (Blair),
David Hayon-Jones (Hobson), Nick Cornish (Guy),
Don Dowe (Construction Worker)

As her eighteenth birthday approaches Buffy suffers dizzy spells and weakness that suggests she is losing her powers. In reality she is being drugged by Giles as part of the *Cruciamentum*, a ritual that The Slayer undergoes to prove their resourcefulness. The weakened Slayer must survive an encounter with a vampire, in Buffy's case the insane Zackary Kralik. All does not go according to the plans of Chief Watcher Quentin Travers, Kralik escaping and abducting Joyce. Giles tells Buffy the truth, to her disgust. Buffy goes in search of Kralik, despite her lack of strength. She cleverly manipulates Kralik into drinking holy water. Travers commends Buffy on her successful passing of the test. However, since Giles demonstrates a relationship with Buffy that the Council deems too close, he is relieved of his Watcher duties.

Dudes and Babes: Giles is at his most toe-curlingly sexy in this episode, while there's an extremely gratuitous shot of Boreanaz's rippling biceps. If that had been one of the girls, everybody would be crying 'exploitation'!

Authority Sucks!: Quentin's treatment of Giles. I wasn't aware that the Watchers' Council was a subdivision of some small fascist dictatorship.

A Little Learning is a Dangerous Thing: Cordelia has a paper to research on Bosnia.

Mom's For Dinner: Kralik killed and ate his own mother, something he takes great delight in telling Joyce.

It's a Designer Label!: Buffy's All Saints-style combat pants. Another triumph for Willow: a pair of suitably horrible hats (a red tea-cosy-bobble one and a yellow abomination), a nasty yellow jumper and pink miniskirt.

References: The 1988 Olympic figure-skating champion Brian Boitano, Bizet's opera *Carmen* and *Superman* are all referenced. Angel's present for Buffy is *Sonnets from the Portuguese* by Elizabeth Barrett Browning (see **3**, 'The Witch') inscribed 'Always'. *Cruciamentum* is Latin for torture or torment.

Bitch!: Cordelia tells one potential suitor that he shouldn't take her flirting seriously as she is on the rebound (from Xander).

Awesome!: Buffy and Angel working out, Kralik's death sequence and Xander and Oz's discussion on what sort of kryptonite is deadly to Superman (Oz is right: green is deadly, red mutates him and gold drains his power!).

The Drugs Don't Work: The pills that Kralik so desperately needs get both Blair and Kralik himself killed.

'You May Remember Me From Such Films, TV Series and Adverts As . . .': Jeff Kober played Bear in the memorable *X-Files* episode 'Ice', was Dodger in *China Beach* and Booga in *Tank Girl*. Readers may recognise him as 'Ray, the voice of Reef Radio' in those annoying Bacardi adverts. Harry Yulin is a character actor *par excellence*, appearing in *Bean*, *Clear and Present Danger*, *Scarface* and *Ghostbusters II*. In one of those coincidences that seem to crop up only in the crazy world of TV books, on the day that I viewed this episode, I stopped the video tape and playing on TV at that moment was an episode of *Ironside*, featuring a younger Mr Yulin.

Valley-Speak: Xander: 'Maybe we're on the wrong track with the whole spell, curse and whammy thing?'

Buffy: 'Did I zone out on you?' And she gives Quentin that old standby: 'Bite me!'

Cordelia: 'First of all, *posse*? *Passé!* Second of all, anyone with a teaspoon of brains knows not to take my flirting seriously. Especially with my extenuating circumstances.'

Logic, Let Me Introduce You to This Window: The last knife that Buffy throws in the library breaks a glass object. However, whenever the camera angle focuses on the target, there's nothing made of glass nearby. Were Hobson's and Blair's deaths part of Quentin's plan from the beginning? Kralik can be photographed (see **M1** the movie) despite a camera using mirrors as part of its focusing mechanism (see **11**, 'Out of Sight, Out of Mind', **21**, 'What's My Line?' Part 1). Buffy says she and her dad go to the Ice Show every year for her birthday, but there was no mention of this last year during **25**, 'Surprise'. Buffy seems to push the bookcase on to Blair rather easily considering how weak she is. She must have switched Kralik's water with the holy water amazingly quickly.

I Just *Love* Your Accent: Exactly where is Quentin from? He doesn't sound English, that's for sure. Giles says he doesn't give 'a rat's arse' about the Council's orders, and refers to the *Cruciamentum* as a dozen-century-old 'archaic exercise in cruelty'.

Quote/Unquote: Angel on Buffy's heart: 'I could see that you held it before you for everyone to see and I worried that it would be bruised or torn. More than anything in my life, I

wanted to keep it safe, to warm it with my own.' Buffy:
'That's beautiful. Or, taken literally, incredibly gross.'

Buffy: 'Hummers. Big turnoff. I like guys who can remember the lyrics.'

Notes: 'I don't *know* you.' A sadistic episode that manages to
rise above its voyeurism just long enough to become a hymn
to the power of intelligence over superstition. Betrayal is the
key theme in a modern 'Little Red Riding Hood' variant that
relies on the old fan-fiction standby of setting a character up
to be hurt, so that they can then be comforted.

Willow went to see *Snoopy on Ice* when she was small (her
father took her backstage and she got so scared she threw up
on Woodstock). Faith is on one of her 'unannounced walkabouts'. There are numerous continuity references, including
Giles saying Buffy may have a 'bad flu bug' (see **30**, 'Killed
By Death'), Angel telling Buffy he saw her before she
became The Slayer (see **33**, 'Becoming' Part 1), references to
the parties in **25**, 'Surprise', and **36**, 'Dead Man's Party',
Buffy's love of skating in **25**, 'Surprise', 'Mr Pointy' the
stake from **33**, 'Becoming' Part 1, and Buffy's birthday
present last year being 'a severed arm in a box' (see **25**,
'Surprise'). Amy is still a rat (see **45**, 'Gingerbread'). There
is no evidence that Blair fed on Kralik to become a vampire
(Kralik's dialogue with both Blair and Buffy suggests that
the process has more to do with the quantity of blood the
vampire takes rather than on cross-feeding as stated in **1**,
'Welcome to the Hellmouth' – see **33**, 'Becoming' Part 1, **56**,
'Graduation Day' Part 2). Blair also rises remarkably
quickly and seems very focused for someone who has undergone such a radical change (see Angel's observation in **15**,
'School Hard', about how confusing it all is for a vampire at
first). Quentin says The Slayer must undergo the *Cruciamentum* '*if* she reaches her eighteenth birthday', which suggests that most Slayers are called before that age (Buffy was
sixteen). However, as both Kendra and Faith have proved,
older girls *have* been called. This also suggests that the calling is not, necessarily, in any fixed order and that had Buffy
not 'died' in **12**, 'Prophecy Girl', and lived for several years

thereafter, Kendra would not have automatically been the next choice.

Electra on Azalea Path: What's going on in the Buffy–Giles relationship? Quentin says Giles has 'a father's love' for Buffy and the implication from Buffy's (unsubtle) attempt to get Giles to take her to the Ice Show in her dad's place indicates her (possibly subconscious) need for a father substitute. She spends a lot of time trying to get Giles and Joyce together, only to be *horrified* when they *do* (see **40**, 'Band Candy', **52**, 'Earshot'). The poet Sylvia Plath (1932–63) was a great exponent of Electra (the female equivalent of the Oedipus Complex proposed by Freud based on the Greek myth of Agamemnon's daughter). In such poems as 'Full Fathom Five', 'Electra on Azalea Path' and 'Daddy' she explored her own relationship with her father, and (particularly in the third poem) her search for a replacement figure in her life.

47
The Zeppo

US Transmission Date: 26 Jan. 1999

Writer: Dan Vebber
Director: James Whitmore Jnr
Cast: Channon Roe (Jack O'Toole), Michael Cudlitz (Bob),
Darin Heames (Parker), Scott Torrence (Dickie),
Whitney Dylan (Lysette), Vaughn Armstrong (Cop)

Combining their talents, Giles, Willow, Faith and Buffy defeat a group of female demons, the Sisterhood of Jhe. Xander, however, can only watch. Stung by Cordelia's jibes that he is a passenger in a group of superheroes, Xander attempts to find his own speciality and borrows his uncle's car, but succeeds only in coming to the attention of a local psychopath, Jack O'Toole. O'Toole, however, needs a 'wheels man' for his quest to raise his three friends from the dead and leads Xander into one of the strangest nights of his life – the night on which he will lose his virginity and prove to himself that he is the equal of his friends. Unfortunately, they're too busy with the End of the World to notice.

Dreaming (As Blondie Once Said) is Free: Every nightmare that Willow has that doesn't involve academic failure or public nudity concerns the Hellmouth creature seen in 12, 'Prophecy Girl'. In fact, she once dreamed it attacked her while she was late for a test *and* naked.

Dudes and Babes: Lysette, the girl Xander takes out to the Bronze, seems to prove the old theory about it being a guy's car that's the biggest turn-on for the girls. The ridiculousness of his liaison with Faith is emphasised when he's pushed out of her room semi-clothed, with his pants in his hands and an idiot grin on his face. Yeah, we've *all* had those sorts of nights . . .

It's a Designer Label!: What on Earth is up with Buffy's hair? It looks like a perm's gone wrong somewhere. Xander's pink jumper takes few prisoners.

References: Superman's pal Jimmy Olsen is mentioned twice. There are references to the fast-food chain Taco Bell, the Beastie Boys' 'Hello Nasty' and Michael Jackson's 1983 hit 'Wanna Be Startin' Something'. Bob's overriding concern after eight months in his grave is 'Whoa! *Walker, Texas Ranger*. You been taping 'em?' Nice to see even the undead have their priorities right. The title, as alluded to by Cordelia, refers to Herbert 'Zeppo' Marx (1901–79), the fourth Marx Brother and the one everybody always forgets alongside his illustrious siblings Groucho, Chico and Harpo. (Does that make Cordy herself Gummo, the fifth – and even more obscure – member?)

Bitch!: Cordelia to Xander: 'Boy, of all the humiliations you've had that I've witnessed, that was the latest.' And: ' "Cool". Look it up. It's something that a subliterate that's repeated twelfth grade three times has and you don't. There was no part of that that wasn't fun.'

Xander tells Cordy: 'Feel free to die of a wasting disease in the next twenty seconds.'

Awesome!: The Xander/Oz 'essence of cool' scene. Plus the sequence in the boiler room with some of Xander's dialogue seemingly inspired by *Dirty Harry*.

'You May Remember Me From Such Films As . . .': Channon Roe played Surfer in *Boogie Nights*.

Don't Give Up The Day Job: Michael Cudlitz worked as a construction co-ordinator on *American History X* and *Beverly Hills 90210*, a series he also starred in as Tony Miller.

Valley-Speak: Faith: 'These babes were wicked rowdy, what's the deal?' ('Wicked' is an all-purpose slang adjective of New England origin cementing Faith's Boston background. See **55**, 'Graduation Day' Part 1.)

Logic, Let Me Introduce You to This Window: The cafeteria scene begins with a shot of the lunch counter. The camera rises and we see Xander in the background along with Buffy and Willow. Oz is nowhere to be seen and Xander is wearing completely different clothes from the rest of this scene. (This is footage from **31**, 'I Only Have Eyes For You'. The episode also features that stock shot from **5**, 'Never Kill a Boy on the First Date', with Owen again.) Jack says he couldn't raise his dead friends earlier because he 'had to wait eight months for the stars to align', but he died three weeks ago himself and yet his grandpappy (presumably) raised him the same night. Throughout the scene in the boiler room, the bomb can be heard beeping as the seconds tick by. But the digital countdown is all over the place, jumping from 10 up to 13, then down to 7, and taking many more than six beeps to reach 2, at which point Jack finally disarms the bomb.

Motors: Xander's green 1957 Chevrolet Bel Air.

Quote/Unquote: Willow: 'Occasionally, I'm callous and strange.'

Xander, on his car: 'It's my thing.' Buffy: 'Is this a penis metaphor?'

Cordelia: 'It must be really hard when all your friends have, like, superpowers. Slayer, werewolf, witches, vampires . . . You must feel like Jimmy Olsen.'

Jack brandishes a knife: 'Are you scared?' Xander: 'Would that make you happy?'

Notes: 'Did I mention I'm having a very strange night?' I'm a real sucker for Xander-led episodes and, as with **28**, 'Bewitched, Bothered and Bewildered', and **32**, 'Go Fish', the decision to use Nick Brendon's comic talents to the fore is an inspired one. 'The Zeppo' was *hated* by many online *Buffy* fans, who completely missed the point and demanded to know why we kept cutting back to Xander and his trivial chase through the school when the fate of the whole world was at stake. I love the way everything keeps happening just out of Xander's reach and we see the world for once through his eyes. Great music too.

Giles says most of his sources have dried up since he was relieved of his duties by the Watchers' Council. He tries to contact the Spirit Guides, who 'live outside of time' and 'have knowledge of the future', but he gets no luck there either. Giles is always the one who asks for jellied doughnuts in the mix during research sessions and is horrified when Buffy eats the last one (*top* bit of snitching by Willow on Buffy: 'She ate *three*!'). Xander asks Oz if learning the guitar is hard. Oz says, 'Not the way I play' (see **22**, 'What's My Line?' Part 2), which proves that Xander's dream in **4**, 'Teacher's Pet', *was* just a dream and the guitar we see in his bedroom *is* just for show. He reveals some musical talent, having played the flugelhorn in eighth grade. Xander tells Jack he is *not* retarded. 'I had to take that test when I was seven. A little slow in some stuff, mostly math and spatial relations, but certainly not challenged.' He mentions his Uncle Rory again (see **20**, 'The Dark Age'). He loses his virginity to Faith.

Soundtrack: 'G-Song' by Supergrass and 'Easy' by Tricky Woo. The acoustic-guitar riff played as Xander walks away from Cordelia at the end sounds like the opening chords of Oasis's 'Talk Tonight'. But it's not.

48
Bad Girls

US Transmission Date: 9 Feb. 1999

Writer: Douglas Petrie
Director: Michael Lange
Cast: Christian Clemenson (Balthazar),
Alex Skuby (Vincent), Wendy Clifford (Mrs Taggert)

The arrival of a replacement Watcher sees Buffy and Faith question to whom their loyalties belong. Hunting a vampire sect called El Eliminati, the girls become reckless, despite Angel's warning that the Demon Balthazar is not as dead as the new Watcher, Wesley, believes. In need of weaponry, The Slayers break into a hunting-equipment shop, but their shop-lifting spree is cut short by two cops who arrest them. Though they escape, Buffy recognises the dangerous game she is playing and that the large amount of time she's spending with Faith has upset Willow and Xander. But, when Giles and Wesley are captured by Balthazar's vampires, Buffy helps them before she can deal with the consequences of Faith's most irresponsible act of all – the staking of the Deputy Mayor. Mayor Wilkins performs a ritual in his office and becomes invincible. Buffy visits Faith's motel room to discuss their crime but is disturbed by Faith's lack of guilt.

Dudes and Babes: In the opening scene, Faith is astonished that Buffy and Xander have never . . . you know. ('Not even *once*?') Buffy says they are just friends, to which Faith replies, 'What else are friends for?' Faith is very descriptive about her need for sex ('A little after-hours [grunt]') and about how 'sweaty' Slaying makes her (see **37**, 'Faith, Hope and Trick', **38**, 'Beauty and the Beasts'). Xander's eye twitches whenever Buffy mentions Faith (see **Notes**).

The Conspiracy Starts at Home Time: The strands of innu-endo that have been building all season start to come together. The Mayor, who again hints at a nonhuman longevity, says that it will be one hundred days to his 'ascension', during which time nothing can harm him (not even getting his head sliced in half). After this process Earthly affairs will not concern him as he will be on 'a higher plane'. Balthazar seems to know what is coming, telling Buffy and her friends, 'When *he* rises, you'll wish I'd killed you all.'

A Little Learning is a Dangerous Thing: Having been accepted for 'early admission' to university, Willow is being 'wooed' by both Harvard and Yale (see **50**, 'Doppelgäng-land'). She says chemistry is a lot like witchcraft, 'only less newt'. Xander, meanwhile, is hoping to get into 'appliance-repair or motel management' post-school, though he has yet to hear back from the Hot-Dog Emporium. Buffy cuts class in the middle of a chemistry test (a silly thing to do considering that Snyder is looking for any excuse to expel her again).

Mom's Waffles: Joyce is on a diet, though she seems to be seeking any excuse to break it and have some waffles. When Buffy says she doesn't want any, Joyce notes that they don't have calories only if she's making them for Buffy. ('Mom logic.')

It's a Designer Label!: Is that underwear Faith is washing in her sink at the end? Why does Willow's jumper look like the Swiss national flag?

References: Wesley's middle name is a reference to the king of British science fiction, John Wyndham (1903–69) author of *The Day of the Triffids*, *The Midwich Cuckoos*, *The Kraken Wakes* and *Random Quest* among others. There's a lengthy discussion on the comic strips *Family Circus, Marmaduke* and *Cathy* (*Family Circus* by Bill Keane, a rather twee story of family life, started in 1960 and is the most widely syndicated strip in the world; *Marmaduke* by Brad Anderson is about a troublemaking Great Dane; *Cathy* by Cathy Guisewite concerns the trials of a single woman). Also name-checked are *Sesame Street, Magnum Force*, Kipling's *Captains Courageous* and Hot Chocolate's 'Every One's a Winner'.

Bitch!: Judging by a horrible comment Cordy makes to Xander, his father seems to have recently become unemployed. Oh, *that's* nasty (see **54**, 'The Prom'). Mind you, his suggestion that she start modelling her own line of 'hooker-wear' is almost as bad.

Awesome!: Buffy and Faith shaking their funky stuff in the Bronze. Balthazar is the most disgusting villain we've had in a while, with the scariest face this side of Keith Richards. His scenes with Giles and Wesley ('Stay calm, Mr Giles', 'Thank God you're here, I was planning to panic') are funny, though the action sequence that follows seems to go on for *ever*.

'You May Remember Me From Such Films and TV Series As . . .' Alexis Denisof was Richard Sharpe's love rival, Lord Rossendale, in *Sharpe*. Christian Clemenson has a blink-and-you'll-miss-him part in *Armageddon* and more substantial roles in *Apollo 13* (as Dr Chuck), *The Big Lebowski*, *The Fisher King*, *Broadcast News* and *Hannah and Her Sisters*.

Valley-Speak: Faith, on dead vampires: 'They're toast.'
And on Buffy and Slaying: 'Like, you *don't* dig it?'
Willow: 'I can *totally* handle myself.'

Not Exactly A Haven For The Bruthas: Mr Trick thinks El Eliminati should use Uzis instead of swords: 'Would've saved your ass right about now.'

Cigarettes and Soft Drinks: The Mayor and Mr Trick are about to share a root beer at the end.

Logic, Let Me Introduce You to This Window: When Buffy breaks into the display case containing the dagger, the weapon falls and she catches it between her index and middle fingers. In the next shot it's between her thumb and index finger. Why didn't Buffy bandage her wound before going to the Bronze with Faith? When telling Wesley about the three vampires she and Faith killed, Buffy says, 'One of them had swords. I don't think he was with the other two.' All three of the vampires were dressed in the same Eliminati uniform, so why would she think they weren't together?

I Just *Love* Your Accent: *Two* British Watchers. (Love the bit where Giles and Wesley simultaneously clean their spectacles). Giles uses the *very* British insult 'twerp' to Wesley. The new Watcher's three most important words ('preparation, preparation, preparation') could be a reference to Tony Blair's famed speech during the 1997 election campaign when he said that the three most important things in Britain were 'education, education, education'. The song that Faith and Buffy dance to is 'Chinese Burn' by the British indie band Curve.

Quote/Unquote: Buffy on Wesley: 'Is he evil?' Giles: 'Not in the strictest sense.'

Buffy: 'Whenever Giles sends me on a mission, he always says "please". And afterwards I get a cookie.'

Wesley says that El Eliminati were a fifteenth-century duellist cult whose numbers dwindled after, among other things, 'a lot of pointless duelling'.

Notes: 'Want. Take. Have.' An up-and-down trip. 'Bad Girls' has lots of good ideas that, sadly, aren't followed up in the next episode so it's guilt by association. The introduction of Wesley allows Giles to get into the action more, which has both positive and negative aspects (attempting to turn him into 'Bruce Willis in Tweed' is a definite negative, as his OTT stunts in the warehouse prove). However, Alexis Denisof's performance is genuinely funny – it was amusing to see Internet fans getting annoyed at how 'irritating' Wesley is. That's the whole *point*, kids, he's *supposed* to be.

Mind you, another inclusion in the growing family of characters means that Oz, Cordelia and Xander hardly appear. There are continuity references to **41**, 'Revelations', and Gwendolyn Post and an oblique reference to Xander and Faith's liaison in **47**, 'The Zeppo'. Giles's first entry in the Watcher Diary noted that Buffy was wilful and insolent and that her abuse of the English language was such that he understood only 'every other sentence'. Wesley says he has faced two vampires himself, under controlled conditions (no word on whether he killed them – was this, perhaps, a Watcher equivalent of Cruciamentum?). There seem to be girl gangs in Sunnydale. Just how stupid *are* the police in Sunnydale (see **33**, 'Becoming' Part 1)? The complete mayoral 'Things to Do' checklist is: 'meet scouts', 'Lumber Union reschedule', 'call temp agency', 'become invincible', 'meeting with PTA', 'haircut'. Mrs Haggard is the chemistry teacher.

49

Consequences

US Transmission Date: 16 Feb. 1999

Writer: Marti Noxon
Director: Michael Gershman
Cast: Amy Powell (TV News Reporter),
Patricia Place (Woman)

The Deputy Mayor's murder is discovered. Buffy tries to persuade Faith to confess, but without success, but they break into his office and spot the Mayor and Mr Trick together. Buffy is concerned by Faith's lack of conscience, though Faith says Slaying puts them above the law. Buffy confesses to Willow, who advises that she see Giles. When she gets to the library, she finds Faith has told Giles that Buffy was responsible. Giles assures Buffy that he's aware of Faith's lies and they ask Angel to help Faith face up to the horror of what she has done. Unfortunately, Wesley overhears the conversation and he and his men subdue Angel and capture Faith. She escapes and seems to have gone rogue, but Buffy finds her at the docks and Faith saves Buffy from an attack by Mr Trick, whom she kills. However, the Mayor gets a visit from Faith at his office. With Mr Trick out of the picture, Faith wants the available job.

Dreaming (As Blondie Once Said) is Free: Buffy's nightmare has her drowning, with Finch holding on to her foot. When she struggles to the surface, Faith pushes her back under.

Dudes and Babes: Faith and Xander are (but for Angel's intervention) at it again, only this time there's more strangulation involved. Presumably, this is the sequence that got the TV-14 rating. Faith's use of the term 'safety words' suggests a knowledge of the BDSM community!

A Little Learning is a Dangerous Thing: Cordelia checks out books from the library by Sigmund Freud (see **23**, 'Ted') and Carl Gustav Jung (1875–1961) for her psychology class.

Mom's Apple Pie: The pained expression on Joyce's face when Buffy arrives home to find a policeman waiting for her speaks volumes. Joyce cuts a lonely figure watching TV alone in the early hours of the morning.

Denial, Thy Name is Faith: Faith attempts to shift the blame for the murder on to Buffy (Giles notes that Faith may be good at a lot of things, but lying isn't one of them).

It's a Designer Label!: Faith's leather strides previously seen, plus a pair of incredibly tight jeans, and her 'Motor City Baby' T-shirt. Buffy's pink overcoat is also worth a mention.

References: Obliquely, *Star Trek: The Next Generation*, plus name checks for MasterCard, the Troggs' 'Wild Thing', England's most underrated band the Kinks, Carolyn Crawford's Motown classic 'My Smile Is Just a Frown Turned Upside Down' and 'Zip a Dee Doo Dah' from *Song of the South*. 'We *are* the Law' refers to *Judge Dredd*.

Bitch!: When Buffy says Cordelia is 'a friend', Cordy replies, 'Let's not exaggerate.'

Awesome!: Xander confessing that he slept with Faith to Giles, Buffy and Willow and their different reactions to it. The Wesley/Cordelia introduction is intriguing and the capture of Faith by Wesley's men (and the brutal subduing of Angel) is astonishingly violent.

Surprise!: Faith turning up at the Mayor's office at the end. Didn't see *that* coming at all.

Valley-Speak: Faith: 'You'd dig that, wouldn't you? To get up in front of all your geek pals and go on record about how I made you my boy-toy for the night.'

Logic, Let Me Introduce You to This Window: The day after Finch's murder (see **48**, 'Bad Girls'), Buffy went to Faith's motel (in daylight and a clean outfit). 'Consequences' begins with Buffy waking up from a nightmare; then she goes to school. This means that it is at least the second day since the murder. But the detective questioning the witness at the scene of the crime says, 'You heard the man scream at about what time last night?' (Finch didn't scream.) Later, Buffy tells Faith, 'Less than twenty-four hours ago, you killed a man,' when it's closer to forty-eight hours. When Angel watches the police at the crime scene, you can see the blood on the dumpster where Finch was killed. The traces start at the top of the dumpster and smear down to the bottom. However, in **48**, 'Bad Girls', Faith didn't stab Finch until he had already slumped to the ground. Is Detective Stein the only officer in the police department making house calls on a regular basis? (Or, more to the point, is he part of the ongoing police conspiracy?) How does Wesley know where Angel is living? The calendar in Giles's office is for April 1997.

I Just *Love* Your Accent: The Watchers' Council is referred to by Wesley as 'The Watchers' Council of Britain'. Is it just me or did anyone else feel really sorry for Wesley when he's left alone in the library after Buffy's caustic put-down?

Quote/Unquote: Mr Trick's death line: 'Oh no, this is no good at all.'

Notes: 'We're warriors, we're built to kill.' An awful episode that attempts to look at what creates human weakness and depravity, but fudges it completely. Even the best bits of 'Consequences' feature heavy-handed moralising and bad characterisation that would be unacceptable from a series novice let alone one of its most accomplished writers.

Giles says this isn't the first time a Slayer has killed a human ('It's tragic, but accidents happen'). The Council, however, take a dim view of such events, suggesting that

Faith will be locked up for a long time (that would have been self-defeating if this was their approach to previous cases – locking up your only Slayer!). Wesley speaks to Quentin on the telephone (the password is 'monkey'). Angel's entrance into Faith's room isn't the first time we've seen this phenomenon (in **26**, 'Innocence', Angel was able to enter Uncle Enyos's hotel room without an invitation). Presumably hotels and motels are public domain (see **30**, 'Killed By Death'). There's a reference to the Scooby Gang's confrontation with Buffy over her keeping Angel's return a secret in **41**, 'Revelations'. Michael is mentioned; he and Willow are *still* trying to 'de-rat' Amy (see **45**, 'Gingerbread').

Soundtrack: 'Wish We Never Met' by Kathleen Wilhoite.

50

Doppelgängland

US Transmission Date: 23 Feb. 1999

Writer: Joss Whedon
Director: Joss Whedon
Cast: Michael Nagy (Alfonse),
Andy Umberger (D'Hoffryn), Megan Gray (Sandy),
Norma Michaels (Older Woman),
Corey Michael Blake (Waiter),
Jennifer Nicole (Body-Double Willow)

Desperate to end her time as a mortal, Anyanka begs a demon to create a temporal fold that would allow her to retrieve her amulet, but the demon refuses. So she seeks Willow's help. The spell is broken before the necklace is returned, but it does have one unexpected side effect: the calling into this dimension of the vampire Willow from the world created by Cordelia's wish. After various confusing meetings in which her friends believe that Willow has become a vampire, the truth is discovered and the two Willows meet. Evil-Willow persuades some vampires to work for her and restore chaos to

Sunnydale and Anya promises to help in the hope of getting her necklace back. But their plans are defeated by Willow, who pretends to be her evil self in a game of double bluff. However, she cannot bear to see her evil twin killed and arranges to send her back to her own dimension.

Dreaming (As Blondie Once Said) is Free: Evil-Willow wakes up in a pink cardigan: 'Oh no, this is like a *nightmare*.'

Dudes and Babes: There are numerous references to sex (even more than **43**, 'The Wish', 'Doppelgängland' is *full* of lesbian overtones). The Mayor tells Faith: 'No Slayer of mine is gonna live in a fleabag hotel. That place has a very unsavoury reputation. There are immoral liaisons going on there.' Faith notes, 'Yeah, plus all the screwin'.' When Evil-Willow finds Xander in the Bronze, they embrace, much to Xander's discomfort: 'This is verging on *naughty touching* here. Don't want to fall back on bad habits. Hands! Hands in new places!' When Evil-Willow is discovered, a conversation ensues on how she is *exactly* like Willow, except, as Buffy says, 'Your not being a dominatrix. As far as we know.' Willow replies, 'Oh, right. Me and Oz play Mistress of Pain every night.' Which leads Xander to ask, 'Did anyone else just go to a scary visual place?' Willow finds her other self: 'So evil and skanky. And I think I'm kind of gay.' Buffy tells her to remember that a vampire's personality 'has nothing to do with the person it was'. Angel says, 'Well, actually . . .' Then, thankfully, he shuts up.

Authority Sucks!: Snyder, as in **32**, 'Go Fish', manipulates Willow, in this case to help Percy with his history paper on Roosevelt: 'I just hate the way he bullies people. He just assumes everyone's time is his,' notes Willow as Giles emerges from another room and says, 'Willow, get on the computer. I want you to take another pass at accessing the Mayor's files.' And, meekly, she does!

A Little Learning is a Dangerous Thing: Xander gets Willow's new nickname 'Old Reliable' mixed up with the film *Old Yeller* and the geyser 'Old Faithful'.

It's a Designer Label!: Oz's yellow 'El Speedo' shirt is a sight for sore eyes. Or a cause of them. Willow's pink fluffy jumper puts in another appearance, as do Evil-Willow's leathers.

References: *Vanity Fair* magazine, *Bill and Ted's Excellent Adventure* ('No way', 'Yes way'), *Old Yeller, The Creature from the Black Lagoon,* PlayStation, *Arts & Entertainment Channel's Biography*, the psychiatry of Rorschach patterns, John Wayne.

Bitch!: Cordelia finds Evil-Willow in the book cage: 'It occurs to me that we've never really had the opportunity to talk. You know, woman to woman, with you locked up . . . What could we talk about? How about the ethics of boyfriend stealing?'

Awesome!: Willow finding Giles, Xander and Buffy in the library mourning her death and their reactions to, first seeing her and then to discovering that she's not a vampire (Xander seems to think there's something wrong with the cross he's holding!). And her reaction to their reaction. This is closely followed by the subsequent scene when Angel tries to give them the bad news about Willow and the facial expressions of Buffy, Giles and Xander at his double take. Xander's line 'We're right there with you, buddy' sums up the whole thing. In an episode full of such tiny gems, there's also that wonderful bit where Willow, pretending to be Evil-Willow, asks Anya and Alfonse, 'Could a human do this?' and then screams loudly. Not forgetting Xander's joy that in Evil-Willow's world he's a 'bad-ass vampire'; the special-effects sequence as Willow and Anya attempt to bring forth the amulet ('Have you tried looking behind the sofa – in Hell?'); Willow's discovery of her breasts ('Gosh, look at *those*!'); her control of a pencil (see **45**, 'Gingerbread'); and Percy's apple-for-teacher bit.

The Drugs Don't Work: Willow on Xander, Buffy and Giles acting strangely: 'Say, you all didn't happen to do a bunch of drugs, did you?'

Valley-Speak: Willow: 'Aren't you sort of naturally buff, Buff?'

Cigarettes and Alcohol: Anya, despite being 1,120 years old, still can't get a beer in the Bronze without ID and has to settle for a Coke instead.

Logic, Let Me Introduce You to This Window: When Evil-Willow throws Willow over the library counter, Willow lands on her right side when she rolls off the edge. In the following shot, Willow is on her left side. The entire episode is based on a *huge* logic flaw. Episode **43**, 'The Wish', created 'Dark Sunnydale' not as an alternative dimension but to *replace* normal Sunnydale. With the destruction of the amulet, things snap back into place and version two of reality never existed. Either one Sunnydale can exist, or the other, but not both. So, at the end of **43**, 'The Wish', Evil-Willow and all of the other 'Dark Sunnydale' characters never existed. Pure 'paradox theory'. Explain *that*, Einstein. How did Wesley get into the bathroom before Cordelia and Evil-Willow? He was running towards them in the hallway, but somehow got in there first and came from behind Cordelia.

I Just *Love* Your Accent: Faith sarcastically refers to Wesley as 'Princess Margaret'.

Quote/Unquote: Anya: 'For a thousand years I wielded the power of the Wish. I brought ruin to the hearts of unfaithful men. I brought forth destruction and chaos for the pleasure of the lower beings. I was feared and worshipped across the mortal globe. And now I'm stuck at Sunnydale High. Mortal. A child. And I'm flunking math.'

A bewildered Willow as Buffy and Xander, realising she's not a vampire, hug her: 'Oxygen becoming an issue.'

Oz: 'Professional bands can play up to six, sometimes seven, completely different chords.' Devon: 'That's just, like, fruity jazz bands.'

Evil-Willow: 'This is a dumb world. In my world, there are people in chains and we can ride them like ponies.'

Notes: 'Aren't you gonna introduce me to your . . . *Holy God,* you're Willow.' Odd, isn't it, that it's the 'funny' episodes that contain the best characterisation? 'Doppelgängland' is a superb example. It's about loss on several levels (Anya's lost her power, Evil-Willow's lost her world, Cordelia's lost her boyfriend) and also about how reality is sometimes less 'real' than fantasy. ('This world's no fun,' says Evil-Willow. 'You noticed that, too?' replies Willow.) This is a genuinely groundbreaking piece of work in any context – all the way to the suddenly explained 'oh f–' reprise from **43**, 'The Wish'.

Buffy has been undertaking sessions with the Watchers' Council psychiatrist after the events of **49**, 'Consequences'. Willow once wanted to be a florist. Evil-Willow remembers that Oz was a 'white hat' in her world. Dingoes Ate My Baby had a gig in Monterey on Sunday night. They don't have a roadie. Snyder refers to the 'swim team debacle of last year' (see **32**, 'Go Fish') and says that Willow has a letter of acceptance from 'every university with a stamp'. The Mayor tells Faith he is a family man. The movies playing at the Sunnydale cinema are an R-rated film, the last word of which is *Hotel*, and one that begins *The Goose Ran* . . .

Soundtrack: 'Virgin State of Mind' by k's Choice and 'Priced 2 Move' by Spectator Pump.

51
Enemies

US Transmission Date: 16 Mar. 1999

Writer: Douglas Petrie
Director: David Grossman
Cast: Michael Manasseri (Demon),
Gary Bullock (Shrouded Man)

Buffy and Faith encounter a demon who offers to sell them the Books of Ascension. Faith reports to the Mayor, who orders her to retrieve the books and kill the demon. Faith and the Mayor plan to banish Angel's soul and, with the aid of a mysterious Shrouded Man, succeed. Angelus and Faith plan to torture Buffy. At the Hall of Records, Oz locates a photograph of Mayor Wilkins taken a century ago. Xander reveals the return of Angelus. Buffy taunts Faith, but when an angry Faith blurts out more information about the coming events Angel tells her that his 'Angelus' role is an act. Faith escapes and is comforted by the Mayor, who reminds her that, once the Ascension takes place, her broken friendship with Buffy will be irrelevant.

Dudes and Babes: The movie that Buffy and Angel see is *Le Banquet D'Amelia*, which seems to be a sexy art-house affair ('I thought it'd be about food,' notes Buffy, and Angel remarks that there was some food involved). 'Check out the lust-bunny,' says Faith when she sees Angel and the episode sees the pair almost becoming entangled (it gets explicit when Faith is astride Angel and he says, 'I should have known you'd like it on top,' before asking her to 'wriggle'). There's also lots of bondage allusions.

The Conspiracy Starts at Home Time: The Ascension will happen on Graduation Day (see **56**, 'Graduation Day' Part 2). Faith notes that the Mayor 'built this town for demons to feed on'. Oz discovers that Mayor Wilkins is over one hundred years old and Wesley guesses that he isn't human. The implication is that, far from being a recent phenomenon, demonic activity has been rife in Sunnydale for decades, hence it *is* possible to rationalise people turning a blind eye to the town's mortality rate (see **37**, 'Faith, Hope and Trick', **45**, 'Gingerbread'). They've never known any different. (See, for instance, Oz's comments in **25**, 'Surprise', on vampires existing.)

A Little Learning is a Dangerous Thing: Cordelia is doing an English paper and wants Wesley's help . . . because he's English.

Mom's Apple Pie: Joyce seems to have reduced every aspect of Buffy's life into two categories: 'vampire problem', and 'nonvampire problem'. When Angel flirts with her, we find that she's recently had highlights added to her hair.

It's a Designer Label!: Some disastrous stuff like the demon's orange shirt and Willow's sheepskin coat (see **53**, 'Choices'). Buffy's blue dress and Faith's tarty leather jacket are better.

References: *Reader's Digest*, the Hanna-Barbera cartoon *Super Friends*, the final words of the murderer Gary Gilmore before his execution ('Let's do it'), another allusion to *Scooby Doo Where Are You?* and to Samuel Beckett's *Waiting for Godot*. The music is reminiscent of *The Omen*.

Awesome!: Angel punching Xander ('That guy just *bugs* me!'). Most of the best bits of the episode involve Giles, particularly the scene with the Shrouded Man where he informs everyone that the 'debt' settled was over the introduction of the Shrouded Man to his wife.

Surprise!: Faith: 'What can I say? I'm the world's best actor.' Angel: 'Second best!'

'You May Remember Me From Such Films As . . .': Gary Bullock was in *RoboCop 2* and *3* and also appeared in *Species* and *The Handmaid's Tale*.

Valley-Speak: Willow: 'Faith would *totally* do that.'
Buffy: 'So, "Ascension", possibly *not* a "love-in"?'
Faith: 'Sure. Fine. Whatever.'

Logic, Let Me Introduce You to This Window: When Cordelia enters the library to ask Wesley to dinner, the sound effect of her shoes on the floor doesn't match the action on screen. When Angel slides the Mayor's letter opener across the desk, you can see the reflection of his hand on the nameplate. After Faith runs from the mansion, we cut to a nighttime exterior shot of the high school. However, the following scene – in which Giles thanks the Shrouded Man – takes place during the day (sunlight is pouring through the windows). Exactly how much of Buffy, Angel and Giles's scheme was preplanned and how much was improvised? For instance, did Angel know about the Mayor's invincibility, or was he aiming to kill him?

I Just *Love* Your Accent: Buffy wears a Union Jack shirt.

Xander refers to Wesley as a 'limey bastard'. Giles uses the expression 'sod all'.

Cruelty to Animals: The Mayor knows that the saying 'there's more than one way to skin a cat' is a factually accurate statement.

Quote/Unquote: Giles: 'Demons after money? Whatever happened to "the still-beating heart of a virgin"? No one has any standards any more.'

Mayor Wilkins's two words that will make all of Faith's pain go away: 'Miniature golf!' (What is it with *Buffy* villains and miniature golf? See **23**, 'Ted'.)

Notes: 'You had to tie me up to beat me. There's a word for people like you, Faith. Loser.' The story of a Slayer going rogue should have been the crowning jewel in this often brilliant season. Sadly, 'Enemies' never begins to hit the mark – the ideas are good, but the script is tired and slow moving. With hindsight and some artistic licence it *is* possible to read aspects of the back-story into the narrative, but this is a long-winded 'one-joke' story that runs out of steam well before the climax.

It's been a while since Angel went to the movies. Buffy doesn't own a kimono. Xander says he 'applied some pressure' to Willy the Snitch (so he *did* survive **47**, 'The Zeppo') for information on where the demon lives. He subsequently reveals that he bribed Willy with $28. The Watchers' Council don't reimburse without a receipt. Faith's mother was a drunk who never loved her and wouldn't let her have a puppy (see **37**, 'Faith, Hope and Trick').

52

Earshot

Original Scheduled Transmission Date: 27 Apr. 1999[3]
US Transmission Date: 21 Sep. 1999

Writer: Jane Espenson
Director: Regis B Kimble

Cast: Keram Malicki-Sanchez (Freddy),
Justin Doran (Hogan), Lauren Roman (Nancy),
Wendy Worthington (Lunch Lady), Robert Arce (Mr Beach),
Molly Bryant (Ms Murray), Rick Miller (Student),
Jay Michael Ferguson (Another Student)

While battling a demon Buffy is infected by its blood, making her telepathic. At first it seems the only drawback for The Slayer is that she knows exactly what her friends are thinking. However, as the horror of being able to read *everyone's* thoughts threatens to overwhelm her, Buffy overhears someone in the cafeteria planning a killing spree. Angel, Giles and Wesley battle to find a cure, while the rest of the gang try to discover who would be alienated enough to commit such an atrocity. Buffy recovers in time to save Jonathan from a foolish act and stop the real would-be assassin.

The Caption: 'Mindful of the tragic events last week at Columbine High School, the originally scheduled episode of *Buffy the Vampire Slayer* will air at a later date.'

Dudes and Babes: Buffy says the boys of Sunnydale are seriously disturbed. The thoughts of the lad who wants to 'shove her against that locker right now . . .' suggest she's right.

A Little Learning is a Dangerous Thing: 'Maybe I'll take French. How hard can it be? French babies learn it!' *Othello* is used as a metaphor in the same way that *The Merchant of Venice* was in **11**, 'Out of Sight, Out of Mind'. Buffy uses her power to read both Nancy Doyle's and Ms Murray's minds in English class. (Ms Murray: 'Jealousy's merely the tool that Iago uses to undo Othello. But what is his motivation? What reason does Iago give for destroying his superior officer?' Buffy: 'He was passed over for promotion. Cassio was picked instead, and people were saying that Othello slept with his wife.') Xander thinks that four times five is thirty and six times five is thirty-two (see **1**, 'Welcome to the Hellmouth', **47**, 'The Zeppo').

Mom's Apple Pie: Joyce asks, 'How about some soup?

Chicken and stars?' while Buffy notices that her mother seems nervous about spending any time with a telepath.

Then . . . 'You had *sex* with *Giles*?' (See **40**, 'Band Candy'.)

Denial, Thy Names are Joyce and Rupert: Which leads to . . . 'It was the candy! We were teenagers!' Buffy: 'On the hood of a police car? *Twice!*' As she later informs Giles: 'We can work out after school. If you're not too busy having *sex with my mother*!'

It's a Designer Label!: Buffy tells Giles, 'When I walked in a few minutes ago, you thought, "Look at her shoes. If a fashion magazine told her to, she'd wear cats strapped to her feet".' Check out Willow's pussycat T-shirt and sun hat, Oz's 'Eater' shirt, Xander's tasteful yellow sweater and Buffy's white miniskirt. Buffy tells Giles she has a hard time finding jeans that fit her.

References: Principal Snyder has the Bangles' hit 'Walk Like an Egyptian' stuck in his head. Oz misquotes René Descartes, while there are references to *Othello* and Pierce Brosnan. The clock-tower finale shares conceptual and visual links with Hitchcock's *Vertigo*, the *X-Files* episode 'Blood' and the 1966 Charles Whitman murders. Mr Beach's history class are doing Henry VIII judging from the blackboard.

Bitch!: Giles: 'I was just filling Buffy in on my progress regarding the research of the Ascension.' Wesley: 'What took up the rest of the minute?'

Oz on the Sunnydale cheerleaders: 'Their spelling's improved.'

Awesome!: The opening as Buffy battles two demons. Angel's fight with one of them later is equally impressive. *All* of the Scooby Gang's 'thought' sequences are wonderful and Oz's are extremely Zen. (Xander's are the funniest, naturally, though Cordelia's are a bit disturbing – can she *really* be that shallow?) Best bit of a clever climax (full of red herrings) is Nancy's unimpressed reaction to Buffy's astounding gymnastic feat ('*I* could have done that'). *Love* the box of rat poison with RAT POISON! written on it.

'You May Remember Me From Such Films And TV series As . . .': Lauren Roman was Laura English in *All My Children*. Keram Malicki-Sanchez appeared in *American History X*.

Valley-Speak: Buffy: 'Scabby demon number two got away. Scabby demon number one, *big check* in the slay column.'

Geeky student: 'Wait till I'm a software *jillionaire* and you're all flipping burgers. Who's the loser then?'

Buffy: 'Mass murder. Not really doctor-recommended for that type of pain. Besides, prison, you know, it's a lot like high school. But instead of *noogies . . .*'

Not Exactly A Haven For The Bruthas: Nancy says race is an issue. In *Othello*.

Logic, Let Me Introduce You to This Window: If the demons are telepathic, how come they don't anticipate Buffy's attack? What's all that rubbish Angel spouts about vampires' thoughts being unreadable for the same reason that their reflections can't be seen? Abject nonsense! Isn't a high-velocity rifle a bit of an ostentatious suicide weapon? Couldn't Jonathan find a handgun?

I Just *Love* Your Accent: A jealous Xander refers to Wesley's 'Pierce Brosney-eyes' being all over Cordelia. When we hear what Wesley actually *thinks* about Cordelia, we're forced to agree ('I'm a *bad, bad* man!'). Giles calls Wesley a 'berk'.

Cruelty to Animals: Buffy: 'I thought I saw a four-legged demon, but it was just a dog.'

Quote/Unquote: Willow: 'According to Freddy's latest editorial, "The pep rally is a place for pseudo-prostitutes to provoke men into a sexual frenzy which, when thwarted, results in pointless athletic competition." ' Xander: 'And the downside being?'

Buffy: 'I'm suddenly gonna grow this demon part . . . It could be claws, or scales . . .' Willow: 'Was it a *boy* demon?'

Angel: 'No matter what, I'll always be with you. I'll love you even if you're covered in slime.' Buffy: 'I liked everything until that part.'

Buffy: 'God, Xander! Is that *all* you think about?'

Cordelia tries to discover if Mr Beech is the would-be murderer: 'I was just wondering, were you planning on killing a bunch of people tomorrow?'

Jonathan: 'Stop saying my name like we're friends . . . You all think I'm an idiot. A *short* idiot!'

Notes: 'Man, you read my mind.' A glorious meditation on isolation, regret and the belief that knowledge is power. That such an epic, lyrical episode fell victim to its own prophecy merely adds to its greatness. In twenty years' time there'll be *legends* about 'Earshot'. Quality, in every department, from start to finish. *Love* the music too.

Willow is still tutoring Percy (see **50**, 'Doppelgängland'). Giles says that Angel's charade in **51** 'Enemies' was important in bringing Faith's treachery into the open. When Oz reads the school newspaper he goes straight to the obituaries (in any other school I'd think he was joking). Angel says he's been with dozens of bad girls like Faith but that in 243 years he's loved one person. Larry is much happier since Xander helped 'out' him in **27**, 'Phases'. These days even his grandma is fixing him dates with guys. The demon Azareth is mentioned as having been ritually flayed. The headlines of various issues of *Sunnydale High Sentinel* are: TEACHERS FAIL COMPETENCY EXAM; DROPOUTS FIND HAPPINESS; APATHY ON THE RISE, NO ONE CARES and BIG GAME DRAWS MINDLESS BRAIN DEAD MOB. Freddy also writes, 'Dingoes Ate My Baby play their instruments as if they have plump Polish sausages taped to their fingers.' Oz agrees this is fair! The Sunnydale basketball team is in the divisional championships.

Despite the best intentions of all concerned, WB still managed to put their foot in it when replacing the postponed episode with, of all things, **48**, 'Bad Girls'. As the TV critic in the *St Paul Pioneer Press* noted, 'Tonight's regularly scheduled new episode . . . has been pulled by the WB Network in the wake of the Littleton High-School shootings. The episode centred on Buffy's clairvoyant ability in which she read the thoughts of someone who was contemplating killing other students . . . Instead, WB airs a repeat, "Bad Girls", in which Buffy craves a taste of the wild side and follows the character Faith into her reckless world. *The repeat seems about as bad as the scrapped one*' (my italics). The first broadcast of 'Earshot' occurred in some regions of Australia a week before the US finally got to see the episode.

Reality Bites: The reaction of some online *Buffy* fans to the postponement of 'Earshot', in light of the terrible events that took place in Colorado, says much about TV fans' occasional lack of priorities. WB's decision to delay broadcast was supported by Joss Whedon, who said, 'We're taking it out of the order. It's about how lonely everybody is . . . and how somebody just snaps.' (Whedon also noted, 'Oddly enough, when we were shooting it I thought it felt like the final High School episode. The last three are very personal, but "Earshot" sort of contains the show's *thesis statement* in a way, though I wish it could have aired in order.') Seth Green added, '[It was] the right decision to postpone . . . It would have seemed really callous and inappropriate. But the actual episode has nothing to do with school violence. It's a red herring in the story.' WB's main concern was one exchange: Xander: 'I'm still having problems with the fact that one of us is just gonna gun everyone down for no reason.' Cordelia: 'Yeah, because that *never* happens at American high schools?' Oz: 'It's bordering on trendy'. There's also Xander's: 'Who hasn't just idly thought about taking out the whole place with a semiautomatic?' A study of the *Buffy* newsgroups following the decision showed some posters allowing their disappointment to cloud both judgement and taste. The sad fact is that fifteen unfortunate people in Colorado were unable to watch 'Earshot' when it was eventually transmitted, whether they were fans or not. At the end of the day, it's still *just* a TV series.

53

Choices

US Transmission Date: 4 May 1999

Writer: David Fury
Director: James A Contner

Cast: Keith Brunsmann (Vamp Lackey),
Jimmie F. Skaggs (Courier),
Michael Schoenfield (Security Guard #1),
Seth Coltan (Security Guard #2),
Jason Reed (Vamp Guard), Brett Moses (Student)

The final preparations for the Mayor's Ascension are under way but the last piece of the jigsaw, the Box of Gavrok, comes to the attention of Buffy and her friends. An attempt to capture the Box from the Mayor's office succeeds, but Willow is taken hostage by Faith and a swap is arranged in the school cafeteria at night. Snyder unwittingly interferes and the Box is briefly opened, revealing its deadly contents. Meanwhile, Buffy and Willow have some hard choices to make about where they will go to college, and Cordelia faces an uncertain future.

Authority Sucks!: Wesley gives a little Masonic-type crossed-fingers sign when he starts his 'by the power invested in me by the Council' bit. But nobody takes any notice of him.

The Conspiracy Starts at Home Time: The Mayor receives the Box of Gavrok from Central America. It contains 'fifty billion' of the spider-crab creatures. He finally meets Buffy (although they were in the same room in **45**, 'Gingerbread', and almost met in the sewers in **40**, 'Band Candy').

A Little Learning is a Dangerous Thing: Buffy has received acceptances from Northwestern University in Illinois and UC Sunnydale. Willow, inevitably, has the pick of 'every school in the country' (Harvard, Yale and MIT are mentioned) and 'four or five in Europe' (including Oxford). Cordelia's include USC, Colorado State and Columbia.

Mom's Apple Pie: Joyce's pride in Buffy's university acceptances is touching.

Denial, Thy Name is Joyce: Willow: 'Sounds like your mom's in a state of denial.' Buffy: 'More like a continent.'

Denial, Thy Name is Willow: When Buffy says her mother has to realise that she can't leave Sunnydale, Willow says,

'Maybe not now, but soon ... Or maybe I too hail from Denial Land.'

It's a Designer Label!: *What* is Willow wearing? (The pink dress thing with nonmatching sheepskin jacket and Doctor Martens.) Also on display, Xander's 'Bean Sprout' T-shirt and Giles's kipper tie. Buffy's green dress and Faith's *incredibly* revealing top are worthy of a second glance, however.

References: Buffy's line about Faith turning to 'the dark side of the Force' is a reference to Darth Vader in the *Star Wars* trilogy. There are nods to the 'Duck and Cover' campaign (see **35**, 'Anne'), *Batman* ('Think about the future', see **24**, 'Bad Eggs') and Nancy Drew. Xander is reading Jack Kerouac's *On the Road* preparing for his sojourn as a backpacking bohemian. Willow refers to Friedrich W Moller's song 'The Happy Wanderer'.

Bitch!: Xander: 'I think it'll be good for me, help me to find myself.' Cordelia: 'And help us to lose you. Everyone's a winner.' Xander: 'Look who just popped open a fresh can of venom!' Plus Cordy's memorable put-down of all the schools Willow has been accepted for: 'Oxford? Whoopee. Four years in teabag central, sounds thrilling. MIT is a Clearasil ad with housing and Yale is a dumping ground for those who didn't get into Harvard.' When Buffy tries to intervene with 'You guys, don't forget to breathe between insults,' Cordy's comeback is, 'I'm sorry Buffy, this conversation is reserved for those who actually *have* a future.' 'She was just being Cordelia, only more so,' notes a conciliatory Willow. Later, Cordelia and Xander have another go. Xander: 'Ten minutes with you and the admissions department decided that they'd already reached their mean-spirited, superficial-princess quota.' Cordelia: 'And once again the gold medal in the Being Wrong event goes to Xander "I'm as stupid as I look" Harris.'

Awesome!: Willow leaving Oz and Xander a diagram on how to mix the ingredients for her spell: Oz: 'There's you, there's me.' Xander: 'How can you tell which is which? They both kind of look stick-figurey.' Oz: 'This one's me. See the little guitar?' Oz's violent outburst, Angel and Buffy taking on two vampires in the Mayor's office and Snyder with the chair clamped to his chest. The Mayor telling Angel and Buffy their relationship is doomed is a defining moment in the series. Given that so much of the show is about denial (from Buffy's continual denial of who she is to the populace's denial of their surroundings) it's interesting that it needs the series' most heinous villain to make the point . . .

Denial, Thy Names are Buffy and Angel: . . . But, of course, they don't take any notice. It'll all end in tears. (See **54**, 'The Prom'.)

Surprise!: The revelation that Cordelia is *working* in that dress shop (see **54**, 'The Prom').

The Drugs Don't Work: Snyder: 'OK, what's in the bag?' Student: 'My lunch.' Snyder: 'Is that the new drug lingo?' Snyder's new quest seems to be a single-handed campaign to stamp out drugs even where they don't exist. As he asks the Scooby Gang, 'Why couldn't you be dealing drugs like *normal* people?'

Valley-Speak: Buffy: 'I gotta have a plan? Really? I can't just be proactive with pep?'

Logic, Let Me Introduce You to This Window: Did David Boreanaz dye his hair? It looks a lot darker than usual. When Cordelia shows Xander her acceptance letters, she hands him three envelopes and says, 'USC, Colorado State, Duke.' She then produces two more, one with a USC logo, and says, '. . . and Columbia.' After the Gavrok spider-crab thing is killed by Buffy, Angel helps her up, but where has the dead creature gone?

I Just *Love* Your Accent: Buffy: 'I can't believe you got into Oxford.' Oz: 'There's some deep academia there.' Buffy: 'That's where they make Gileses!' Willow: 'I could learn and have scones.' If *Inspector Morse* is to be believed, Oxford's got a mortality rate higher than Sunnydale.

Quote/Unquote: Mayor Wilkins on his present to Faith: 'You be careful not to put somebody's eye out with that thing. Till I tell you to.'

Buffy, when Wesley reminds her that she is The Slayer: 'I'm also a person. You can't just define me by my Slayer-ness. That's . . . "something-ism".'

Faith on the courier: 'I made him an offer he couldn't survive.'

Willow to vampire: 'Hey! Did you get permission to eat the hostage?'

Mayor Wilkins: 'This is exciting, isn't it? Clandestine meetings by dark of night, exchange of prisoners . . . I feel like we should all be wearing trenchcoats.'

Notes: 'Now we're supposed to decide what to do with our lives.' A fine way to snuggle into the Ascension story-arc. 'Choices' isn't the greatest of episodes (there's not much plot, for a start), but it has much energy and humour.

Buffy's Aunt Arlene lives in Illinois. She and Angel recently found a fire demon's nest in a cave by the beach (which Angel considered 'a nice change of pace'). There's a reference to 'Mr Pointy' (see **33**, 'Becoming' Part 1). It's established that Buffy will 'live in' at college next season. The Mayor had an Irish setter called Rusty. He married his wife, Edna Mae, in 1903 and was with her until she died, wrinkled and senile and cursing him for his youth, which indicates she, at least, was human.

54

The Prom

US Transmission Date: 11 May 1999

Writer: Marti Noxon
Director: David Solomon
Cast: Brad Kane (Tucker Wells),
Andrea E Taylor (Sales Girl), Mike Kimmel (Butcher),
Tove Kingsbury (Tux Boy),
Michael Zlabinger (AS Student at Microphone),
Monica Serene Garnich (Pretty Girl), Joe Howard (Priest),
Damien Eckhardt (Jack Mayhew),
Stephanie Denise Griffin (Tux Girl)

The Senior Prom is coming and Xander has an interesting date. Anya. By chance he discovers Cordelia's part-time job and is shocked to learn that her family have lost all of their money. But they are interrupted by an attack from a creature Giles describes as a 'hell hound'. A bitter classman, Tucker, has captured and trained the creatures to attack anyone wearing a tuxedo, after his failure to get a date to the prom. Buffy, angry after a breakup with Angel, averts the attack by the creatures and arrives in time to receive a surprise award from her classmates. And to enjoy a dance with her former lover.

Dreaming (As Blondie Once Said) is Free: The king of *all* dream sequences: Angel dreams that he and Buffy marry in church, walk down the aisle and out on to a beautiful sunny day at which point she, rather than Angel, bursts into flames. A photo of the pair in their wedding attire appeared in *TV Guide*, leading to all sorts of weird fan rumours.

Dudes and Babes: Anya says she has witnessed a millennium of treachery and oppression by the male species and she has nothing but contempt for the gender. But she'd like Xander to go to the prom with her. (Anya: 'I have all these feelings ... I know you find me attractive. I've seen you looking at my breasts.' Xander: 'Nothing personal, but when a guy does that it just means his eyes are open.') Buffy writes, 'Buffy and Angel 4ever' on one of her school books.

Mom's Apple Pie: Joyce finally has a heart-to-heart with Angel (probably half a season too late), which, along with much of the rest of this episode, sets up the parameters for *Angel*. As with Mayor Wilkins in the previous episode and Spike in **42**, 'Lover's Walk', Joyce tells Angel that there *can* be no future for him and Buffy as a couple. The crucial difference, of course, is that she's putting the onus on Angel, saying that if he *really* loves Buffy he must make the hardest choice of all.

It's a Designer Label!: Check out Willow's pussycat T-shirt. All the cast look gorgeous in their prom outfits (especially Buffy's Pamela Dennis dress). When everyone gets obsessed with what they'll be going to the prom in, Giles says, 'I shall be wearing pink taffeta, as chenille will not go with my complexion. Now can we *please* talk about the Ascension!'

References: Buffy's 'Giles, we get it: miles to go before we sleep' is a reference to Robert Frost's poem 'Stopping By Woods on a Snowy Evening'. There are allusions to *Carrie*, *Psycho*, Prince's '1999' ('tonight I'm going to party like it's . . .') and Sister Sledge's 'We Are Family'. The videos that Tucker has forced the hell hounds to watch are *Prom Night* (1 and 4!), *Pump Up the Volume*, *Pretty in Pink*, *The Club* and *Carrie* (most of which concern disastrous events on prom nights). Many mythologies have 'hell hounds', the most famous being the three-headed dog Cerberus in Greek myth, who stood guard over the entrance of the Underworld. The creatures in this episode, however, seem more like werewolves, doglike demon foot-soldiers left over from 'the Makhesh War'.

Awesome!: Xander's disgust when someone else wins the 'Class Clown' award. Oz's reaction to Xander's prom partner ('Interesting choice'). Plus Buffy doing her job on the hell hounds while everybody else has fun.

Don't Give Up The Day Job: In addition to playing Larry in *Starship Troopers*, Brad Kane was the singing voice for Aladdin in Disney's *Aladdin*.

Valley-Speak: Buffy and Angel share a 'post-Slayerage nap thing'.

Buffy on the prom: 'End-of-school, rite-of-passage thingy.'

Cigarettes and Alcohol: Buffy describes the prom to Angel as a 'cotillion with spiked punch and Electric Slide'. (A cotillion is a formal ball, usually given for debutantes to be introduced to society, although it originated as an eighteenth-century formation dance in France. The Electric Slide is a line dance, often performed at weddings.)

Logic, Let Me Introduce You to This Window: The positioning of Angel's bed – facing a huge panoramic window – is majorly stupid. True, the window is covered by a thick drape, but all it needs is for Buffy or Angel himself to get a bit careless with opening the curtain at the wrong time (as here), or to come in a bit drunk the night before and forget to close it (we've all done that), and it's a question of how they'll get the ash stains from the bedsheets. Similarly, when Joyce calls at Angel's during the day why does he answer the door in clear sunlight? It could have been anybody asking him to step outside. In **52**, 'Earshot', the entrance to Angel's place was covered by a black drape (as the windows are), so when did he have the doors installed? When the hell hound bursts through the store window, the boy it attacks remains calmly adjusting his tuxedo. When Buffy takes her prom dress out of her bag she leaves the bag (full of lethal weapons) outside the school. We never saw Buffy put a knife in her jacket, yet she stabs one of the hell hounds with one. Does she carry it around all the time? (It looks like the knife she got at the library, but she put that one in her bag, not her jacket.) 'Blueberry scones', though very common in the California, are rare (and virtually unknown) in England. Derby or fruit scones are a more likely object of a conversation between Giles and Wesley. Where did Angel get his tuxedo from? Is there an all-night tux-hiring shop in Sunnydale?

I Just *Love* Your Accent: Aside from half the songs being by British artists (Fatboy Slim, the Sundays), there's Giles's rant at Wesley (see **Quote/Unquote**). Cordy thinks that Wesley will look 'way-007 in a tux'.

Cruelty to Animals: Buffy says she killed her goldfish (presumably accidentally) when Angel talks about her possibly wanting to have children one day.

Quote/Unquote: Anya (asking Xander to the prom): 'You're not quite as obnoxious as most of the alpha males around here.'

Giles (on Buffy's breakup with Angel): 'I understand this sort of thing requires ice cream of some kind.'

Wesley asks Giles's opinion on whether he should ask Cordelia to dance: 'For God's sake, man, she's eighteen. And you have the emotional maturity of a blueberry scone. Just have at it, would you? And stop fluttering about!'

Notes: 'Once again, the Hellmouth puts the special into special occasion.' Simply beautiful, a story about hidden feelings in which Buffy loses Angel but learns how appreciated she is, even if it's sometimes unspoken. Cordelia discovers how much Xander cares for her and where love ultimately triumphs. Interestingly, two weeks before this episode, **52**, 'Earshot', (which concerned a student apparently planning a spree-killing) was withdrawn and yet this episode (which *does* concern a student planning a spree-killing) escaped completely unchallenged. Maybe it was the modus operandi (hell hounds are acceptable, guns aren't).

There are references to the 'weird stuff' that goes on around Sunnydale including 'zombies' (see **36**, 'Dead Man's Party'), 'hyena people' (see **6**, 'The Pack') and 'Snyder' (student humour, seemingly). Jonathan says that the Class of '99 has the lowest mortality rate of any class in Sunnydale High's history, which fits in with supernatural nastiness having gone on for decades rather than starting when Buffy arrived (see **51**, 'Enemies'). Given the events of **52**, 'Earshot', Jonathan's personal endorsement of Buffy's award is sweet and touching. Buffy is given the title of 'Class Protector'. The clothing store where Cordelia works is called April Fools (see **53**, 'Choices'). Her family have lost all of their money after her father made 'a little mistake on his taxes – for the last twelve years'. (One fan theory is that Cordelia's medical bills from her injury in **42**, 'Lover's Walk', didn't help and this may explain her continued blaming of all of her problems on Buffy – see **43**, 'The Wish'.) Xander pays for Cordy's prom dress with money from his 'road-trip fund' (see **53**, 'Choices'), a selfless act that makes me want to grow up to be Xander Harris. Giles states that there are thousands of species of demons (see **55**, 'Graduation Day' Part 1). Angel has no mirrors at home (which stands to reason, despite Buffy's surprise). He gets his blood from a local meat factory (see **21**, 'What's My Line?' Part 1). He doesn't drink coffee because it makes him jittery. Anya still hasn't got her powers back (see **43**, 'The Wish', **50**, 'Doppelgängland'). Wesley went to an all-male preparatory.

An unconfirmed rumour is that the winner of the '1-800-

Collect' competition (see **42**, 'Lover's Walk'), Jessica Johnson of Maryland, appears in this episode. The prize was a three-day trip for two 'to participate in the taping of an upcoming episode' and $2,000 cash.

Soundtrack: One of the best: 'Praise You' by Fatboy Slim, 'The Good Life' by Cracker, 'El Rey' by the Lassie Foundation and the Sundays' beautiful version of 'Wild Horses'. A ten-second snatch of Kool & The Gang's 'Celebration' brings a less than enthusiastic response from Buffy ('that song *sucks*!').

Did You Know?: A highlight of *The 1999 MTV Movie Awards* was the appearance of Alyson Hannigan in a series of spoofs used to introduce the various categories. Among the films parodied were *I Know What You Did Last Summer, The Breakfast Club, Varsity Blues, She's All That, Say Anything* and (brilliantly) *Cruel Intentions*. The show, hosted by Lisa Kudrow, also saw Seth Green reprise his role as Scott Evil in an *Austin Powers* sketch. Around this time Seth also appeared on the *Conan O'Brien* chatshow and revealed that, although he is seldom pestered by fans, he *is* continually asked by shady characters if he would like some of their drugs! A couple of weeks later Sarah Michelle Gellar hosted the season finale of *Saturday Night Live*, going (almost) topless for a 'Holding Your Own Boobs' sketch.

55
Graduation Day Part 1
US Transmission Date: 18 May 1999

Writer: Joss Whedon
Director: Joss Whedon
Cast: Hal Robinson (Professor Lester Worth),
John Rosenfeld (Vamp Lackey #2),
Adrian Neil (Vamp Lackey #1)

With the Mayor's transformation at hand, the Scooby Gang prepare for what they believe may be their last day on Earth.

Angel walks into a trap and is shot with a poisoned arrow by Faith. Buffy is told that only the blood of a Slayer will be enough to save his life. Buffy goes to Faith's apartment and The Slayers fight to the death on the rooftop. Buffy stabs Faith with Faith's own knife, but, as a final desperate act, Faith topples on to a passing truck.

The Conspiracy Starts at Home Time: The Mayor tells Snyder that his help in maintaining order at Sunnydale High will be rewarded. He's dead meat, right?

A Little Learning is a Dangerous Thing: Mr Miller's class are playing 'Hangman' instead of studying (a last-day-of-school tradition the world over).

Mom's Apple Pie: 'Looking back,' notes Joyce, 'maybe I should have sent you to a different school.' There's a great scene as Buffy tells Joyce she wants her to leave town until after the graduation as she won't be able to concentrate on fighting the demon if she's also worrying about Joyce.

It's a Designer Label!: Cordelia: 'I can't believe this loser look. I lobbied so hard for the teal. No one ever listens to me. Lone fashionable wolf.' Xander: 'I like the maroon. It has more dignity.' There are a whole bunch of cool clothes: Faith's pink dress, Buffy's red leather pants, Wesley's mauve shirt and the reappearance of Buffy's blue frock coat.

References: 'Big Sister's Clothes' is an Elvis Costello song (see **42**, 'Lover's Walk'). Willow asks if the commencement speaker will be 'Siegfried? Roy? One of the tigers?' referring to 'The Masters of the Impossible'. 'This is mutiny' is from *Mutiny on the Bounty*. Xander quotes from *Jaws* ('We're gonna need a bigger boat'). The motto on the school year-book is 'The Future is Ours', a possible reference to the Stone Roses song 'She Bangs A Drum'.

Bitch!: Cordelia to Xander: 'Dignity? You? In relation to clothes? I'm awash in a sea of confusion.' Willow says she'll miss Harmony. Buffy: 'Don't you hate her?' Willow: 'Yes, with a fiery vengeance. She picked on me for ten years. Vacuous tramp!'

Awesome!: *Love* Willow's chopper bike. Giles and Wesley's fencing is hilarious, while Oz and Willow's final surrendering to intimacy was well worth waiting for. Buffy and Faith's five-minute fight in Faith's apartment is a Hong Kong action movie in miniature.

Valley-Speak: Faith: 'I feel *wicked* stupid in this.'

Xander, to Anya: 'That humanity thing's still a "work in progress", isn't it?'

Angel: 'Are you mad at me for being around too much, or for not being around enough?' Buffy: '*Duh*, yes!'

Logic, Let Me Introduce You to This Window: Anya mentions her car. Where did she get the money? Indeed, where does she live? As Angel and Buffy argue in the street, he's holding a cardboard box with two hands. The camera moves to Buffy, but you can still see Angel at the edge of the shot and he doesn't move. When it cuts back to him, he has the box in only one hand. When Buffy tends to Angel's wound in the library, the shots from the front show sweat on his face, but from the side it looks dry. Buffy says that the Mayor will have a hundred helpless kids to feed on at graduation. That's a pretty small graduating class for a city with a population of 38,500 (see **15**, 'School Hard', **42**, 'Lover's Walk') and a university. (There are other high schools in Sunnydale – see **14**, 'Some Assembly Required', and **17**, 'Reptile Boy' – and this *is* a place where teenage mortality is on the high side.) When Angel is shot with Faith's arrow Giles notes that he is bleeding. If Angel is a walking corpse (in **54**, 'The Prom', Buffy confirms that his heart doesn't beat; see also **12**, 'Prophecy Girl', **26**, 'Innocence') this is impossible.

I Just *Love* Your Accent: Xander refers to Wesley as 'Monarchy Boy'. Wow, *top* insult. When Wesley says Buffy can't turn her back on the Council she replies, 'They're in England. I don't think they can tell which way my back is facing.'

Cruelty to Animals: The Mayor eats some of the Gavrok spider-crab things.

Quote/Unquote: Xander on Anya's perception of men: 'Yes men like sports. Men watch the action movie. They eat of the beef and enjoy to look at the bosoms. A thousand years of avenging our wrongs and that's all you've learned?'

Buffy: 'The whole senior class has turned into the 60s. Or what I would've imagined the 60s would've been like, you know, without the war and the hairy armpits.'

Anya: 'I've seen some horrible things in my time. I've been the cause of most of them actually.'

Mayor Wilkins after Giles stabs him: '*That* was a little thoughtless. Violent outbursts like that in front of the children. You know, Mr Giles, they look to you to see how to behave.'

Anya: 'When I think that something could happen to you, it feels bad inside, like I might vomit.' Xander: 'Welcome to the world of romance.'

Mayor Wilkins to vampire: 'We don't knock during dark rituals?'

Notes: 'That's one spunky little girl you've raised. I'm gonna eat her.' A fine example of how to move pieces into position without losing narrative cohesion. There *are* contrived elements (why turn Buffy into a murderer so pointlessly?) but, as a series of mini-climaxes, the episode works. The characterisation of the Mayor is interesting. Trouble is he's so *sympathetic* – it's a bold thing for the series to have its most dangerous character *not* going around eye-gouging subordinates or doing over-the-top baddy things that undermine credibility. Wilkins is someone who one feels *would* kill without a second thought if he felt it necessary, rather than spend time boasting like a hackneyed Bond villain. He gets two glorious scenes with the Scooby Gang in **53**, 'Choices', and this episode, which give the impression of a slightly eccentric but basically decent family man who just has a hobby of wanting to rule the world. Well, it's more sane than stamp collecting, isn't it? (Albeit, more time-consuming . . .)

Willow says she'll miss PE, though this seems to be a touch of temporary insanity. Her scene with the 'trusty soda machine', which gives her Coke instead of root beer, could be a reference to the mistake with the Dr Pepper can in **18**, 'Halloween'. Percy thanks Willow for helping him with his history and for not kicking his ass like she did in the Bronze (see **50**, 'Doppelgängland'). The implication of the Willow/Oz bed scene could be that both were previously virgins, though Oz's postcoital 'Everything feels different' may simply mean that Willow is the best he's ever had. He's certainly mentioned having groupies before and claimed in **44**, 'Amends', to have previously 'done it'. When Oz and Willow get intimate they do so without covering Amy's cage (*this* could be considered 'cruelty to animals'?), which is an incentive to keep Amy rat-like if *ever* there was one. Faith's childhood in Boston is mentioned (see **37**, 'Faith, Hope and Trick', **47**, 'The Zeppo'). About 800 years ago in the Urals, a sorcerer achieved Ascension becoming the embodiment of the demon Lohesh (a four-winged soul killer). Anya witnessed this while cursing a local shepherd. All of the demons that walk the Earth are tainted, human hybrids like vampires. Those demons not of this realm are different. They're certainly *bigger*.

Soundtrack: Spectator Pump's 'Sunday Mail'.

Did You Know . . .?: The first – four-second – trailer for *Angel* appeared during the initial US broadcast of this episode. Against a red background, David Boreanaz turns towards camera with the words '*Angel. This Fall*' superimposed.

56
Graduation Day Part 2

Original Scheduled US Transmission Date: 25 May 1999
Canadian Transmission Date: 23 May 1999
US Transmission Date: 13 July 1999

Writer: Joss Whedon
Director: Joss Whedon
Cast: Paolo Andres (Dr Powell), Susan Chuang (Nurse), Tom Bellin (Dr Gold), Samuel Bliss Cooper (Vamp Lackey)

Buffy saves Angel's life by offering herself for him to feed on, although he is still determined to leave her. Surviving (with the subconscious help of the comatose Faith), Buffy, the Scooby Gang and the students of Sunnydale High surreptitiously arm themselves against the Mayor's coming Ascension. The Mayor begins to transform during his speech and kills Principal Snyder. The students attack using what weapons they have at their disposal and, ultimately, Buffy destroys the demon, though at the cost of many lives. As she and her friends prepare for college, Angel leaves Sunnydale and Buffy behind.

The Caption (Slight Return): 'Mindful of recent tragic events affecting America's schools, the conclusion to *Buffy the Vampire Slayer*: Graduation Day, originally scheduled for tonight's broadcast will air at a later date.'

Dreaming (As Blondie Once Said) is Free: The shared coma/dream/whatever-it-is between Buffy and Faith takes on the dream in **54**, 'The Prom', for weirdness and beats it hollow. (Sample dialogue: Buffy: 'A higher power guiding us?' Faith: 'I'm pretty sure that's not what I meant.') The sequence's climax is among Whedon's most beautifully realised scenes: Faith places her hand on Buffy's cheek; in a flash of light Buffy wakes up in her hospital bed. She slowly gets up and walks across the room to Faith, still in a coma, and kisses her. Stunning.

Question: was this a psychic transference of Slayer powers from one Slayer to the next (or, in this case, previous)? Some of the dialogue suggests as much, with Buffy saying, 'How are you going to fit all this stuff?' and Faith replying, 'Not gonna, it's yours.'

Dudes and Babes: One final moment of greatness for Cordelia. In many ways she was at the core of why *Buffy* is so special. In *any* other series Cordy would have been a two-dimensional cardboard cipher. A hollow archetypal bad girl, laughed at and given her comeuppance once per episode. That's probably how the character was devised, but, in the hands of a gifted actress and sympathetic writers, she blossomed. Of course, it was getting difficult to convince *anybody* that Charisma Carpenter is eighteen. An interesting fan idea is that over the summer Cordelia will be sent to Hell and return somewhat older. The sexuality in Angel's drinking Buffy's blood is the clearest link in *Buffy* between vampirism and sexual awakening. Joss Whedon has suggested that he was unsure if he'd get away with this scene but that, in the furore over the students attacking the Mayor, WB missed it completely.

Authority Spanks!: Mayor Wilkins to his vampire minions: 'No snacking. I see blood on your lips, it's a visit to the woodshed for you boys!'

Authority Sucks!: Snyder, begrudgingly: 'Congratulations to the class of 1999. You all proved more or less adequate. This is a time of celebration so sit still and be quiet. Spit out that gum!' When the Mayor ascends: 'This is simply unacceptable . . . This is not disciplined. You're on my campus, buddy, and when I say I want quiet . . .' Followed, inevitably, by death.

A Little Learning is a Dangerous Thing: Giles saves Buffy's diploma from the flames. As Oz notes they survived not just the battle but also high school, leading Buffy to ask if someone will 'wake me up when it's time to go to college'.

It's a Designer Label: Difficult to work out which is worse, Buffy's leather pants or Jonathan's red anorak.

References: The Mayor's line concerning Angel eating spinach refers to Popeye the Sailor. There's a dialogue allusion to Little Miss Muffett and another reference to Frost's 'Stopping By Woods On a Snowy Evening' (see **54**, 'The Prom').

Bitch!: Cordelia to Xander: 'So very funny. Any minute now I'm sure to laugh.'

   Xander: 'I need to talk to you . . .' Harmony: 'You mean in front of other people?'

Awesome!: Angel feeding on Buffy. The scene where Wilkins ascends into a sixty-foot serpent-like demon. The following battle sequences are breathtaking. My favourite bit of the episode is Xander's sarcastic line about how much he'll miss Angel.

The Drugs Don't Work: When Angel takes Buffy to hospital, Dr Powell asks, 'You two been doing drugs?' Angel: 'She's clean.'

'You May Remember Me From Such TV Series As . . .': Tom Bellin's impressive CV includes appearances on *The Monkees, Alias Smith and Jones, The Streets of San Francisco, The Rockford Files, The Bionic Woman, Charlie's Angels, Matlock* and *Beverly Hills 90210*.

Valley-Speak: Cordelia: 'My point, however, is, crazy or not, it's pretty much the only plan. Besides, it's Buffy's. Slay gal, you know, little Miss Likes-to-fight?' Xander: 'I think there was a "yea" vote buried in there somewhere.'

Xander: 'Angel, in his "Non-Key-Guy" capacity, can work with me.' Angel: 'What fun.' Xander: 'Hey, "Key Guy" still talking!'

Willow: 'Man, just *ascend* already.'

Surrealism Rules – Fish: Cordelia: 'I personally don't think it's possible to come up with a crazier plan.' Oz: 'We could attack the Mayor with humus.' Cordelia: 'I stand corrected.'

Logic, Let Me Introduce You to This Window: Sunnydale is said to have been founded a hundred years ago by Wilkins. This doesn't square with **2**, 'The Harvest', which suggests that the town is much older, originally settled by the Spanish in the 1700s. If the Mayor set up Sunnydale as demon-feeding ground, then is *he* behind Buffy being there too? Consider the numerous occasions when world-threatening stuff has been averted only because Buffy is on hand. The Master, the Judge, Acathla, the Hellmouth creature in **47**, 'The Zeppo', the thing 'the darkness fears' in **44**, 'Amends', all Armageddon scenarios. Episodes **39**, 'Homecoming', and **42**, 'Lover's Walk', both indicate that the Mayor had full knowledge of what was going on in Sunnydale during the two years prior to his introduction, so one has to wonder if there is something in how he's set the city up that means they will always fail, or if he's been depending on Buffy all along.

I Just *Love* Your Accent: Xander, after his discussion with Giles on tea ('you're destroying a perfectly good cultural stereotype'), makes reference to cricket batting averages. Cordelia demands an 'explanation for Wesley'. 'In-breeding?' suggests Xander.

Cruelty to Animals: Faith believes that cats are able to take care of themselves. You normally have to feed them, though.

Quote/Unquote: Willow on Angel: 'He's delirious. He thought I was Buffy.' Oz: 'You too?'

Cordelia, to Giles concerning Wesley: 'Does he have to leave the country? I mean you got fired and you still hang around like a big loser – why can't he?'

Wilkins: 'I'd get ready for some weeping if I were you. I'd get set for a world of pain. Misery loves company, young man, and I'm looking to share that with you and your whore.'

Xander: 'It's just good to know when the chips are down and things look grim you'll feed on the girl that loves you to save your own ass.'

Cordelia: 'We'll attack him with germs.' Buffy: 'Great, we'll get him cornered, then you can sneeze on him.' Cordelia: 'We'll get a container of Ebola virus . . . It doesn't have to be real: we can just get a box that says "Ebola" on it and chase him. With the box.' Xander: 'I'm starting to lean towards the humus offensive!'

Wesley: 'It's rather a lot of pain actually. Aspirin, anyone . . .? Perhaps I could just be knocked unconscious.'

Giles: 'There's a certain dramatic irony attached to all of this. A synchronicity that borders on predestination, one might say.' Buffy: 'Fire bad, tree pretty!'

Notes: 'The show's not over but there will be a short intermission. Don't want to miss the second act, all kinds of excitement.' A suitably intense finish to a remarkable six months of television. The build-up is well handled though the effects-overload finale lacks some finesse.

Angel says that Buffy has no allergies (how does he

know?). Buffy's amazing healing properties are again demonstrated (see **30**, 'Killed By Death'); indeed she refers to them. The doctor's astonishment that Faith is still alive after her ordeal suggests that this is something all Slayers share. Buffy also notes that Angel heals fast (see **4**, 'Teacher's Pet'). Angel confirms that Buffy will not become a vampire as she did not feed off him (see **46**, 'Helpless'). Xander believes that Giles's coffee is 'brewed from the finest Colombian lighter fluid'. Giles prefers tea, but 'tea is soothing. I wish to be tense'. There's another reference to Xander's military knowledge (see **18**, 'Halloween', **26**, 'Innocence'). Wesley says a solar eclipse is 'standard procedure for an Ascension'. Brief cuts were made to the episode before the first scheduled transmission date – Xander loudly celebrating the blowing up of school, for instance.

Soundtrack: Elgar's *Pomp and Circumstance* March No. 1.

What the Papers Said: A number of newspapers sprang to the defence of *Buffy* when WB's decision was announced. Robert Bianco, TV critic for *USA Today*, naming *Buffy* as one of the ten best shows of 1998–9, noted, 'This consistently surprising and enormously entertaining comic morality play from the incredibly talented Joss Whedon is one of the wittiest, smartest series on TV. Too smart for WB, maybe, which insulted the audience's intelligence and the show's integrity by shelving the season finale because of sensitivity concerns, even though no series has been more adept at teaching teens about responsibility and consequences. Never fear: Buffy will triumph, as she always does.' *Entertainment Weekly* also attacked WB: 'This post-Columbine squeamishness is not just idiotic (not airing one of the few programs that portray teens in powerful, responsible positions is being "respectful" of the tragedy?); it also gives strength to the notion that TV shows should be censored to fit whatever is politically prominent at the moment.' The *Chicago Sun Times*' Richard Roeper added, 'Cloaking itself in a veil of disingenuous good intentions while combining cowardice with stupidity, WB squelched Tuesday's *Buffy the Vampire Slayer* because of fears that impressionable young minds might be influenced by watching teenagers doing battle in the hallways of their High School with the town mayor, transformed into a 60-foot, serpentlike creature ... Here's a thought. If you lose a child or a friend or a loved one in a school shooting, I would imagine your grief would be so overwhelmingly complete that you really wouldn't give a rat's behind about what they're doing on *Buffy* ... Most American TV shows and movies, including stuff like *Buffy* and *The Matrix*, also play in dozens of foreign countries, including places where they have strict gun-control laws. And guess what? It turns out that the lack of access to handguns actually translates to fewer killings, regardless of what's playing on TV or at the local multiplex.' The *Newark Star-Ledger*'s Alan Sepinwall said, 'Virtually every episode of *Buffy* features some plot or another to kill students, their parents, their dogs, etc. If you start pulling every episode in which a massacre either happens or is planned, you won't have a show left. But if anything in television is an unwitting culprit, it's not the likes of *Buffy*, but TV news. Kids aren't stupid; they see the way CNN, MSNBC, *Dateline, 20/20*, etc., descend on these tragedies and cover them wall-to-wall for weeks at a time. If some troubled teenager decides he wants to go out in a blaze of glory, the cable news channels and news magazines have clearly established that they will make him famous.' The final word should go to Buffy herself: Sarah Michelle, in a dignified statement, said, 'I share WB's concern and compassion for the recent tragic events ... I am, however, disappointed that the year-long culmination of our efforts will not be seen by our audience. *Buffy the Vampire Slayer* has always been extremely responsible in its depiction of action sequences, fantasy and mythological situations. Our diverse and positive role models battle the horror of adolescence through intelligence and integrity and we endeavor to offer a moral lesson with each new episode. There is probably no greater societal question we face than how to stop violence among our youth. By cancelling intelligent programming like *Buffy the Vampire Slayer*, corporate entertainment is not addressing the problem.'

When the episode finally did air, Matt Roush wrote an

impassioned *TV Guide* article, concluding with his assessment that, 'If Emmy voters weren't such snobs about fantasy and youth genres, *Buffy* and its gifted creator Joss Whedon . . . would merit recognition. The writing is that sharp, the performances that good, the tone that consistent – a unique blend of ironic whimsy and tumultuous passion amid the carnage.'

Joss Whedon's Comments: On 27 May, Joss Whedon told the BtVS posting board, 'How about that season finale, eh? Although, looking at it objectively, it WAS a little like "Band Candy".' ('Graduation Day' Part 2 was replaced by a repeat of **40**, 'Band Candy'.) Whedon continued, 'For the record, I don't think the WB had to pre-empt the episode, but I understand why they did. When those of you who haven't seen it do, you'll wonder what all the fuss was about. But one violent graduation incident and the WB and I would feel like collective @$~%. So, July. At least we won't be up against the final *Home Improvement*. Crazy people with guns bother me.' Whedon also noted, 'It's nice to see how much people care about seeing the episode – although there were threats made against WB execs which is most creepy. Look to poor Britain who get it [the series] in clumps, out of order, on different networks or not at all.'

Nice to see somebody's aware of what we have to put up with over here.

But then Joss Whedon is a remarkable man. When told by *USA Today* that there was a flourishing black market in videotapes and computer downloads of the withheld episodes, his advice to fans was simple: 'I'm having a Grateful Dead moment here . . . Bootleg the puppy!'

The Buffy Novels

Published in the US by Pocket Books, the novels arrived in Britain before the series did, via import book stores like Forbidden Planet. Although they often contradict established continuity, most are well written (notably Christopher Golden and Nancy Holder's impressive characterisation). It's tempting to wonder whether some of the ideas from the books influence the series itself (there are certainly some coincidences, as noted below).

Halloween Rain

Writers: Christopher Golden and Nancy Holder
Published: November 1997
Tagline: He walks . . . He talks . . . He kills . . .
Setting: 30–1 October 1996

It's Halloween and Giles expects trouble. Sure enough, the vampires are out in force, but the biggest danger comes from Samhain, who raises the Sunnydale dead as zombies, fulfilling a local legend concerning walking scarecrows. Buffy almost loses her nerve, while Willow, Giles and Xander face a zombie attack . . .

Authority Sucks!: 'Xander, do not argue with me. I'm your school librarian.'

A Little Learning is a Dangerous Thing: We're subjected to a lecture on the origins of Halloween and the druid feast of Samhuinn.

Mom's Apple Pie: Buffy and Joyce indulge in a horror-movie fest on Showtime.

Denial, Thy Name is Sunnydale: 'The rest of the town is psycho,' says Willow. 'They all want to pretend Sunnydale is as sunny as Sunnybrook Farm . . . The stories are all there . . . but nobody connects the dots.' 'Because nobody wants to,' Buffy says.

References: 'Sometimes it concerned [Buffy] that her head was filled with so many pop-culture references.' *The Twilight Zone, Heathers, Indiana Jones* ('if adventure has a name, my dear, it's Xander Harris'), Jackie Chan, *The X-Files, Mission: Impossible, Pinky and the Brain, The Pirates of Penzance, The Addams Family, The Wizard of Oz, Star Trek: The Next Generation,* James Bond, *Star Wars, Superman, The Jetsons, Grease, Back to the Future III, Dawn of the Dead, Nightmare Before Christmas, The Terminator,* Roy Rogers and Dale Evans ('popular American cowpeople'), *Zorro, Macbeth*.

Logic, Let Me Introduce You to This Window: Giles expects Halloween to be a big time for vampires, though **18**, 'Halloween', tells us exactly the opposite. Buffy is sixteen, although her seventeenth birthday in **25**, 'Surprise', comes after Halloween 1997. As this is set during the first season, Buffy must have been fifteen when she arrived in Sunnydale. Buffy has a phobia about clowns – it's actually Xander who has this. (See **10**, 'Nightmares'.)

Notes: The first original novel could easily be a television script, if it didn't contradict so many later-established concepts. Xander and Willow discuss whether vampires can enter public places long before **30**, 'Killed By Death'; Mr Flutie is one of the raised zombies. Samhain claims to be the instigator of all the nightmares that Buffy suffered as a child. Buffy originally runs away from Samhain, before realising that her destiny is to be The Slayer. She promises Giles that she'll never shirk her duty again.

Coyote Moon

Writer: John Vornholt
Published: January 1998
Tagline: Humans by day . . . Evil by night . . .
Setting: Late August 1997

A carnival comes to town, at the same time as a coyote pack. When Willow and Xander fall under the spell of the carneys, Buffy and Giles must prevent the resurrection of Spurs Hardaway, a 'werecoyote' buried in Sunnydale, and save their friends from sacrifice.

References: Bela Lugosi's *Dracula*, Stephen King's *Cujo*.

Logic, Let Me Introduce You to This Window: Buffy is in Sunnydale during the summer. Not according to **13**, 'When She Was Bad', she wasn't (and babysitting at that). Willow is allergic to dogs (does Oz know?). Giles doesn't recognise candy floss.

I Just *Love* Your Accent: Giles raised hounds for a local fox hunt.

Notes: A werewolf story, competently told, but done much better in **27**, 'Phases'. There are some nice continuity touches – Angel is mentioned but not present; Xander doesn't like clowns. One line stands out: 'We need to start using trickery, though, or the next mayor of Sunnydale is going to be a werebear!'

Night of the Living Rerun . . .

Writer: Arthur Byron Cover
Published: March 1998
Tagline: The stage is set for a killer performance . . .
Setting: Late 1996

Buffy has weird dreams, linking her to Samantha Kane, one of the Salem witch-hunt victims. Xander and Giles suffer similar nightmares and four ghost hunters arrive in Sunnydale hot on the scent. Buffy has to discover why history is repeating itself and what it has to do with a statue in her mom's gallery.

A Little Learning is a Dangerous Thing: We learn far more than we ever want to about the Salem trials, mixing rather too much fiction with the facts.

Denial, Thy Name is Sunnydale: It's stated – as a fact – that there is a 'forgetfulness spell' over Sunnydale. Joyce worries that Buffy won't keep her skin's 'youthful quality' if she keeps getting bruised.

References: *Kolckak: The Night Stalker* (one of the ghost hunters is a reporter called Darryl MacGovern), Taster's Choice coffee commercials, *Romeo and Juliet*, the game show *Jeopardy*.

Logic, Let Me Introduce You to This Window: When told to prepare for death, Buffy says, 'Been there, bought the T-shirt.' Her 'death' doesn't occur until a later date in 1997.

Notes: The Master was responsible for the events of the Salem witch trials, apparently. Lora Church (one of the hunters) was at Oxford with Giles and remembers his great interest in the paranormal, though they lost touch after graduation. The theme of possession is handled far better in **31**, 'I Only Have Eyes For You', while a possessed artefact would later feature in **36**, 'Dead Man's Party'. Buffy disguises herself in a burger-joint uniform – as she would do in **35**, 'Anne'.

Blooded

Writers: Christopher Golden and Nancy Holder
Published: August 1998
Tagline: Buffy's new enemy is close to her heart . . .
Setting: Impossibly, after **34**, 'Becoming' Part 2, but before **35**, 'Anne'

On a school trip to the museum, Willow cuts herself on a Japanese artefact and she is possessed by an ancient Japanese vampire, Chirayoju. When Xander is possessed by Chirayoju's ancient enemy, Sanno, a fight to the death ensues . . .

A Little Learning is a Dangerous Thing: We learn a lot about Japanese customs.

References: *Pulp Fiction, William Shakespeare's Romeo and Juliet, Hamlet, Casper, Rocky, Poltergeist, ER, Deep Space 9*

('Principal Snyder looked only slightly more human than one of the Ferengi on *Star Trek*'), *The Absent-Minded Professor, Batman, Star Wars, Mission: Impossible*.

Bitch!: 'You could use some time on self-improvement, Cordelia. Maybe then people would stop mistaking you for Barbie's friend Skipper turned crack-ho.' And this, from Willow!

Logic, Let Me Introduce You to This Window: Angel has stopped being Angelus and everyone is friendly with him – even Giles! Cordelia says Xander 'doesn't usually snore', suggesting they have slept together (Xander is still a virgin until **47**, 'The Zeppo').

I Just *Love* Your Accent: 'It was times like this that Giles wished he was back in the land of tea, crumpets and baked beans for breakfast.' As Giles would say, 'Americans!'

Notes: The first book to try to deal with the aftermath of Season Two is hampered by clearly not knowing what happened in **33/34**, 'Becoming'. Additionally, it's set within 1998 – SATs are next year – but Angel is, critically, one of the gang after 'the Angelus crisis'. We meet Willow's mom for the first time in another tale of possession (this time much closer to **31**, 'I Only Have Eyes For You', in form). Oz is experimenting with heavy chains as a werewolf-containment system. Buffy's driving is as excruciating as her attempts in **40**, 'Band Candy'.

Child of the Hunt

Writers: Christopher Golden and Nancy Holder
Published: October 1998
Tagline: Only his soul was human . . .
Setting: Autumn 1998

As Joyce becomes involved with parents searching for their missing children, a Renaissance Faire comes to Sunnydale – bringing with it the Elf Hunt and its leader Herne the Hunter. When Giles, Willow, Xander and Buffy are captured, it's up to Cordelia to save the day.

Mom's Apple Pie: Joyce insists on some quality time with Buffy, Slayer or not.

Denial, Thy Name is Sunnydale: 'Typical Sunnydale denial,' Willow says when Cordelia wonders why no one noticed 'spooky horse guys snatching people and . . . killing babies'.

Denial, Thy Name is Joyce: Joyce still can't understand why Buffy has been chosen and ends up clutching a stake as a comforter and moaning 'It wasn't meant to be like this.'

References: *Camelot, Who Framed Roger Rabbit?, Jeopardy, Star Trek, Rain Man, The Addams Family, Hamlet, Batman, Mary Poppins, Something Wicked This Way Comes, Hansel and Gretel, The Hobbit, Bewitched, The Wizard of Oz, The Silence of the Lambs.*

Cigarettes and Alcohol: Giles remembers escaping into the bottle in **20**, 'The Dark Age': 'The one and only time he had gotten drunk in Sunnydale he had so badly frightened Buffy that he had vowed never to be so self-indulgent again.'

Logic, Let Me Introduce You to This Window: Although Buffy's disappearance to LA is mentioned, Angel is still part of the team and even agrees to share a beer with Giles.

Notes: Another story that could work on screen (it's similar in places to **45**, 'Gingerbread'), bringing fantasy into the Buffy universe. Willow's parents (and their disapproval of Oz), Xander's parents (who ignore him) and Cordelia's parents (who disapprove of Xander) all appear. Giles uses a phone card to avoid questions about all the long-distance calls from the library. Cordelia has visited England and seen a fox hunt.

Return to Chaos

Writer: Craig Shaw Gardner
Published: December 1998
Tagline: Under the cover of Darkness . . .
Setting: Spring 1999

All the signs point to a major event at the Hellmouth. Plans for the Spring Formal Dance are put aside when a group of Druids invade Sunnydale and Cordelia is bitten by a former rival, who is now a vampire, under the thrall of a British demon called Eric . . .

A Little Learning is a Dangerous Thing: The origins of the Druids are explained.

References: *Batman, Sesame Street, Masterpiece Theater, Lost in Space, Mad* magazine, *Mission: Impossible, The Man From UNCLE, Rebel Without a Cause, Jeopardy, Superman.*

Logic, Let Me Introduce You to This Window: The relationship between Buffy and Angel is not as on screen by this time – and Xander and Cordelia are still an item.

Notes: A much simpler novel than the two predecessors, although for once the British contingent are portrayed accurately. Cordelia beat Naomi to become chief cheerleader. Research shows that Drusilla was a regular user of a spell that would explain how she killed Kendra so easily. The high mortality rate of principals is referred to: 'Cordy hadn't gotten in real trouble at Sunnydale High for at least the last three principals. That was probably close to two years around here.' The most prophetic line is, 'An alliance between us [a vampire and a druid] will allow you to control the Hellmouth for a hundred years.' Ascension, anyone?

The Gatekeeper Trilogy Book One: Out of the Madhouse

Writers: Christopher Golden and Nancy Holder
Published: January 1999
Tagline: Evil is eternal . . .
Setting: Spring 1999

Weird things start happening in Sunnydale, with the arrival of Springheel Jack, the Kraken, storms of toads *and* a mysterious brotherhood stalking Buffy. Giles believes the Gatehouse

– a mystical gateway between dimensions – is under attack and he, Buffy, Cordelia and Xander head to Boston, where they discover that the Gatekeeper is dying. The Brotherhood of the Sons of Entropy (who are killing Watchers around the world) nearly destroy the Gatehouse and the only hope is the Gatekeeper's son – who is in the hands of Spike and Drusilla!

Denial, Thy Name is Sunnydale: Xander: 'Maybe [my parents] live on the Hellmouth, but like everyone else in Sunnydale, they somehow manage to get by without acknowledging how crazy that is.'

Denial, Thy Name is Joyce: 'Mom had been in denial ever since Buffy told her the truth.'

References: The Energizer Bunny, *Rocky the Flying Squirrel, The Beverley Hillbillies,* Elmer Fudd, *My Private Idaho, Dawson's Creek, Reservoir Dogs, Jeopardy, Thelma & Louise, Supergirl, Sabrina The Teenage Witch, The Wizard of Oz, Alice's Adventures in Wonderland, Peanuts* and Charlie Brown, *Batman, Ricochet Rabbit, Star Wars.* Oz's infrequent gigging with Dingoes Ate My Baby is causing rifts (the band refer to Willow as 'Yoko'). There's an oblique reference to Golden's excellent vampire trilogy, *The Shadow Saga.*

Logic, Let Me Introduce You to This Window: Giles seems to think that all nurses are called 'Sister' in Britain. They aren't. This is set in the same alternate universe as 'Child of the Hunt', with Giles accepting Angel and Cordy and Xander still dating in spring 1999.

Notes: Lot of running around and action sequences that would make this a terrific movie, but they just don't work on paper. Half the fights are unnecessary and the chapters within the Gatehouse go on far too long. However, it's a continuity-fest both to the series and to the books, with Roland from *Child of the Hunt,* and Kobe Sensei from *Blooded* both appearing. Travelling the ghost roads between dimensions, Oz meets Kendra, while Angel sees Jenny.

The Gatekeeper Trilogy Book Two: Ghost Roads

Writers: Christopher Golden and Nancy Holder
Published: March 1999
Tagline: Last exit before fear . . .
Setting: 30–1 October 1996

Buffy, Angel and Oz travel the ghost roads around Europe, visiting London and Paris, before a dream guides them to the Sons of Entropy in Florence, where they are saved by Il Maestro's daughter, Micaela, and rescue the Gatekeeper's son from Spike and Dru. Meanwhile, Giles visits the *Flying Dutchman* and Joyce is captured by the Sons of Entropy in a bid to get Buffy to surrender. Xander is shot during a rescue attempt . . .

References: *Casper, E.T., Little Shop of Horrors, The Addams Family, Batman, Someone's Killing the Great Chefs of Europe, Casablanca,* Daffy Duck, *Superman,* Xander misquotes John Masefield, *Star Trek, Star Wars, West Side Story,* TS Eliot's *The Wasteland, Man of La Mancha, Invasion of the Body Snatchers, The X-Files, Armageddon,* the game Cluedo.

Cigarettes and Alcohol: In an effort to fit in, Angel smokes a cigarette at a Paris café, while Giles gets drunk on board the *Flying Dutchman*.

Logic, Let Me Introduce You to This Map: There's some weird geography going down. The Cotswolds are apparently to the east and slightly south of London. Travelling from there, they arrive on Hampstead Heath!

Logic, Let Me Introduce You to This Window: Joyce moves in with Giles for safety, with absolutely no reference to **40**, 'Band Candy'.

Notes: Middle books of trilogies tend to drag, and this is no exception. The whole *Flying Dutchman* incident is pure padding and Spike and Dru are underused. Like episode three of your average *Doctor Who* story – loads of running around, and the plot barely progresses. One neat reference is Amy

Madison helping out in Sunnydale, since there's no Slayer around.

The Gatekeeper Trilogy Book Three: Sons of Entropy

Writers: Christopher Golden and Nancy Holder
Published: May 1999
Tagline: The final battle has begun . . .
Setting: Spring 1999

Willow and Cordelia take Xander to the Gatehouse, where he is saved. When the Gatekeeper is killed, Xander becomes acting Keeper. With Ethan Rayne's help, Buffy rescues Joyce, and Angel and Oz escort Jacques, the new Keeper, to Boston. Il Maestro is in alliance with the demon Belphegor, but realises that he's on the wrong side as Buffy defeats Belphegor.

References: *Batman, The Wizard of Oz*, Ethan refers to Buffy as 'Slayer Spice', *Spider-Man, Star Trek* (Xander realises he is now 'Picard, Kirk, Sisko and – God help him – Janeway, all rolled into one'!), *Alice's Adventures in Wonderland, Apollo 13, I Was A Teenage Werewolf, Sliders, Silent Night, The Addams Family, The X-Files* and *The Shining* novel, *Pleasantville*.

Logic, Let Me Introduce You to This Window: Despite no mention being made of Joyce's and Giles's exploits in **40**, 'Band Candy', Buffy refers to this episode when talking to Ethan.

I Just *Love* Your Accent: Ethan: 'Good Lord. Who died and made you Xena?' Buffy: 'Same people who made you Dr Smith.' 'Sorry, I don't follow,' Ethan told her. '*Lost in Space*?' Buffy prompted. 'The cowardly bad guy?' 'We're from Britain, Buffy,' Giles informed her. 'We had *Dr Who*.'

Notes: More running about, and the cue for some great special effects, but they don't work on paper. There are a couple of neat ideas (Xander as the Gatekeeper), but none of it lives up to the promise of the first book.

Visitors

Writers: Laura Anne Gilman and Josepha Sherman
Published: April 1999
Tagline: The Slayer is being stalked . . .
Setting: Spring 1999

Buffy has problems when a group of student teachers get the hots for Giles and infest the library; Ethan Rayne returns to Sunnydale; the Watchers' Council sends a Watcher to watch Giles, and the korred – a creature that makes people dance themselves to death – arrives.

Mom's Apple Pie: Buffy and Joyce have a weekly quality time set aside, which seems to be painful for both sides.

References: *Batman*, Leonardo DiCaprio, *Wheel of Fortune*, *Macbeth*, *Gunfight at the OK Corral*, *West Side Story*, *All's Well That Ends Well*.

Logic, Let Me Introduce You to This Window: Ethan's return here takes place not long after **40**, 'Band Candy' – just as in *The Gatekeeper Trilogy*. A wonderful mistake that went unspotted: Willow refers to 'The Dingoes' *Ate My Babies*'. Cordy and Xander are *still* together.

Notes: Back to the younger-readers range, with a weak plot. The Council sending someone to check out Giles had been seen on the series (although not before this was delivered) and the possibility of Willow becoming a Watcher is one that fans have debated.

Unnatural Selection

Writer: Mel Odom
Published: June 1999
Tagline: An environmental evil haunts Willow . . .
Setting: Spring 1999

Gallivan Industries' plans for a local park disturb the inhabitants – a bunch of Soviet faeries, who need a witch's blood for one of their rites. The faeries start stealing babies, Buffy and Angel have to pose as a married couple, Xander discovers that a new friend is not all he appears to be and Willow must be rescued from the middle of a faerie civil war.

A Little Learning is a Dangerous Thing: Lot of faerie folklore.

Denial, Thy Name is the Summers Family: 'Both [Buffy and Joyce] knew that each time [Buffy] stepped out the door to go Slaying could be the last time they saw each other, but they couldn't act that way.'

References: The works of James Fenimore Cooper, *Dragnet, NYPD Blue,* Jerry Springer, *Good Housekeeping,* Bugs Bunny, *Scream* (Willow is babysitting for the Campbells when their baby is taken), *The Godfather, Dirty Harry, The Smurfs, Scooby Doo, Duck Tales, Yogi Bear, The X-Files, Dick Tracy, Small Soldiers, Butch Cassidy and the Sundance Kid, Pinky and the Brain,* Superman's foe Brainiac, *The Twilight Zone, Lassie,* 'Santa Claus Is Coming To Town', *Star Trek: The Next Generation.*

Logic, Let Me Introduce You to This Window: Cordy and Xander are *still* dating! Do the editors of the two ranges talk to each other? Buffy encountered the faerie folk in 'Child of the Hunt', and briefly in 'Out of the Madhouse', yet here she's never heard of them.

Notes: A convoluted plot that just about manages to keep going for 210 pages – but there's precious little of The Slayer, compared with normal. Notable for being the first original novel *not* to feature Sarah Michelle Gellar on the cover.

The Outsiders

*'The brilliant thing about Joss is he's got all these people
sucked in watching this fantasy, but in the meantime he's
making them think about the kid that they've ostracised and
the kid who's in trouble . . . He explores a lot of things that
are going on with kids today.'*

– Kristine Sutherland

'I don't want him to be lonely. I don't want anyone to.'

– 'Passion'

For some people memories of school are as Muriel Spark
describes them in *The Prime of Miss Jean Brodie*: 'the happi-
est days of their lives'. For most of us, however, it was a time
of intense pressure and loneliness when, cruelly, we were
nowhere near mature enough to deal with these emotions.
That's the central paradox of the teenage years that *Buffy the
Vampire Slayer* articulates. Many TV series have talked about
how hard growing up can be (from *Happy Days* and *The
Wonder Years* to *Press Gang*). Few, however, have been as
honest or as painfully accurate as *Buffy*. When Buffy is over-
whelmed by the thoughts of her fellow students in **52**,
'Earshot', from the cacophony certain phrases stand out: 'It's
got to get better. *Please* tell me it gets better'; 'I *hate* my
body'; 'What if I *never* get breasts?'; 'I *hate* her'; 'No one's
ever gonna love me'.

'I was a pathetic loser in high school,' confesses Joss
Whedon but, despite his stated intention to make Buffy's con-
flict with the monsters she fights 'a metaphor about just how
frightening and horrible high school is' there are few
metaphors in *Buffy*'s treatment of the high school years themselves. Here, an outsider *is* an outsider. The aspirations of
parents and teachers place a burden on young shoulders that

needs no subtext to amplify it. Self-doubt, especially in those with identity or image problems, is never far from the surface. (Xander acknowledges his shortcomings in **3**, 'The Witch', saying, 'For I am Xander, King of Cretins. May all lesser cretins bow before me.') The fear of failure and peer rejection is a topic of many conversations. As Willow tells Xander in **6**, 'The Pack', 'You fail math, you flunk out of school. You end up being the guy at the pizza place that sweeps the floor and says, "Hey, kids, where's the cool parties this weekend?" ' The obsessions of sex and peer acceptance are crucial to the way that characters regard themselves. Cordelia's dream in **3**, 'The Witch', is: 'Me on the cheerleading squad, adored by every varsity male as far as the eye can see. We have to achieve our dreams, or else we wither and die.' In **11**, 'Out of Sight, Out of Mind', Cordelia seems sympathetic towards Marcie, the Invisible Girl saying, 'It's awful to feel that lonely.' When Buffy asks how *she* would know, Cordy replies, 'You think I'm never lonesome 'cause I'm so cute and popular? I can be surrounded by people and be completely alone. It's not like any of them really know me. I don't even know if they like me half the time. People just want to be in the popular zone.' When Buffy asks why, if Cordelia feels like this, she works so hard at being popular, Cordelia says simply that it 'beats being alone all by yourself'.

'The anger of the outcast', central to **11**, 'Out of Sight, Out of Mind', is a touchstone for the entire series. 'On the exterior it's about demons and vampires and the mythology of The Slayer, but underneath it is strictly about growing up and all of that stuff just becomes a metaphor,' said Kristine Sutherland in a recent interview with Paul Simpson. And most *Buffy* episodes do concern one form of outsider or another. Buffy herself, from the first episode, is a textbook example. A girl in a new town and school, struggling to keep her head above waves that could drown someone with less mental toughness (as it does Marcie). Battling the preconceptions of others, whether those of hated authority figures like Snyder, or of her friends.

In **23**, 'Ted', after she has apparently killed her stepfather-in-waiting, Cordelia asks Willow, 'Shouldn't there be different rules for her?' 'In a fascist society,' notes Willow. 'Right!' continues Cordy. 'Why can't we have one of those?' Others deal with the pressure in different ways. Willow keeps her head down and hopes to avoid Cordelia's sarcasm. Xander becomes the class clown, with a witty comeback for every 'loser' put-down. When Willow asks Giles why Marcie is doing the terrible things she does, he replies, 'The loneliness, the constant exile. She's gone mad.' It's a simplistic answer but, in essence, it describes a heightened version of a form of trauma that many teenagers go through.

In 3, 'The Witch', Amy is seen as a victim of the aspirations of her 'Nazi-like' mother. The issue of parental pressure here (the implication of Amy as a little fat girl beaten into agreeing to Catherine's mad schemes), along with 23, 'Ted' (a potential stepfather who likes to slap young girls about), and 24, 'Bad Eggs' (Joyce at the nadir of her *Mommie Dearest* period), reaches a violent climax in 45, 'Gingerbread'. Here, it's no longer a case of 'I want my kids to be just like me' but rather 'what are my children up to behind my back, and how can I put a stop to it?' The episode's witch hunt is an analogy of censorship, but the belief systems into which Buffy and Willow find their mothers trying to push them are frighteningly real. As Buffy tells Joyce when the demon manifests itself, 'Mom, dead people are talking to you. Do the math.'

Bullying is also a central prop. 'Every school has them,' notes Xander in 6, 'The Pack'. 'You start a new school, you get your desks, your blackboards, and some mean kids.' Whether it's Jack O'Toole pulling a knife on Xander in 47, 'The Zeppo', or Larry's outrageous sexual innuendo in 27, 'Phases' ('Be still, my shorts'), the threat of humiliation and pain is never far from the minds of the audience. 'Testosterone is a great equaliser', notes Giles in 6, 'The Pack'. 'It turns all men into morons.' In 27, 'Phases', Buffy tells Willow, 'Welcome to the mystery that is men . . . It goes something like, "They grow body hair, they lose all ability to tell you what they really want." ' 'That doesn't seem like a fair trade,' says Willow. Ultimately, the theme is examined to breaking point in 38, 'Beauty and the Beasts', which fudges the tricky subject of male domestic violence, but accurately captures the confusion on both sides when trying to maintain relationships.

The second year of *Buffy* was the point at which a promising idea suddenly (and, given the formulaic nature of American series TV, quite unexpectedly) grew up and got serious. If the initial episodes had been a dip of the toe into a pool of delicious irony, in which teenagers fought vampires between homework and dates, then the second season was a fully clothed dive into the murky waters of the adult world. We had no reason to expect anything so daring, so *challenging*, as this. Previously, *Buffy* had been about teenage dreams and desires: Xander's helpless love life, Willow's quest to make Xander notice her. The great taboo 's' word ('sex') was finally spoken (by of all people Joyce) in **29**, 'Passion', after the heroine's virginity was lost in **25**, 'Surprise'. Even Giles was not immune to the great hormonal upheaval going on around him, first winning Jenny Calendar, then mourning her.

Giles is another outsider. The Englishman abroad, lost in a school situation he doesn't understand, working with a girl who speaks a language he doesn't, having to put aside all his preconceptions about what a Watcher is, to deal with the realities of life in Sunnydale. 'But Giles is not a fool,' says Tony Head. 'He's deeply learned. One of the choices I made at the beginning was that [Giles has] prepared for this for some time. There's a lot of theory gone into it, but that [he's] had absolutely no practical experience. So when we first get into the affray, it's a bit of a shock.'

In **42**, 'Lover's Walk', Buffy tells him that, when her mother saw her SAT scores, 'her head spun around and exploded'. Giles asks, 'I've been on the Hellmouth too long. That was metaphorical, yes?' Episode **41**, 'Revelations', sees Buffy keeping Angel's return from Giles and, upon discovering this, Giles is furious at her betrayal: 'I won't remind you that the fate of the world often lies with The Slayer. What would be the point? Nor shall I remind you that you've jeopardised the lives of all that you hold dear by harbouring a known murderer. But, sadly, I must remind you that Angel tortured me. For hours. For pleasure. You should have told me he was alive. You didn't. You have no respect for me or the job I perform.'

But he *knows* Buffy and is able to spot Faith's lies about her in **49**, 'Consequences'. Of course Giles was an outsider even as a teenager and in **40**, 'Band Candy', we see evidence of his way of dealing with responsibility: 'I'm your Watcher, so you do what I tell you. Now, sod off!' And: 'Let's find the demon and kick the crap out of it!' 'Did anyone ever tell you you're kind of a fuddy-duddy?' Jenny asks him in **20**, 'The Dark Age'. 'Nobody ever seems to tell me anything else,' he replies.

In Xander we have a paradox. Someone who is (according to **47**, 'The Zeppo') 'not challenged', but who finds school such hard going that he has surrendered his intellect to the clouds and spends his days dreaming about sex (hinted in **10**, 'Nightmares', **26**, 'Innocence', and **47**, 'The Zeppo', and confirmed in **52**, 'Earshot'). But Xander is, as Oz notes in **52**, 'Earshot', 'a very complex man'. 'You are strange,' Ampata tells him in **16**, 'Inca Mummy Girl'. 'Girls always tell me that,' notes Xander, 'right before they run away.' The only time we see Xander enraged about the abject unfairness of a system of which he is a crushed victim is in **32**, 'Go Fish', when Willow is told by Snyder to up the failing grades of one of the swim team. This causes Xander to rant, 'That's wrong. Big fat spanking wrong.' Xander knows, however, that life is seldom fair (it's a system that, he acknowledges, 'discriminates against the uninformed'). In **17**, 'Reptile Boy', having suffered from a ritual frat-party humiliation, his way of dealing with his feelings is mind-numbing violence.

Willow's story is different. In **1**, 'Welcome to the Hellmouth', she is simply looking for a friend to call her own. ('Aren't you hanging out with Cordelia?' she asks. Buffy responds, 'I can't do both?' 'Not legally,' Willow replies). Willow never surrenders to the cruelties of life (not even Xander's failure to notice her increasingly desperate advances), but sometimes longs for change. By **50**, 'Doppelgängland' she is bemoaning the one quality she can be proud of: 'Yeah, that's me. Reliable Dog Geyser Person.'

There's also Faith, whose way of dealing with the 'outsiderness' of being a Slayer is radically different from Buffy's – as shown in **18**, 'Bad Girls', and her random sexual exploits. 'How many people do you think we've saved by now. Thousands? And didn't you stop the world from ending? Because, in my book, that puts you and me in the plus column,' she says in **49**, 'Consequences', as the cracks begin to open. Faith turns to the dark side because she's an outsider within the Scooby Gang – none of them really want her around. Whereas, with the Mayor, she's cherished in a home rather than alone in a motel room ('This place is the kick,' she says when entering her new apartment). In **51**, 'Enemies', her sleeping with the enemy is revealed as she tells Buffy, 'I'll be sitting at his right hand. Assuming he has hands after the transformation. I'm not too clear on that part. And all your little lame-ass friends are gonna be Kibbles and Bits.'

Ultimately it could have been so different if only she'd had any love in her life. But at every step, from her mother's rejection onwards, it was not to be. In **38**, 'Beauty and the Beasts', Buffy calls her 'all men are beasts' view cynical. 'It's not . . . It's realistic. Every guy, from *Manimal* to Mr "I Love *The English Patient*", has *beast* in him. I don't care how sensitive they act. They're all still just in for the chase.'

Angel doesn't fit in either. He's shaken to his core by Buffy's arrival. (In **19**, 'Lie to Me', he tells Willow, 'A hundred years just hanging out feeling guilty, I really honed my brooding skills. Then *she* comes along.') His curse puts him on the outside of his own kind *and* humanity. 'The last time I looked in on you two,' says Spike in **42**, 'Lover's Walk', 'you were fighting to the death. Now you're back to making googly eyes at each other again like nothing happened. Makes me want to heave.' When Angel loses his soul in **26**, 'Innocence', note how happy Angelus is to be back with Spike and Drusilla.

For Buffy, the constant struggle is to balance the different elements of her life. In **40**, 'Band Candy', she challenges Joyce and Giles saying, 'You're both scheduling me twenty-four hours a day. Between the two of you, that's forty-eight hours.' But her rebellion against her destiny is only a tiny part of the complicated double life she is forced to lead. On occasions (**3**, 'The Witch', **17**, 'Reptile Boy', **37**, 'Faith, Hope and Trick') she longs for a life free of the burden of her Slayer duties. In **39**, 'Homecoming', she even tries to put it into practice: 'This is just like any other popularity contest. I've done this before. The only difference being this time I'm not actually popular.'

And with her off-on-off-on-again relationship with an older man (old enough, in fact, to be her ancestor) Buffy's confusion reaches critical meltdown. Even when she *tries* to find a normal boy (Owen or Scott), Slaying gets in the way. 'Obviously my sex appeal is on the fritz today,' she notes in **32**, 'Go Fish', when Gage calls her a 'psycho bitch'.

It's the five episodes that detail the climax and breakdown of the Buffy–Angel relationship (**25**, 'Surprise', **26**, 'Innocence', **29**, 'Passion' and **33/34**, 'Becoming') that identify the biggest change to *Buffy*. These are episodes in which we see a teenage girl being given some heartbreaking lessons in the horrors of the adult world. In the teen-suicide drama **31**, 'I Only Have Eyes for You', Buffy spends the episode believing that the haunting of the school by the restless soul of James is just retribution for what he did to Grace, until Giles tells her, 'To forgive is an action of compassion. It's not done because people deserve it. It's done because they *need* it.' It's only when she realises, in **54**, 'The Prom', that what she is doing has not gone unnoticed that Buffy's defences crumble. 'It was a hell of a battle,' she says at the end of **56**, 'Graduation Day' Part 2. She could be talking about her own struggle to find a purpose in the madness around her.

In **52**, 'Earshot', Buffy finds Jonathan alone on the top of the school clock tower with a gun in his hand. We've seen him in several episodes before, always the butt of cruel jokes by the likes of Harmony, or intimidated and bullied by others. Buffy tells Jonathan that she's never thought much about him: 'Nobody here really does. Bugs you, doesn't it? You have all this pain, all these feelings, and nobody's really paying attention . . .' Jonathan says, 'You think I just want attention?' 'No,' replies Buffy sarcastically, 'I think you're up in the clock tower with a high-powered rifle because you want to blend in! Believe it or not, I understand about the pain.' Jonathan is incredulous: 'Oh, right! Because the burden of being beautiful and athletic, that's a crippler!' he says, echoing Buffy's own disbelief at Cordelia in **11**, 'Out of Sight, Out of Mind'. 'I was wrong,' says Buffy. 'You *are* an idiot. My life happens, on occasion, to suck beyond the telling of it. Sometimes more than I can handle. Not just mine. Every single person down there is ignoring *your* pain because they're dealing with their *own*. The beautiful ones, the popular ones, the guys that pick on you, everyone. If you could hear what they're feeling, the loneliness, the confusion. It looks quiet down there. It's not. It's deafening.'

Analysing the success of *Buffy the Vampire Slayer* requires us to look hard at our own experiences in our teens. Joss Whedon and the other writers, in using the clichés of horror movies – vampires, demons, possession, robots and so on – to represent the terrors of being a teenager, have managed to tap into something buried deep within all of us. It's the subtext stuff – parental pressure, bullying, fear of sex, social exclusion. The characters in *Buffy* are characters that we empathise with, because we were all once like them. Outsiders.

> *Cordelia: 'Are we killing something tonight?'*
> *Buffy: 'Only my carefree spirit.'*
>
> – 'Band Candy'

Demonising America

'This is not gonna be pretty. We're talking violence, strong language, adult content.'

– 'Welcome to the Hellmouth'

Shortly after *Buffy*'s BBC debut, the media critic AA Gill wrote a hysterically overblown review of the series in the *Sunday Times*:

> This is a High School where even the plain girls are models . . . And they're all remorselessly Anglo-white. If I were writing a communication studies thesis on *Buffy* . . . I might go so far as to say the allegory of vampirism has been subtly shifted from sex to outsiders. The monsters have the look of the underclass, the leather-jacketed, dangerous drifting denizens of street corners and recreation areas, the gangs of lost youth that prey on middle-class America.

Opinionated stuff but not without an element of truth. In Sunnydale there are not only no drug dealers but also no homeless people (Spike mentions one in **42**, 'Lover's Walk', but we never see him) and frequently no ethnic diversity – something Mr Trick spotted in **37**, 'Faith, Hope and Trick'. Not a haven for the bruthas, indeed. Instead, these pariahs of society have been replaced by 'the forces of darkness'. A new underclass of demonised nightmares. When we *do* see the underbelly of Sunnydale (the prostitute in **26**, 'Innocence', for example) it's the cosiest underbelly imaginable. This is a small town with no sleaze, no junkies and no dog shit. In any sort of real-world-type scenario, Cordelia should be doing five lines of cocaine a day, Xander would be asking serious questions about his sexuality and Buffy would be living on the street selling her body to finance her smack addiction. 'Buffy's school', added Gill, 'is an embattled fortress of learning and the old Eisenhower American way of life, full of beautiful, rich middle-American kids. It doesn't take a huge stretch of the imagination to see that this is how a lot of Americans view their current predicament, and there's no doubt where the real power lies.'

In other words, American small-town *gothica* in the dying days of the millennium, and America is *scared*. If you tolerate this, your children will be next. 'Pre-wedlock humping isn't the fate worse than death that keeps American mothers awake worrying about their daughters,' Gill concluded, and continued:

> It's crack and gun control and the waves of ethnic visigoths that are sucking the blood right out of the nation. And it's no great stretch of the imagination to set *Buffy* in the long line of separatist white xenophobia that is a continuing riff in American films and television. In fact, she has a lot more in common with John Wayne than she does with Peter Cushing.

In many ways this view of contemporary America is *de rigeur*. One doesn't have to be a genius to spot the link between series that use science fiction and horror as an audience grabber while simultaneously pointing the finger at politicians and the media and the paranoia of many of the people who are vocal in their admiration of such series. Some people may watch *The X-Files* for revelation. More watch it as, they believe, an act of rebellion. In the words of one of the true philosophers of the age, Bruce Willis, 'You're either part of the solution or you're part of the problem.' *Buffy* is part of the solution, even if this is sometimes *in spite* of itself. Its agenda is specific, measurable, achievable, realistic and time-bound.

'It's a very ambitious show,' says Charisma Carpenter, and she's right. Put simply, *Buffy the Vampire Slayer* may (just) be a series about post-millennium neuroses but, unlike *First Wave*, *Dark Skies*, *Millennium*, *Brimstone* and (during its po-faced early days) *The X-Files*, it *knows* that. In this regard, *Buffy* is closer to the spirit of Homer Simpson, *Friends* and *Ally McBeal* than it is to Mulder and Scully or the kids of its

WB network neighbours *Dawson's Creek* and *Felicity*.

Self-awareness is not, in itself, something to shout about too loudly. Being self-aware simply means that, when you're bad, you *know* you're bad. (The volume of television-industry one-liners that Xander is given suggests that self-awareness *is* a deliberate part of the mix.) Where *Buffy* scores again, and more tellingly, is that, in addition to the knowing glances it gives to viewers and critics alike (let's remember, at one time the series' critical standing was far higher than its audience appreciation), it seems to have an uncanny knack of hitting weak spots at the heart of the intellectual demonisation process of American youth culture, the era's great trio of evil – television, rock music and the Internet. All of the elements, in other words, that *Buffy* itself satirised as 'evil' in **37**, 'Faith, Hope and Trick' (the 'hankering for the blood of a fifteen-year-old Filipina' sequence) and **45**, 'Gingerbread'. But sometimes we must pay the price for being ahead of the game.

In April 1999, two students from Littleton High School in Denver took guns into their school cafeteria and opened fire. It wasn't the first such incident to shock America in recent years and it won't be the last (indeed, within weeks, a similar if less fatal event had taken place in Georgia). That evening on *Newsnight*, the BBC's America correspondent Gavin Esler gave a critical summation of the mood of the country when he reported that, as with previous incidents of this kind, America was in a collective state of shock but with an equally collective determination that such a thing should never, ever be allowed to happen again. However, when it came to the actual apportioning of *blame*, this consensus had quickly evaporated. Each time something like this happens, noted Esler, within hours the TV screens are filled with people with easy answers and easy solutions. Blame the violence on TV or in the cinema. Blame the power and lack of control of the Internet. Blame satanic messages in rock music. (In the particular case of Littleton, all three were combined by media desperate to make some *sense* out of the tragedy, though it's noticeable that the Marilyn Manson angle was quickly pushed to one side when the controversial rock star actually stood up and defended his right to freedom of speech under the First Amendment of the Constitution). Sadly, noted the reporter, this deflects the argument away from the *real* cause of such cases and, after much wringing of hands, everybody quietly forgets about such events until the next one happens. As Elizabeth Wurzel wrote in *Bitch*, discussing the case of Amy Fisher, a sixteen-year-old high school girl who in 1992 shot her lover's wife, 'Bad people and bad parenting are what made Amy bad, not rock music or the Internet.'

None of this stopped the *Buffy the Vampire Slayer* episode 52, 'Earshot', from being postponed a few days after the Littleton incident. By a horrible irony, the episode concerned just such a scenario. The decision to pull the episode by WB executives *was* understandable – indeed, given the circumstances, it was probably the only thing to do. Sometimes we do the right things for the wrong reasons. Sometimes, we can't even manage that. WB's subsequent decision to also postpone the *Buffy* season finale, 56, 'Graduation Day' Part 2, four weeks later was a knee-jerk reaction which probably did more harm than good. In doing headline-making things like initiating cancellations, one tends to draw media attention *to* such episodes that may otherwise have passed by unnoticed. When Associated Press's Ted Anthony called *Buffy* 'a vivid piece of hip TV splatterpunk, a hybrid of *Fast Times at Ridgemont High*, gothic romance and one of the video games you might think was favoured by Columbine's "Trench Coat Mafia" ', at least he tempered this with an interesting observation: 'White peppered with cartoonish violence – choreographed kung-fu, blood rites and the occasional stabbing or vampire-related blood feast – *Buffy* is actually pacifist in many ways.'

That *Buffy the Vampire Slayer* touched a raw nerve in the American psyche with these episodes and others is evidenced by the very nature of the episode cancellations themselves. They were pulled because they had *predicted* events rather than reacted to them. One should, perhaps, be grateful that 52, 'Earshot', wasn't shown a week earlier, as there would be those who would have used such a coincidence to suggest that *Buffy* had actually *caused* Littleton. Appearing on CNN,

Sarah Michelle Gellar was asked whether she thought the violence in *Buffy* and programmes like it was in any way responsible for such acts. She responded, 'Our show is broadcast in England, throughout Europe and throughout the world. And apparently only in America do we have this problem. Why?' Why indeed?

Seth Green also expressed anger at the suggestion that controversy should be avoided just for the sake of it: 'The simple fact is, this is a topical issue,' noted Green. 'It's a growing problem and Colorado isn't the only place it's happened. We just don't want to think these things happen, but they happen all the time.' The actor was bothered that the shootings had *again* provided a target for criticism on violence in entertainment. 'Instead of focusing on the real issues and the fact that guns are so easily and readily available to kids and that people aren't watching their kids carefully enough or monitoring the emotions of their students, they'd rather say, "Oh, that guy's got a Mohawk," or "That guy's got a leather jacket on, and *Natural Born Killers* is a film I don't like, and Marilyn Manson scares me, so all that shit should be put on a funeral pyre." I think that's the wrong way to go.'

Ultimately, we need television series and films that tackle issues that concern society. Sometimes the medium genuinely *is* the message and, if only briefly, a well-written teenage horror-comedy-soap-drama can have its finger so on the pulse of a nation that it hurts. In the spring of 1999 *Buffy the Vampire Slayer* for one brief moment got to the absolute heart of what currently makes America tick. What it found was *fear*.

In the preface I said that *Buffy the Vampire Slayer* has more in common with *Hamlet* than a blond hero and death on a large scale. Shakespeare too was writing his stories at a time of great change and his audience were presented with plays that dealt with things that they could recognise in their own lives. In *Hamlet* (Act III, Scene II), the Prince tells the First Player that the purpose of drama is 'to hold, as 'twere, the mirror up to nature'.

Sometimes we need that mirror very badly.

Buffy and the Internet

Jenny: '*In the last two years, more e-mail was sent than regular mail. More digitised information went across phone lines than conversations.*'
Giles: '*That is a fact that I regard with genuine horror.*'

– 'I Robot . . . You Jane'

Buffy the Vampire Slayer is TV's first *true* child of the Internet age. Even more *The X-Files* and *Babylon 5*, *Buffy* not only saw its fans embrace the new technology to (articulately) spread the gospel, but the Net itself became a part of the series' iconography. Within weeks of *Buffy* beginning a flourishing Net-fan community had spawned newsgroups, posting boards and websites. As with most fandoms there is a lot of good stuff and a little bad in what's emerged. This is a rough guide to get you started.

Newsgroups: The main *Buffy* usenet newsgroup, alt.tv.buffy-v-slayer, is generally a fine open-discussion forum, although some posters seem to have an obsession with the sex lives of the characters (the logistics of the Buffy–Angel coupling in **25**, 'Surprise', occupies an *awful* lot of bandwidth). The group features a lively and intelligent cross-section of views, though some contributors let themselves – and the series – down with their reaction to the postponement of **52**, 'Earshot'. Other major discussion topics are reviews, 'spoilers' for forthcoming episodes and other assorted minutiae (a huge debate centred on Buffy's Wonder-Woman-esque leap from the sewer in **32**, 'Go Fish'. One faction was disappointed that she was unable to clear the trapdoor. Another thought it amazing that she managed to jump that high, while soaking wet and waist-deep in water). As with most fandoms, *Buffy*'s contains a small but vocal elitist group who are unhappy with the current direction of the show (childishly dubbing season three 'BufLite'). Remarkably, there are even some 'where were you in '92?' fans who prefer the original movie to the series itself. There are also newsgroups for both Sarah Michelle Gellar and Alyson Hannigan (although neither alt.fan.sarah-m-gellar or alt.fan.hannigan at present generates large numbers of posts). alt.fan.buffy-v-slayer. creative is a fan-fiction forum and carries a range of 'missing adventures', character vignettes, erotica and slash (same-sex) erotica, some of it of a very high standard. A UK newsgroup, uk.media.tv.buffy-v-slayer features gossip and spoilers from the States, arrangements for pub meetings and an individual who openly sells copies of new US episodes for profit. *Naughty*. And illegal.

Among the (seemingly) erroneous rumours that began on the Internet during the writing of this book have been:

- Buffy is having a gay affair with either Willow or Faith (see **39**, 'Homecoming', for Joss Whedon's reaction to that).
- Giles/Oz/Wesley will die in the last episode of Season Three.
- In an episode called 'Pinocchio', Angel gets the chance to become human again.
- Faith will become a vampire.
- The Watchers' Council tries to recruit Willow.
- Lifelike statues of students and teachers appear at school. Giles suspects gorgons.
- Buffy is seriously hurt in a battle that leaves Angel devastated. He swears vengeance on the demon responsible and tearfully leaves her in the hospital to hunt him down in LA.
- Amy, in her ratlike existence, will chew through a rope that will, in some way, destroy the Mayor's plans. (What *idiot* thought that one up?)

Posting boards: http://board.buffy.com/bronze/postingboard. shtml is the web address for the official *Buffy the Vampire Slayer* [BtVS] posting board, which includes regular contributions from Joss Whedon and other members of the production team and cast (Seth Green has been known to post). This is an excellent forum for fans (particularly as it features a direct line to the production office and some official input). The only problem is the sheer size of the thing.

Websites: There are literally hundreds of sites on the World Wide Web relating to *Buffy the Vampire Slayer*, full of interesting material. What follows is a (by no means definitive) list of some of my favourites, which should give you an idea of where to start your Net surfing. Many of these are also part of web rings that contain links to other related sites.

(Disclaimer: websites are transitory things at the best of times and this information, though accurate when it was written, may be woefully out of date by publication.)

UK sites: http://www.users.globalnet.co.uk/~fraxis (*The Watcher's Web*) is an invaluable source of information and analysis with a largely British perspective. Includes interviews, reviews, probably the most up-to-date *Buffy* news service on the Net, ratings figures and fan fiction (including some by this author). You can get lost in it for days.

http://www.btvs.freeserve.co.uk (*Planet Buffy*) is also a good British-based site, including a similar range of information.

http://www.soft.net.uk/buffyuk/ (*Bring Back Buffy Campaign*) is, as the name suggests, a site dedicated to getting Buffy back on to Sky and to get the BBC to show the series at a more sensible time, uncut and without interruptions from sporting events (some hope). This had early success in March 1999 when, after an impressively co-ordinated e-mail campaign, James Baker at Sky contacted one of the campaigners to announce, 'I give in. You win'! A clear demonstration of the power of both fans' voices *and* the Internet.

US sites: http://www2.uic.edu/~ahufan1/btvs (*Domain of the Slain*) is a terrific general site featuring episode breakdowns in great detail, along with reviews and sections on errors and goofs. Contains many links to other sites and lots of other fun stuff.

http://members.tripod.com/~Little_Willow/index.html (*Little Willow's Slayground*) is a real treasure trove of multimedia extracts and photos. Includes 'Who Says?', the VIP archive of the BtVS Posting Board and fun sections like 'The Xander Dance Club' and 'A Tribute to Willow's Frog Fear'. Another site where it's possible to find something new each visit.

http://www.buffyguide.com (*The Complete Buffy the Vampire Slayer Episode Guide*) is one of the best and certainly most enthusiastic general review sites, with excellently written, intelligent summaries of all the episodes and lots of photos.

http://www.geocities.com/Hollywood/Lot/8864/music.htm (*Buffy the Vampire Slayer: The Music*) is a beautiful site devoted to the music on *Buffy* (indexed by artist, episode and song), plus interviews, tour dates for bands that have appeared, musical allusions, etc. A gem.

http://www.enteract.com/~perridox/SunS/ (*Suns – The Sunnydale Slayers*) was, according to the authors, set up by 'a gang of people . . . who wanted to talk about, lust after and discuss in depth *Buffy the Vampire Slayer*.' It's great fun, including fiction, sound clips and well-written reviews. Love the FAQ, where they answer the question, 'So, it's not just a bunch of women who want to drool at Anthony Stewart Head, David Boreanaz, Seth Green and Nicholas Brendon then?' with 'Oh no, we've got a few guys too!'

http://www.geocities.com/TelevisionCity/Lot/7330/index2.html (*Beneath the Bronze*) is another impressive general site featuring a bit of everything. This was one of the first places on the Net to transcribe the script of **52**, 'Earshot'.

http://www.hannigan.com/altar/ (*The Alyson Hannigan Altar*) is a lovely fan site dedicated to all things Alyson, and includes news, quotes, trivia and lots of photos and sound clips. Well worth dropping in.

http://www.smgfan.com (*The Unofficial Sarah Michelle Gellar Page*) has numerous pages dedicated to Sarah's career both inside and outside *Buffy*.

http://homes.acmecity.com/buffy/spike/297/index.html (*The

Buffy Shooting Script Site) features fascinating background details on many scripts, including **U1**.

http://www.geocities.com/Hollywood/Boulevard/4065/ (*For Every Generation There is Only One Slayer!*) features a real plethora of information, including quotes from episodes, photo galleries and biographies for all the stars and a list of facts about characters and episodes.

http://www.angelfire.com/wa/SpikesPrincess/ (*He's To Die For: James Marsters Fan Page*) is a charming site, with amusing subsections like 'All I Needed to Know in Life I Learned from Spike' ('If you're going to hit a girl, make sure her mother isn't standing behind you with an axe') and the bitchy 'Why Spike is Better than Angel'!

http://www.geocities.com/~angelsecrets/ (*Angel's Secrets*) – not that the creator of this excellent site would agree. *Angel's Secrets* is a charming and well-produced site, full of all things Boreanaz. Contains lots of interesting speculation about *Angel*.

http://www.geocities.com/TelevisionCity/7728/gaspers.html (*The Official Giles Appreciation Society Panters Home Page*) includes a list of appearances, many quotes and a section devoted to Tony's legendary stage performance as Frank N Furter in *The Rocky Horror Show* (with photos). Nicely put together, imaginative and easy to navigate, a labour of love.

http://come.to/Buffy-timeline (*BtVS Series Timeline*) is an attempt to pull together the entire back-story of *Buffy* into a chronology. A fascinating idea, well presented.

http://slayerfanfic.com (*The Slayer Fanfic Archive*) is, as the name suggests, a terrific site dedicated to *Buffy the Vampire Slayer* fan fiction with links to lots of related sites offering all sorts of fan writing.

http://www.synapse.net/~dsample/BBC/ (*The Buffy Body Count*) contains 'an ongoing count of the number of dead bodies which have shown up on school property'.

http://buffyfiles.com/cbcc/sounds.html (*The Chris Beck Cameo*

Committee) an enthusiastic fan site for the *Buffy* composer Christophe Beck. Includes samples of Beck's Season Two scores (including the Emmy Award-winning work on 'Becoming'). You may need to download some additional software to listen to these MP3s.

http://www.geocities.com/stakeaclaim (*The Keeper Sites*) is a handy web ring containing numerous fan sites on some of Sunnydale's more obscure characters and institutions, with lots of enthusiastic humour and articles.

Selected Bibliography

The following books, articles, interviews and reviews were consulted in the preparation of this text:

Anthony, Ted, '12 Weeks After Columbine, Delayed "Buffy" airs', *Associated Press*, 12 July 1999.

Atkins, Ian, 'Fallen Angel', *Cult Times*, issue 47, August 1999.

Baldwin, Kristen, 'Green's Day', *Entertainment Weekly*, May 1999.

Bergstrom, Cynthia, 'Slaying With Style', interview by Matt Springer, *Buffy the Vampire Slayer*, issue 3, Spring 1999.

Boreanaz, David, Landau, Juliet, and Marsters, James, 'Interview with the Vampires', interview by Tim Appelo, *TV Guide*, September 1998.

Boreanaz, David, 'Leaders of the Pack', interview (with Kerri Russell) by Janet Weeks, *TV Guide*, November 1998.

Boreanaz, David, 'City of Angel', interview by David Richardson, *Xposé*, issue 35, June 1999.

Brendon, Nicholas, 'Evolving Hero', interview by Paul Simpson, *DreamWatch*, issue 53, January 1999.

Brendon, Nicholas, and Miller, Craig, 'Xander the Survivor', *Spectrum*, issue 17, March 1999.

Bunson, Matthew, *Vampire: The Encyclopaedia*, Thames and Hudson, 1993.

Carpenter, Charisma, 'Charismatic', interview by Jim Boutlier, *SFX*, issue 40, July 1998.

Cornell, Paul, Day, Martin, and Topping, Keith, *The Guinness Book of Classic British TV*, 2nd edition, Guinness Publishing, 1996.

Cornell, Paul, Day, Martin, and Topping, Keith, *X-Treme Possibilities: A Comprehensively Expanded Rummage Through the X-Files*, Virgin Publishing, 1998.

DeCandido, Keith RA, *The Xander Years, Vol. 1*, Archway Paperback Publishing, 1999.

Fairley, Peter, 'Last Night's View' ('The Puppet Show' review), *The Journal*, 4 March 1999.

Fretts, Bruce, 'City of Angel', *Entertainment Weekly*, April 1999.

Gabriel, Jan, *Meet the Stars of Buffy the Vampire Slayer: An Unauthorized Biography*, Scholastic Inc., 1998.

Gellar, Sarah Michelle, interview by Sue Schneider, *DreamWatch*, issue 42, February 1998.

Gellar, Sarah Michelle, 'Star Struck Slayer', interview by Jenny Cooney Carrillo, *DreamWatch*, issue 55, March 1999.

Gellar, Sarah Michelle, interview by Jamie Diamond, *Mademoiselle*, March 1999.

Gill, AA, 'A Teeny Pain in the Neck', *Sunday Times*, 24 January 1999.

Golden, Christopher, and Holder, Nancy (with Keith RA DeCandido), *Buffy the Vampire Slayer: The Watcher's Guide*, Pocket Books, 1998.

Hannigan, Alyson, 'Slay Belle', interview by Sue Schneider, *DreamWatch*, issue 43, March 1998.

Hannigan, Alyson, 'Net Prophet', interview by Paul Simpson, *DreamWatch*, issue 55, March 1999.

Head, Anthony Stewart, 'Bewitched, Bothered & Bewildered', interview by Paul Simpson, *DreamWatch*, issue 54, February 1999.

Hensley, Dennis, 'Sarah Michelle Gellar Vamps it Up', *Cosmopolitan*, June 1999.

Hughes, David, 'Slay Ride', *DreamWatch*, issue 42, February 1998.

Johnson, Kevin V, 'Fans Sink Teeth into Bootlegged "Buffy" ', *USA Today*, May 1999.

Johnson, RW, 'The Myth of the 20th Century', *New Society*, 9 December 1982.

King, Stephen, *Danse Macabre*, Futura Books, 1981.

Lane, Andy, *The Babylon File*, Virgin Publishing, 1997.

Lowry, Brian, 'Actresses Turning Down Roles of Teens' Mothers', *Los Angeles Times*, 29 April 1999.

Marsters, James, 'Sharp Spike' interview by Cynthia Boris, *Cult TV* Special 9, Spring 1999.

Metcalf, Mark, 'Buffy's Master', interview by Mark Wyman, *Starburst*, issue 245, January 1999.

Newman, Kim, *Nightmare Movies: A Critical History of the Horror Movie From 1968*, Bloomsbury Publishing, 1988.

Peary, Danny, *Guide For the Film Fanatic*, Simon & Schuster, 1986.

Pirie, David, *The Vampire Cinema*, Galley Press, 1977.

Plath, Sylvia, *Collected Poems*, Faber and Faber, 1981.

'Queen of the Damned', *FHM*, issue 114, July 1999.

Richardson, David, 'Snyder Remarks', *Xposé*, issue 37, August 1999.

Roeper, Richard, 'Buffy Crackdown Won't Strike Heart of Problem', *Chicago Sun Times*, 27 May 1999.

Roush, Matt, 'The Roush Review', *TV Guide*, 3 April 1999.

Roush, Matt, 'The Roush Review – Buffy Rocks: Better Late Than Never', *TV Guide*, 10 July 1999.

Sepinwall, Alan, 'Delaying Episode Could Make "Buffy" Target of Witchhunt', *Network Star-Ledger*, May 1999.

Simpson, Paul, 'Red Shirt Robia', *DreamWatch*, issue 59, Summer 1999.

Spragg, Paul, 'Welcome to the Hellmouth', *Cult Times* Special 9, Spring 1999.

Springer, Matt, 'Crusin' Sunnydale', *Buffy the Vampire Slayer*, issue 3, Spring 1999.

Stanley, John, *Revenge of the Creature Features Movie Guide*, Creatures Press, 1988.

Summers, Montague, *The Vampire, His Kith and Kin*, Kegan Paul, Trench, Truber & Co., 1928.

Sutherland, Kristine, 'Source of Denial', interview by Paul Simpson, *DreamWatch*, issue 58, July 1999.

'Today's Trout' ('Earshot'/'Bad Girls' preview), *St Paul Pioneer Press*, 27 April 1999.

'The Top Fifty SF TV Shows of All Time!', *SFX*, issue 50, April 1999.

Topping, Keith, 'Buffy the Vampire Slayer Season One', *DreamWatch*, issue 55, March 1999.

Topping, Keith, 'Buffy the Vampire Slayer Season Two', *DreamWatch*, issues 57, 58, May, July 1999.

Topping, Keith, 'The Way We Were', *DreamWatch*, issue 58, July 1999.

Topping, Keith, 'Buffy the Vampire Slayer Season Three', *DreamWatch*, issues 60, 61, August, September 1999.

Wagner, Chuck, 'Punk Shocks', *SFX*, issue 49, March 1999.

Wilson, Steve, 'Web Sucks TV's Blood – Buffy Fans Bite Back', *Village Voice*, May 1999.

Wurtzel, Elizabeth, *Bitch*, Quartet Books, 1998.

Wyman, Mark, 'The Buffy Guide Season Two', *Xposé*, issue 29, December 1998.

Wyman, Mark, 'Anno I', *Cult Times* Special 9, Spring 1999.

Grrr! Arrrgh!

September 1999: *Buffy the Vampire Slayer*'s third season has just ended, several weeks later than expected and with some major hitches along the way. October will see Buffy and friends now at UC Sunnydale, but it will be without both David Boreanaz and Charisma Carpenter, who will be starring in the spin-off *Angel*, set in Los Angeles. Boreanaz told *TV Guide* that Angel 'goes to L.A. and fights for humanity. He fights inner demons . . . I'll have an interesting sidekick. A lot of people from *Buffy* will come visit me and I'll come back and visit them.' (Sarah Michelle Gellar told *Sci-Fi TV Magazine*, 'I probably won't be making crossovers. I may do one at the beginning of *Angel*, but that will be it. You have to realise that with my schedule the way it is on *Buffy*, there's no room left for that kind of thing.')

Angel will also star Glenn Quinn as Doyle – one of the undead who serves as Angel's spiritual mentor at a detective agency. According to Joss Whedon in *Entertainment Weekly*, 'the higher powers have called Doyle to be Angel's guide, and he's the last person in the world who wants to – or should – be doing this. He really just wants to play the ponies and drink a lot. But he has unexpected wisdom in the midst of his extreme foibles.'

Whedon has managed to get *Angel* and *Buffy* scheduled side by side, though he notes that *Angel* will be more of an anthology show than *Buffy*: 'There's not a soap opera at the centre of it.' We should also see a more humorous side to Angel ('Dry and sarcastic,' says Boreanaz) but no necking with Cordelia, who will 'still be somewhat self-involved and in her Cordelia-bubble, which is her charm,' notes Whedon.

Boreanaz has revealed that 'We'll explore Angel's past, maybe flashing back to a period when he . . . [was] wandering the streets in abject misery . . . cursed by the gypsies,' and that some episodes will be shot in Ireland. The actor has also hinted that *Angel* may not be the end of the spin-off line for

Buffy characters, telling *Xposé*, 'You could take the Snyder character somewhere, you could go to Giles's past, you could show what's going to happen to the other Watcher. Are there any other Slayers out there? What happens with these demons? Then you've got Xander, Willow's witchcraft. . . He could probably spin off eight shows from just the one series!'

Joss Whedon is certainly a busy man, as he recently told the BtVS posting board: 'Today's schedule, an example of a typical day: Watch filming. Edit. Production meeting re the next episode. Prep next director, explain tone and meaning in script. Pick song for the Bronze. Casting. Drink huge amount of tea. Talk to Sarah about the script. Discuss directors for next season. Panic. More tea. Work on *Angel*.' And then he goes online for an hour to talk about it! It seems that the actual day-to-day organisation of *Angel* will be in the capable hands of David Greenwalt.

On the future of *Buffy*, it has been confirmed that a new love will enter Buffy's life. Buffy's boyfriend will be Riley Finn (played by Marc Blucas). Casting calls for the character describe him as 'the antithesis to Angel'. Current rumours surround the possible return of Spike and the intriguing possibility that he may actually *join* the Scooby Gang. However, as Whedon commented in the wake of **56**, 'Graduation Day' Part 2, 'The show will not change. I made a couple of trims in the final episodes, but I was on board for that – they just seemed tasteless (by pure coincidence). But nothing will change in the creative process. If someone tries to start interfering with the show, I'll not make it any more. Very simple.'

That would be a tragedy, but it demonstrates the single-mindedness that has made *Buffy the Vampire Slayer* unique.

Notes

First Season

1 Credited as 'Senior Cheerleader' in 'The Witch'.
2 Credited as 'Boy' in 'Never Kill a Boy on the First Date'.
3 Credited as 'Collin' in 'Angel'.

Second Season

1 For episodes 26–34 ('Innocence' to 'Becoming' Part 2) the character is referred to as Angelus – Angel's demonic persona.
2 Credited as appearing in 'Surprise', but the scene was cut before transmission.
3 Credited as 'Hostage Kid' in 'What's My Line?' Part 2.
4 Credited as 'Student' in 'Passion'.
5 Credited as 'Teacher' in 'Innocence' but the scene was cut before transmission.
6 There is considerable debate in the *Buffy* fan community as to whether this character is supposed to be Merrick or not. Certainly the scenes set in Hemery High are conceptually close enough to the movie to suggest that the film's events are canonical. Additionally, at least one 'official' book on the series lists the character as Merrick.

Third Season

1 Credited as 'Teacher' in 'Anne'.
2 Credited as 'Manager' in 'Choices'.
3 'Earshot' was initially advertised in the TV trade press for transmission on 13 April 1999.